OXFORD EARLY CHRISTIAN STUDIES

General Editors

Gillian Clark   Andrew Louth

THE OXFORD EARLY CHRISTIAN STUDIES series includes
scholarly volumes on the thought and history of the early Christian
centuries. Covering a wide range of Greek, Latin, and Oriental
sources, the books are of interest to theologians, ancient historians,
and specialists in the classical and Jewish worlds.

Eusebius of Caesarea's *Commentary on Isaiah*

Christian Exegesis in the Age of Constantine

MICHAEL J. HOLLERICH

CLARENDON PRESS · OXFORD
1999

Oxford University Press, Great Clarendon Street, Oxford OX2 6DP

Oxford New York

Athens Auckland Bangkok Bogotá Buenos Aires Calcutta
Cape Town Chennai Dar es Salaam Delhi Florence Hong Kong Istanbul
Karachi Kuala Lumpur Madrid Melbourne Mexico City Mumbai
Nairobi Paris São Paolo Singapore Taipei Tokyo Toronto Warsaw
and associated companies in
Berlin Ibadan

Oxford is a registered trade mark of Oxford University Press

Published in the United States
by Oxford University Press Inc., New York

British Library Cataloguing in Publication Data
Data available

Library of Congress Cataloging in Publication Data
Eusebius of Caesarea's Commentary on Isaiah : Christian exegesis in the age
of Constantine / Michael J. Hollerich.
(Oxford early Christian studies)
Includes bibliographical references
1. Eusebius, of Caesarea, Bishop of Caesarea, ca. 260–ca. 340. Commentaria in
Hesaiam. 2. Bible. O.T. Isaiah—Criticism, interpretation, etc.—History—Early
church, ca. 30–600. I. Title. II. Series.
BR65.E76H653   1993   224'.107—dc21   98-29123
ISBN 0-19-826368-6

1 3 5 7 9 10 8 6 4 2

Typeset by Best-set Typesetter Ltd., Hong Kong
Printed in Great Britain on acid-free paper by
Bookcraft (Bath) Ltd., Midsomer Norton

CONTENTS

Contents

LIST OF TABLES

LIST OF ABBREVIATIONS

CCL	*Corpus Christianorum, Series Latina* (Turnhout, 1953–)
CH	*Church History*
CSEL	*Corpus Scriptorum Ecclesiasticorum Latinorum*
GCS	Die griechischen christlichen Schriftsteller der ersten Jahrhunderte (Leipzig and Berlin, 1898–)
HTR	*Harvard Theological Review*
LCL	Loeb Classical Library
PG	J. P. Migne, ed. *Patrologia graeca*
PGL	G. W. H. Lampe, ed. *A Patristic Greek Lexikon*
PL	J. P. Migne, ed. *Patrologia latina*
RAC	Theodore Klauser *et al.*, eds. *Reallexikon für Antike und Christentum: Sachwörterbuch zur Auseinandersetzung des Christentums mit der antiken Welt* (Leipzig, 1941–)
RB	*Revue biblique*
RE	Georg Wissowa *et al.*, eds. *Paulys Realencyclopädie der classischen Altertumswissenschaften* (Stuttgart and Munich, 1894–1980)
RSR	*Recherches de science religieuse*
SC	Sources chrétiennes (Paris, 1942–)
SP	*Studia Patristica* (Papers presented at International Conference on Patristics Studies; Berlin, 1957–79; New York, 1982; Kalamazoo, Mich., 1986; Leuven, 1987–)
TU	Texte und Untersuchungen zur Geschichte der altchristlichen Literatur
ZNW	*Zeitschrift für die neutestamentliche Wissenschaft*

Frequently cited works of Eusebius:

CI	*Commentary on Isaiah*
DE	*Demonstratio Evangelica*
EP	*Eclogae Propheticae*
HE	*Historia Ecclesiastica*

LC	*De Laudibus Constantini*
MP	*De Martyribus Palestinae*
PE	*Praeparatio Evangelica*
VC	*De Vita Constantini*

I

Introduction

1. Eusebius, the Bible, and Modern Scholarship

Eusebius, bishop of Caesarea in Palestine (d. 339), was the leading Christian scholar of his age. Caretaker of the theological and scholarly heritage of the great Origen, he became a prolific author in his own right. His scholarly production paved the way for a role as an important actor in the heated ecclesiastical politics of the era following the end of persecution and the conversion of Constantine. Despite the temporary setback of being excommunicated on the eve of Nicaea, he recovered to become in his last years an ecclesiastical elder statesman. He was sufficiently close to the court to exchange several letters with Constantine, to have the honour of delivering a panegyric on the occasion of his thirtieth anniversary as emperor, and to write his biography.

However, it is his books which have won him a permanent place in the history of the church and of human culture, not his engagement in ecclesiastical and secular politics.[1] Had he been less industrious an author, he would be no better known today than his

---

[1] The basic study of his life and works is T. D. Barnes, *Constantine and Eusebius* (Cambridge, Mass., 1981). D. S. Wallace-Hadrill, *Eusebius of Caesarea* (London, 1960), is a sound general presentation, as is J. Moreau, 'Eusebius von Caesarea', *Reallexikon für Antike und Christentum* (hereafter *RAC*) vi. 1052–88. Still valuable are the lengthy encyclopedia articles of Eduard Schwartz, 'Eusebios von Caesarea', in *Paulys Realencyclopädie der classischen Altertumswissenschaften* (hereafter cited as *RE*) (Stuttgart and Munich, 1894–1980), vi. 1370–439, reprinted in *Griechische Geschichtsschreiber* (Leipzig, 1957), 495–598, and J. B. Lightfoot, 'Eusebius of Caesarea', in *Dictionary of Christian Biography*, 4 vols. (London, 1880), ii. 308–48. Shorter encyclopedia articles and other general studies are listed in J. Quasten, *Patrology*, 4 vols. (Westminster, Md., 1983–6), iii. *The Golden Age of Greek Patristic Literature from the Council of Nicaea to the Council of Chalcedon*, 310 f. Quasten, *Patrology* iii. 309–45, and M. Geerard, *Clavis Patrum Graecorum*, 5 vols. (Turnhout, 1974–87), ii. 262–75, nos. 3465–505, contain basic information on modern editions and studies. They may be supplemented by F. Young, *From Nicaea to Chalcedon: A Guide to the Literature and its Background* (Philadelphia, 1983), 355–8, and B. Altaner and A. Stuiber (eds.), *Patrologie: Leben Schriften und Lehre der Kirchenväter*, (9th edn., Freiburg, 1980), 217–21, 591 f.

contemporary namesake Eusebius of Nicomedia, another activist bishop but no scholar. His collected works cover subjects as diverse as universal chronology, church history, biblical geography, exegesis, theology, biography, royal panegyric, and apologetics, a range of accomplishment matched by few patristic authors. Their importance rests on two factors. First, they are supremely valuable witnesses to ecclesiastical and secular history during an era which permanently marked Christianity's character, as it moved from persecution to state patronage. Second, many of his books were composed by compiling material from other sources which have otherwise disappeared. Thanks to Eusebius' use of extracts and quotations, his books are treasure troves for scholars on the trail of lost or fragmentary works. He received his scholarly training in the library and scriptorium of Caesarea, where the rich presbyter Pamphilus was restoring the collection of pagan and Christian literature originally established by Origen during his tenure in Caesarea. After Pamphilus' death as a martyr, Eusebius assumed responsibility as custodian. The resources of the library explain the documentary and archival character of so much of his work.[2]

Modern scholarship on Eusebius has been deeply affected by these features of his books. The historical and panegyrical writings have received the keenest scrutiny, at the expense of the apologetic, dogmatic, and exegetical works. Furthermore, many of them are studied not so much for their own sake as for the source material they contain, with the effect of diverting attention from Eusebius himself.

---

[2] To cite some examples: apologetic works like the *Prophetic Selections* and *The Proof of the Gospel* expand on the old proof text tradition, with often lengthy expositions of texts arranged either topically or by biblical book. *The Preparation for the Gospel* uses the same technique of commenting on excerpts from pagan philosophers, many of which would otherwise be lost. In the *Church History* Eusebius pioneered a tradition of ecclesiastical history which placed a special emphasis on documentary quotation. The *Church History* elaborates the theme of the succession of ecclesiastical writers with rich quotations from their writings, about half of which are otherwise unknown (so the estimate of H. J. Lawlor, cited in Young, *From Nicaea to Chalcedon*, 291). Schwartz saw the emphasis on quotation as a Christian analogue to the pagan scholarly tradition of literary and philosophical history (*RE* vi. 1395 f.). The *Chronology* used extracts from various Hellenistic historians. Although the *Life of Constantine* resembles an encomium as well as a biography, it too relied on the documentary approach. In its present form imperial letters and orders constitute about a fourth of the whole. Works of controversial theology like the *Against Marcellus* and *On the Ecclesiastical Theology* also used the method of quotation and refutation.

There is no difficulty understanding fascination with the historical and panegyrical literature, such as the *Church History*, the *Chronicle*, the *Life of Constantine*, and the composite oration known as *In Praise of Constantine*. The *Life of Constantine* has teased the ingenuity of generations of Roman historians and church historians, who debate its authorship, literary unity, documentation, historical accuracy, and *Tendenz*.[3] Its popularity with scholars arises partly from the inherent importance of its subject and partly from the literary complexity of the work itself, which most agree has undergone some kind of posthumous revision. The *Church History* remains the primary source for the study of Christianity in the first three centuries. Internal evidence and the manuscript tradition show that Eusebius made significant additions and editorial revisions to respond to the rapid pace of events from 303 to 325. Both of these facts have guaranteed the *Church History* a permanent place in research in early Christianity. As the first church history, it has traditionally drawn the attention of classical historians as well as church historians, from Eduard Schwartz to Arnaldo Momigliano and T. D. Barnes.[4] The *Chronicle*, to cite a third example, is still 'one of the fundamental books upon which all research in the past of mankind

---

[3] For partial bibliography see Quasten, *Patrology*, iii. 322–4, and Young, *From Nicaea to Chalcedon*, 14–16. To these add H. A. Drake, 'What Eusebius Knew: The Genesis of the *Vita Constantini*', *Classical Philology*, 83 (1988), 20–38, and Glenn Chesnut, *The First Christian Histories* (rev. edn.; Macon, Ga., 1986), 113–25. Barnes, *Constantine and Eusebius*, 267 ff., argues that the anomalies of the work are to be explained by a change in Eusebius' design, from encomium to true biography, which death prevented him from carrying out thoroughly. Barnes' interpretation has now been extended considerably in 'Panegyric, History, and Hagiography in Eusebius' *Life of Constantine*', in Rowan Williams (ed.), *The Making of Orthodoxy* (Cambridge, 1989), 94–123. See also the brief but suggestive remarks of Averil Cameron in her newly published Sather Lectures, *Christianity and the Rhetoric of Empire: The Development of Christian Discourse* (Sather Classical Lectures, no. 55; Berkeley, 1991), 53–6, 61–4. In her contribution to a festschrift for Arnaldo Momigliano, Professor Cameron emphasized how much can be gained by reading the *Life of Constantine* as a creative work in its own right, not just as a source for understanding Constantine; cf. 'Eusebius of Caesarea and the Re-Thinking of History', in E. Gabba (ed.), *Tria Corda: Scritti in onore di Arnaldo Momigliano* (Como, 1983), 82–8.
[4] The most recent book-length study is Robert M. Grant, *Eusebius as Church Historian* (Oxford, 1980). Among classical scholars who have studied it, we may mention Schwartz, who edited the *Church History* for the critical edition of Eusebius' works: Eduard Schwartz (ed.), *Die Kirchengeschichte*, ii, pts. 1–3, of *Eusebius' Werke* (Die Griechischen Christlichen Schriftsteller der ersten drei Jahrhunderte (hereafter GCS), no. 9; Leipzig, 1903–9); Arnaldo Momigliano, in his contribution on pagan and Christian historiography in the fourth century, in the collection he edited as *The Conflict between Paganism and Christianity in the Fourth Century* (Oxford, 1963),

has been based'.[5] The orations have been fertile sources for students of religious and political ideology in the foundational era of the Christian empire.[6]

Against competition of this calibre, it is not surprising that Eusebius' achievements in the areas of apologetics, theology, and exegesis were for a long time relatively neglected. Of the apologetic works, only *The Preparation for the Gospel* drew much attention, mostly because of the extracts it contained. With rare exceptions scholars were slow to see their relevance to a variety of important subjects, such as the character of pre-Nicene Origenist theology, Christian attitudes to Judaism, and Eusebius' developing view of the Roman Empire.[7]

In recent years the situation has improved considerably. Path-breaking studies such as Erik Peterson's *Monotheismus als politisches Problem*, an analysis of ancient political theology, and Marcel Simon's *Verus Israel*, which reshaped the study of relations between Judaism and Christianity, pointed out the value of Eusebius' apologetic tracts for both topics. Jean Sirinelli and Glenn Chesnut made rich use of them in comprehensive studies of Eusebius' ideas of culture, history, religion, and politics.[8] The whole subject of Eusebius' apologetic programme is being given close examination in the lengthy introductions and annotation of the Sources chrétiennes edition of *The Preparation for the Gospel*.[9] E. des Place, one of the editors, has published a separate study of the nature and function of Eusebius' extracts from pagan philosophers and from scripture.[10] He treats this anthologizing approach as an

79–99; Barnes' book on Constantine and Eusebius; and Glenn Chesnut's *The First Christian Hstories*, in which Eusebius is the major figure. See most recently Andrew Louth, 'The Date of Eusebius' *Historia Ecclesiastica*', *JTS* 41 (1990), 111–23, and the invaluable compendium of articles edited by Harold Attridge and Gohei Hata, *Eusebius, Christianity, and Judaism* (Detroit, 1992).

[5] Quasten, *Patrology*, iii. 313.

[6] Now available in the useful edition, with lengthy introduction and commentary, by H. A. Drake, *In Praise of Constantine: A Historical Study and New Translation of Eusebius' Tricennial Orations* (Berkeley, 1976).

[7] Note Schwartz's shrewd protest against the neglect of *The Proof of the Gospel* (*RE* vi. 1388 f.).

[8] Jean Sirinelli, *Les vues historiques d'Eusèbe de Césarée durant la période prénicéenne* (Dakar, 1961).

[9] J. Sirinelli, G. Schröder, E. des Places, O. Zink (eds.), *Eusèbe de Césarée, Préparation évangélique* (Sources chrétiennes (hereafter SC) nos. 206, 215, 228, 262, 266, 292, 307, 338, 369; Paris, 1974–91).

[10] E. des Places, *Eusèbe de Césarée, commentateur: Platonisme et écriture sainte* (Théologie historique, 63; Paris, 1982).

intelligent and creative enterprise in its own right, which preserves the authentic words of the sources Eusebius is examining, though more in the polemical spirit of ancient intellectual debate than of modern dialogue. P. W. L. Walker's recent *Holy City, Holy Places?* makes Eusebius' apologetics a central focus for a study of changing fourth-century views on Jerusalem and the Holy Land.[11]

Eusebius' theology for long suffered from his association with the resistance against the Council of Nicaea. A valuable 1935 article by H.-G. Opitz, the editor of Athanasius, drew sympathetic attention to Eusebius' importance as a spokesman for the harmony of reason and revelation, and of Christianity and culture.[12] Reformed theologian Hendrik Berkhof, on the other hand, criticized this very aspect of Eusebius' theology in his 1939 study, *Die Theologie des Eusebius von Caesarea*.[13] Berkhof drew extensively on the apologetic and controversial treatises in making the first comprehensive assessment of Eusebius' theology, although he perhaps judged Eusebius too much in terms of Nicene developments.[14] More recent studies have recognized the traditional, pre-Nicene cast of his theology.[15]

Eusebius' biblical scholarship has been served even more unhappily than his apologetics and his theology. This is surprising when we recall that he began his long career as a biblical scholar and remained one until the end of his life. A substantial number of his works are devoted to understanding the Bible, and even the apologetic treatises *The Prophetic Selections* and *The Proof of the Gospel* consist largely of biblical extracts with explanatory glosses.

A quick review will give an idea of the character of Eusebius' scholarship in this area, and the range of subjects and genres in

[11] P. W. L. Walker, *Holy City, Holy Places? Christian Attitudes to Jerusalem and the Holy Land in the Fourth Century* (Oxford, 1990).

[12] H.-G. Opitz, 'Euseb von Caesarea als Theologe', *Zeitschrift für die neutestamentliche Wissenschaft* (hereafter *ZNW*), 34 (1935), 1–19.

[13] H. Berkhof, *Die Theologie des Eusebius von Caesarea* (Amsterdam, 1939).

[14] See Barnes' criticism, *Constantine and Eusebius*, 337 n. 193.

[15] C. Luibheid, *Eusebius of Caesarea and the Arian Crisis* (Dublin, 1978); A. Weber, *ARXH: Ein Beitrag zur Christologie des Eusebius von Caesarea* (Rome, 1963); F. Ricken, 'Die Logoslehre des Eusebius von Caesarea und der Mittelplatonismus', *Theologie und Philosophie*, 42 (1967), 341–58, which is very helpful at setting Eusebius' thought in its middle Platonic context. See the review of recent work in Young, *From Nicaea to Chalcedon*, 16–21, and the balanced assessment of R. P. C. Hanson, *The Search for the Christian Doctrine of God: The Arian Controversy 318–381* (Edinburgh, 1988), 46–59. Walker, *Holy City, Holy Places?*, 51–116, stresses the spiritualizing influence of Origen on Eusebius' theology of time and especially of space (esp. 76–92).

which he was accomplished.[16] His early training in the scriptorium of Pamphilus' library at Caesarea involved the correcting of Septuagint manuscripts according to Origen's amended Septuagint column in the Hexapla. As a result of the work the Hexaplaric recension of the LXX spread throughout Palestine and Syria.[17] For Eusebius himself there was the benefit of a thorough acquaintance with the Hexapla and an initiation to the methods of ancient philology. Colophons in several ancient manuscripts attest to his work.[18] His renown as a biblical scholar was such that Constantine appealed to him for fifty copies of the scriptures for divine services in his new capital city, though scholars disagree about the effect this large book order had on the Old or New Testament text in use in Constantinople.[19]

Eusebius composed four books on the topography of the Holy Land, of which only the last one survives, the alphabetized handbook of biblical place-names and their contemporary locations commonly known as the *Onomasticon*.[20] The preface says that the other three parts of the work dealt with Greek translations of the Hebrew words for the peoples of the world, a topographic description of ancient Judaea with the boundaries of the twelve tribes, and a plan of Jerusalem and the Temple, with annotations. It is still a valuable resource for Palestinian topography.

Eusebius also wrote several monographs on selected subjects from scripture: a treatise called *On the Large Families of the Patriarchs*, which dealt with the polygamous families of the biblical patriarchs; a harmonization of the four Gospels commonly called the *Eusebian Sections and Canons*; and a two-part work called *Gospel Questions and Solutions*. The first of these is not extant, though Eusebius refers

---

[16] I acknowledge in particular my dependence on the fine survey of Barnes in *Constantine and Eusebius*, ch. 7.

[17] Sidney Jellicoe, *The Septuagint and Modern Study* (Oxford, 1968), 134–46.

[18] A. Harnack, *Geschichte der altchristlichen Literatur bis Eusebius*, 2 vols., (repr., Leipzig, 1958), i, pt. 2, 573f.; Schwartz, *RE* vi. 1371–3; Barnes, *Constantine and Eusebius*, 93–5.

[19] Eusebius, *Vita Constantini* (hereafter *VC*), 4. 36–7, ed. F. Winkelmann, i, pt. 1 of *Eusebius' Werke* (2nd edn., GCS; Berlin, 1975). Brief discussion and bibliography in Barnes, *Constantine and Eusebius*, 124 f.; see D. S. Wallace-Hadrill, 'Eusebius and the Gospel Text of Caesarea', *Harvard Theological Review* (hereafter *HTR*), 49 (1956), 105–14.

[20] All references are to the critical edition by E. Klostermann, iii, pt. 1 of *Eusebius' Werke* (GCS, no. 11; Leipzig, 1904). Bibliography in Quasten, *Patrology*, iii. 336 f. Cf. discussion in Barnes, *Constantine and Eusebius*, 106–11.

to it in *The Preparation for the Gospel*, where he says that both literal
and allegorical interpretations of patriarchal marriage customs are
possible.[21] The *Sections and Canons* is a cross-referencing index for
locating similar passages in the Gospels.[22] Eusebius says in a prefatory letter that he got his inspiration from a Gospel synopsis of
Ammonius the Alexandrian, but that the numerical cataloguing system was his own invention.[23] The third work shows a certain kinship
with the second, being devoted to differences in the infancy and
resurrection narratives of the Gospels. It consisted of two parts, one
entitled *Questions and Solutions on the Genealogy of our Saviour
Addressed to Stephanus*, and the other *Questions and Solutions on
the Resurrection of our Saviour Addressed to Marinus*. They are lost
in complete form, but Greek fragments survive in Gospel catenae
and in epitomes in Greek and Syriac.[24] These two works belong
to the second decade of the fourth century, with the treatise to
Stephanus apparently written while *The Proof of the Gospel* was in
composition.[25] The questions that are asked and answered have
mostly to do with discrepancies in the Lucan and Matthean
genealogies and with details of the Resurrection narratives. Eusebius
considers them on a purely historical level, without recourse to
allegorical interpretation, despite occasional edifying conclusions.[26]
Although in Barnes' words 'the basic assumptions . . . are essentially
dogmatic and uncritical', the analysis is literal and philological, recognizing *inter alia* the textual problem of the multiple endings to

---

[21] *Praeparatio Evangelica* (hereafter *PE*), 7. 8. 29. Cf. Harnack, *Geschichte der
altchristlichen Literatur*, i. pt. 2, 572. and ii. pt. 2, 121; Quasten, *Patrology*, iii. 339.
[22] Text in J. P. Migne (ed.), *Patrologia Graeca* (hereafter *PG*) (Paris, 1857–66), xxii.
1275–92. See Harnack, *Geschichte der altchristlichen Literatur*, i, pt. 2, 573, for the
remains. Analysis of contents in H. D. McArthur, 'The Eusebian Sections and
Canons', *Catholic Biblical Quarterly*, 27 (1965), 250–6, and Barnes, *Constantine
and Eusebius*, 120–2.
[23] The letter is translated by Barnes, *Constantine and Eusebius*, 121 f.
[24] On the texts see Harnack, *Geschichte der altchristlichen Literatur*, i, pt. 2, 577–
9, and Quasten, *Patrology*, iii. 337. Discussion in Barnes, *Constantine and Eusebius*,
121–4, and G. Bardy, 'La littérature patristique des Quaestiones et Responsiones sur
l'Écriture sainte', *Revue biblique* (hereafter *RB*), 41 (1932), 228–36.
[25] As noted by Barnes, *Constantine and Eusebius*, 344 n. 126, it is cited in
Demonstratio Evangelica (hereafter *DE*) 7. 3. 18 (all references, except as noted, are
from the critical edition of I. A. Heikel, vi of *Eusebius' Werke* (GCS, no. 23; Leipzig,
1913)), and Question 7.7 to Stephanus in turn refers to the *Demonstratio* (*PG* xxii.
912A). For the date, see Barnes, op. cit., and Harnack, *Geschichte der altchristlichen
Literatur* ii. pt. 2, 124.
[26] Barnes, *Constantine and Eusebius*, 122 f.; Bardy, 'La littérature patristique', 231,
236.

Mark.[27] This is in keeping with the expressly philological nature of the classical and post-classical genre of the *zêtêma*, a limited investigation of problems posed by a literary work.[28]

Eusebius also composed commentaries on complete biblical books, but only from the Old Testament. A possible exception is the disputed fragments on Luke preserved in the catena of Nicetas of Heraclea.[29] Wallace-Hadrill has defended the judgement of Mai, the original editor, that such a commentary existed, but only in scholia form, having originated as the tenth book of the lost *General Elementary Introduction*.[30] Even if this hypothesis is correct, the fact that the text of Luke is only treated selectively, along with texts from Matthew, shows that it is misleading to think of it as an actual line-by-line commentary such as Eusebius wrote on Old Testament books.[31] No other solid evidence exists that he wrote commentaries on the New Testament.[32]

From the Old Testament we have one work on the 150 Psalms and another on Isaiah. In various catenae there are fragments on Proverbs, Song of Songs, Jeremiah, Ezekiel, and Daniel attributed to Eusebius, but since no mention of distinct commentaries on these books is found in other ancient witnesses, it is more likely that they come from other works of Eusebius, if they are genuine at all.[33] Both the Psalms and the Isaiah commentaries are very long works. They come from late in Eusebius' career, the former sometime after 330, the latter sometime after 325.[34] They represent his mature work as a

[27] Question 1 to Marinus, cited by Bardy, 'La littérature patristique', 234 f.
[28] See the remarks by C. Schäublin on pagan and Christian forms of the genre: *Untersuchungen zu Herkunft und Methode der Antiochenischen Exegese* (Theophaneia, 23; Bonn, 1974), 55–60.
[29] MS survey in Harnack, *Geschichte der altchristlichen Literatur*, i, pt. 2, 577. The texts are reprinted in *PG* xxiv. 529–605.
[30] D. S. Wallace-Hadrill, 'Eusebius of Caesarea's *Commentary on Luke*: Its Origin and Early History', *HTR* 67 (1974), 55–63.
[31] As pointed out long ago by Schwartz, *RE* vi. 1431–3.
[32] See ibid. 1437 f., and Harnack, *Geschichte der altchristlichen Literatur*, i, pt. 2, 577, and ii, pt. 2, 123.
[33] See the list of MSS, Harnack, *Geschichte der altchristlichen Literatur*, i, pt. 2, 577, and the brief discussion in Schwartz, *RE* vi. 1437.
[34] Harnack, *Geschichte der altchristlichen Literatur*, ii, pt. 2, 123, dates the *Commentary on the Psalms* sometime after 330. He is followed by other commentators, with the exception of M.-J. Rondeau, who takes up a suggestion first made by Mercati and proposes that the commentary is pre-Nicene, with a final redaction around 325 or 326: see *Les commentaires patristiques du psautier (IIIe–Ve siècles)*, 2 vols. (Orientalia Christiana Analecta, 219, 220; Rome, 1982, 1985), i, *Les travaux des pères grecs et latins sur le psautier: Recherches et bilans*, 66–9. For my date of the *Commentary on Isaiah*, see Ch. II. 1.

biblical scholar. Both were known only through extensive fragments in the catenae, until Ziegler's recent publication of a nearly complete edition of the commentary on Isaiah. No critical edition of the Psalms commentary exists.[35] Both works were widely used and admired in antiquity. The *Commentary on the Psalms* was twice translated into Latin, by Hilary of Poitiers and Eusebius of Vercelli, although according to Jerome the latter omitted passages deemed heretical.[36] The *Commentary on Isaiah* was not translated into Latin, but Jerome used it extensively, as did several Greek patristic writers. The large number of citations in the catenae attest to their popularity.

What has modern scholarship done to evaluate an exegetical achievement of this scope? A check of the bibliographical entries in Quasten's *Patrology* shows that much of the older literature was inspired more by interest in extrinsic subjects such as biblical textual studies or Palestinian geography than by curiosity about the exegesis itself.[37] A sound general appraisal was not available until 1960, when Wallace-Hadrill devoted two chapters to Eusebius' scriptural scholarship in his fine book *Eusebius of Caesarea*. His survey moves quickly through Eusebius' textual work, his thought on the canon, and his interpretive method.[38] Not long afterwards Carmel Sant wrote a Roman dissertation on Eusebius' Old Testament interpretation, the results of which were published in article

---

[35] The printed version of the *Commentary on the Psalms* in *PG* xxiii and xxiv. 9–76 presents material of very unequal reliability, according to the article on Eusebius by M.-J. Rondeau and Jean Kirchmeyer in *Dictionnaire de spiritualité*, iv, pt. 2, 1687–90 (12 vols. to date; Paris, 1932–), from which the following is taken. The commentary on Pss. 51–95: 3 (*PG* xxiii. 441C–1221C) is based on direct tradition from the actual commentary and is authentic. This material was first published by Montfaucon in 1713 and reprinted by Migne. The printed commentary on Pss. 95: 3–150 is not presently usable because of the mixture of authentic and inauthentic material and gaps in the text. An exception to this generalization is Ps. 119, edited separately by G. Mercati in *Opere minori*, ii (Studi e testi, 77; Vatican City, 1937), 58–66). An edition of Eusebius' commentary on Pss. 95: 3–150 is being prepared by C. Curti, preliminary studies of which have already appeared (cited in Rondeau, *Les commentaires patristiques* i. 66 n. 153). The situation is more complicated with Pss. 1–50, also edited by Montfaucon and reprinted in *PG* xxiii. 72D–441C. The most unreliable sections are Pss. 1–15 and 48: 2–50. The intermediate part (*PG* xxiii. 160B–429C) is Eusebian, certain portions excepted which are inauthentic or doubtful (see the exact list in Rondeau-Kirchmeyer, *Dictionnaire de spiritualité* iv, pt. 2, 1689). Rondeau-Kirchmeyer, further bibliography on edited material. See Rondeau's summary of the subject in *Les commentaires patristiques* i. 64–6.

[36] Jerome *Epp.* 61. 2, 112. 20, cited in Quasten, *Patrology*, iii. 337.

[37] Ibid. 334–40.

[38] *Eusebius of Caesarea*, 59–99.

form.[39] Sant focused on exegetical method, but did not relate the substance of the exegesis to Eusebius' other work and to the contemporary setting. These studies were limited somewhat by the unavailability of a complete form of the *Commentary on Isaiah*. The more recent book of des Places, *Eusèbe de Césarée, commentateur*, devotes over half its length to biblical exegesis. Des Places has some useful comparative material on Eusebius' approaches to the Psalms and to Isaiah, but his book is a bit disappointing.[40] Its narrowly textual focus makes no real attempt to advance our understanding of Eusebius' exegesis in the wider context of his thought and his age. A more fruitful contribution has been made by T. D. Barnes in his splendid book *Constantine and Eusebius*, which includes fresh and original appreciations of Eusebius' biblical scholarship. Barnes too recognized the inadequate attention given to works outside the historical and 'political' treatises:

Worse still, most historians of the Roman Empire and its institutions decline to read Eusebius'

theological, exegetical and apologetical works, and even historians of the Christian church overlook precious nuggets of information which lie buried there. I decided, therefore, to redress the balance, and I have tried not only to set Eusebius in his historical milieu, but also to use the full range of his writings to illuminate the age in which both he and Constantine lived.[41]

The exposition of the exegetical works serves his general thesis that Eusebius should be regarded first as a scholar and only secondarily as an apologist: 'Eusebius was by instinct and training a scholar; he became an apologist only because circumstances demanded that he do so, and his style of argument in apology and polemic continually betrays the biblical exegete.'[42] Finally, we should mention M.-J. Rondeau's monograph on patristic exegesis of the psalter, which contains a chapter on Eusebius' *Commentary on Psalms*.[43]

Aside from these longer studies, only scattered articles have appeared. Perhaps the most interesting is Barthélemy's piece on Eusebius' view of the Septuagint and the other Greek versions. Barthélemy argues that Eusebius accepted the other versions of the

---

[39] Carmel Sant, 'Interpretatio Veteris Testamenti in Eusebio Caesariensi', *Verbum Domini*, 45 (1967), 79–90.

[40] See Stead's critical review in *JTS* 35 (1984), 230–2.

[41] Ibid., pp. v–vi.

[42] Ibid. 164.

[43] Rondeau, *Les commentaires patristiques*, i. 64–75.

Hebrew Bible as unveilings of the clear meaning of scripture which were providentially withheld until Christian times. This was Eusebius' rebuttal of the Jewish rationale for discarding the Septuagint once it became tainted as a Christian book.[44] In another article which gave a valuable impetus to the present study, F. E. Cranz used exegetical material to shed light on Eusebius' vocabulary of political community.[45]

A telling indication of the low profile of Eusebius' exegesis is his complete omission in the substantial article on early Christian exegesis in the *Reallexikon für Antike und Christentum*, which found space for characterizations of Clement of Alexandria, Origen, Lucian of Antioch, Methodius of Olympus, Eustathius of Antioch, Cyril of Jerusalem, Didodore of Tarsus, Theodore of Mopsuestia, John Chrysostom, Theodoret of Cyrrhus, Basil of Caesarea, Gregory of Nyssa, Gregory of Nazianzus, Hippolytus of Rome, Tertullian, Hilary of Poitiers, Ambrose, Ambrosiaster, Jerome, Augustine, and assorted Gnostics.[46] It is difficult to see how Eusebius escaped this patristic dragnet. His absence in the relevant section of *The Cambridge History of the Bible* is easier to justify, since the editors granted separate chapters only to Origen, Theodore of Mopsuestia, Jerome, and Augustine, an élite company to which Eusebius cannot claim to belong.[47]

There are several reasons why Eusebius' exegesis has not been studied more closely. Patristic exegesis in general has rarely been the first item on the scholarly agenda, despite recognition of the central role of the Bible in early Christian life and thought. Exegetical methods largely regarded as superseded by modern historico-critical scholarship account for part of the neglect. An often tedious and

[44] D. Barthélemy, 'Eusèbe, la septante, et "les autres"', in André Benoit (ed.), *La Bible et les pères* (Paris, 1971), 51–65.

[45] F. E. Cranz, 'Kingdom and Polity in Eusebius of Caesarea', *HTR* 45 (1952), 47–66. Other articles on Eusebius' exegesis which turned up in bibliographical searches but did not contribute to the present study: T. D. Barnes, 'Origen, Aquila and Eusebius', *Harvard Studies in Classical Philology*, 74 (1970), 313–16; C. Curti, 'L'interpretazione di Ps. 67, 14 in Eusebio di Caesarea', in *Paradoxos Politeia: Studi patristici in onore di Giuseppe Lazzati* (Milano, 1979), 195–207; id., 'Il linguaggio relativo al Padre e al Figlio in alcuni passi dei Commentarii in Psalmos di Eusebio di Cesarea', *Augustinianum*, 13 (1973), 483–506; M.-J. Rondeau, 'Une nouvelle preuve de l'influence littéraire d'Eusèbe de Césarée sur Athanase: L'interprétation des psaumes', *Recherches de science religieuse* (hereafter *RSR*), 56 (1968), 385–434.

[46] 'Exegese, christliche', in Theodor Klauser et al. (eds.), *RAC*, vi. 1217–29.

[47] P. R. Ackroyd and C. F. Evans (eds.), *The Cambridge History of the Bible*, i: *From the Beginnings to Jerome* (Cambridge, 1970).

diffuse style and the lack of critical texts may also be factors.[48] In Eusebius' case the situation was made worse, as noted, by the powerful appeal of the historical and panegyrical works at the expense of the rest, exegesis included. The condition of the texts was also discouraging, especially for his most substantial works, the commentaries on Psalms and Isaiah. Finally, it may have been assumed that Eusebius' commentaries were mostly derived from Origen. Perhaps the author of the *RAC* article ignored Eusebius because he was thought to be merely an Origenist epigone. However, a close comparison of what remains of Origen's exegesis of Isaiah shows that despite his use of Origen Eusebius remained very much his own man. The second problem has been partially resolved with the publication of the Isaiah commentary, though a critical edition of the Psalms commentary is still wanting.

2. Purposes of the Present Study

Eusebius' *Commentary on Isaiah* is the oldest extant Christian commentary on Isaiah, a central biblical text for Christianity's definition of its relationship with Judaism. Along with the *Commentary on the Psalms* it is the most considerable exegetical achievement of a major Christian writer. Since it was written in the immediate wake of the Council of Nicaea, it is a valuable witness to Eusebius' thinking at a critical time in his career and the life of the church. Lastly, it has only recently been made available for research in a form close to its original condition. There is thus solid justification for the present study, which fills a gap in research on Eusebius by fitting the *Commentary on Isaiah* into its contemporary context. Not much has been done since the publication of the critical edition, aside from the appraisals of Barnes and des Places.[49] My research reaches conclusions similar to Barnes' as to the broadly historical character of Eusebius' exegesis. Barnes' general approach, which de-emphasizes Eusebius' direct political involvement with Constantine and sees him first and foremost as a scholar and a bishop, supports the picture

---

[48] See Rondeau's comments on the slowness of patristic exegesis to win its place in the sun, in her *Les commentaires patristiques*, i. 9 ff.

[49] See also J. van Cangh, 'Nouveaux fragments hexaplaires: *Commentaire sur Isaie* d'Eusèbe de Césarée', *RB* 78 (1971), 384–90.

of Eusebius which I have found reflected in the pages of the *Commentary on Isaiah*.[50]

Two distinct but complementary purposes have guided the research and the composition of the present study: to describe and analyse the interpretive techniques and controlling themes of Eusebius' exegesis of Isaiah, and to place the commentary in relation to his thought as a whole and to its contemporary religious and political setting. The present study is thus a contribution to the history of exegesis, with special attention to subjects such as Christian apologetics against the Jews, Eusebius' concept of the church, his view of the relation between the church and the empire, and his eschatology. As a study in the history of exegesis, it offers a detailed portrait of Eusebius' engagement with the text of Isaiah. The *Commentary on Psalms* has not been brought under scrutiny nor have the other works of biblical scholarship, because of the lack of critical editions and the need to keep the investigation within reasonable limits.

I was particularly concerned to answer the following questions about Eusebius' exegesis: First, what interpretive methods did he use to exegete Isaiah? (Ch. III) As a protégé of Origen, he is widely regarded as a member of the Alexandrian school.[51] Yet commentators have also noted the prominence of literal and historical interpretation in his exegesis.[52] Second, what does Eusebius owe to his predecessors and what can be claimed as his own contribution? (Ch. II, sect. 3) The focus here is on Justin's *Dialogue with Trypho* as a representative of traditional apologetic exegesis of Isaiah, and on Origen's works, principally the Isaian homilies, the *Homilies on Jeremiah*, *Against Celsus*, and *On First Principles*.

Had space permitted, it would have been interesting to trace the influence of Eusebius' commentary on his successors. I limit myself to remarks on Jerome's use of Eusebius, which is more extensive than he acknowledges. Jerome claims that apart from Victorinus of Pettau the knowledge of Isaiah in the West was marked by a *grande silentium* when he began his task. Through his mediation Eusebius exercised a significant impact on Latin exegesis. Eusebius' influence

---

[50] Barnes, *Constantine and Eusebius, passim* and esp. at 265 f.

[51] Quasten, *Patrology*, iii. 337.

[52] Wallace-Hadrill, *Eusebius of Caesarea*, 83–7; Carmel Sant, 'Interpretatio Veteris Testamenti', 84–6; F. Young, *From Nicaea to Chalcedon*, 22.

in the East is real but not precisely defined. Greek patristic writers who are known to have written commentaries on all or part of Isaiah are Didymus the Blind (on Isa. 40–66), Cyril of Alexandria (a complete commentary), Pseudo-Basil of Caesarea (Isa. 1–16), Apollinaris of Laodicea, Theodore of Mopsuestia, John Chrysostom (a complete commentary plus homilies), Hesychius of Jerusalem (glosses on Isaiah), and Theodoret of Cyrrhus (a complete commentary).[53] Ziegler has demonstrated Theodoret's use of Eusebius, as well as Procopius of Gaza's strong dependence on him.[54]

The second purpose of this book is to place the commentary in Eusebius' thought as a whole and in its contemporary religious and political setting. (Ch. II) At first sight this did not seem a promising task, despite the dramatic events at the time of the commentary's composition in the wake of Nicaea and the unification of the Roman Empire under a Christian emperor. There is no mention of the Arian controversy in the commentary. Nor is there much in the way of direct references to specific persons and events, although the buoyant optimism of the Constantinian settlement is unmistakable.

An important discovery was Eusebius' habit of referring to the church as 'the godly polity' (*to theosebes politeuma*) and 'the city of God'. These phrases recalled Peterson's monograph on the political theology of monotheism, in which Eusebius enjoys a prominent role as the paradigm of a Christian political theologian, and prompted the question of the significance of applying 'political' terminology to the church. Eusebius is better known for skewing the language of church and state in the other direction, by investing the empire and

[53] Nothing remains of the commentaries of Didymus and Apollinaris (Quasten, *Patrology*, iii. 91, 377), both of whom Jerome mentions in the prologue to his *Commentary on Isaiah*, and only two catenae fragments of Theodore's (ibid. 406). Theodoret's commentary was only discovered in 1899 and then edited by A. Möhle, *Theodoret von Cyrus, Kommentar zu Jesaia* (Berlin, 1932). Annotated edition and French translation by J.-N. Guinot, *Théodoret de Cyr, Commentaire sur Isaie* (SC, 276, 295, 315; Paris, 1980–4). For Cyril's commentary *PG* lxx. 9–1450. The commentary of Hesychius of Jerusalem was rediscovered in 1900 in the form of 2,680 glosses; see M. Faulhaber, *Hesychii Hierosolymitani interpretatio Isaiae prophetae* (Freiburg, 1900). Chrysostom's was discovered in modern times in Armenian translation (Quasten, *Patrology*, iii. 436); six homilies are also extant (*PG* lvi. 97–142). For the commentary on Isa. 1–16 wrongly attributed to Basil of Caesarea (Quasten, *Patrology*, iii. 218 f.), see *PG* xxx. 118–668. On patristic study of Isaiah see now Roger Gryson and Dominique Szmatula, 'Les commentaires patristiques sur Isaïe d'Origène à Jérôme', *Revue des Études Augustiniennes*, 35 (1990), 3–41.

[54] J. Ziegler (ed.), *Jesajakommentar*, ix of *Eusebius' Werke* (hereafter abbreviated *CI*; all references are to the page and line number of this edition) (GCS; Berlin, 1975), pp. xlv–xlvii, xlix.

its ruler with sacred and even eschatological prerogatives. Inspection of the commentary revealed a persistent interest in the institutional church as the central object of Isaiah's prophecies. The church's character as the godly polity thus became the organizing principle for this book. A lexical analysis establishes that Eusebius used *politeuma*, and to a lesser degree *politeia*, to evoke political and civic associations which had become diluted in the imperial period. (Ch. IV) The description of Israel as a godly polity raised the question of the place of Judaism and of Jewish exegesis in the commentary. (Ch. V) Alongside a predictable element of anti-Jewish apologetics, Eusebius showed a willingness to grant validity to Jewish institutions and history and to confine many of Isaiah's prophecies to an Old Testament fulfilment. His treatment of Judaism is explained in terms of the new circumstances created by a Christian emperor.

The last chapter (Ch. VI) explains how Eusebius invested the institutional church, the contemporary embodiment of the godly polity, with the authority of biblical prophecy. In text after text he finds the present structure and situation of the church anticipated literally by Isaiah's prophecies. In certain eschatological and messianic passages the Christian episcopacy displaces the person of Christ himself, to whom the passages were traditionally referred. Since Eusebius had dedicated his life to the church's service as a bishop and a scholar-apologist, his enthusiasm for its triumph is not surprising. But what is the political implication of investing the church and its leadership with eschatological significance? The *Commentary on Isaiah* shows none of the extravagant adulation of Constantine found in the panegyrical literature Eusebius wrote just a few years later. Constantine himself is never named. This study argues that the religio-political perspective of the commentary reflects Eusebius' real priorities better than *The Life of Constantine* and the *Tricennial Oration*, at least if these are read, as they frequently have been, in near isolation from his other works.

3. The New Edition of the *Commentary on Isaiah*

The *Commentary on Isaiah* has traditionally been known only in partial form on the basis of medieval catenae. In 1706 the great Benedictine scholar Bernard Montfaucon edited the remains he found in four Parisian MSS in the series *Collectio nova Patrum et*

Scriptorum Graecorum.[55] This edition, with Montfaucon's preface and translation, was reprinted by Migne.[56] In 1933 R. Devreesse identified elements in the edition wrongly attributed to Eusebius that actually belonged to Basil of Caesarea, Cyril of Alexandria, Theodoret of Cyrrhus, and Theodore of Heraclea, as well as genuine scholia from other sources which Montfaucon had overlooked.[57] The following year A. Möhle, who was doing research for the Isaiah volume of the Göttingen Septuagint, announced that the nearly complete commentary had been discovered in the margin of a Florentine biblical codex.[58] It had escaped identification because the cataloguers failed to recognize that the marginal scholia were not a catena of several authors but only of one. Möhle was able to establish its authorship easily by comparison with the fragments of the commentary which Montfaucon had published. The new material doubled what had previously been available.

When Möhle left the Göttingen Septuagint Project, Joseph Ziegler inherited the task of editing both the commentary and the Isaiah volume. He put the discovery to immediate use in his 1939 edition of Isaiah, by printing the commentary's rich citations of the versions of Aquila, Symmachus, and Theodotion in a separate hexaplaric apparatus.[59] The commentary itself did not appear until 1975, when Ziegler published it as number nine in the Griechische Christliche Schriftsteller edition of Eusebius' works.[60]

The eleventh-century MS (Florentine Codex Laur. 11.4, 'F' in Ziegler's sigla) covers almost all of Isaiah, except for places where it had deteriorated so that it could not be deciphered at all or only with great difficulty.[61] At two places short lacunae in the text could not be corrected by other scholia from the catenae.[62] At two other places

[55] Bernardus Montfaucon, *Eusebiou Tou Pamphilou Hypomnemata Eis Ton Esaian, Eusebii Pamphili Commentaria in Hesaiam,* in *Collectio nova Patrum et Scriptorum Graecorum II* (Parisiis, 1706), 347–593, based on Paris MSS 155, 156, 157, and 159; see Ziegler's discussion of Montfaucon's edition and of the manuscripts in *Jesajakommentar,* pp. x–xvii.

[56] *PG* xxiv. 77–526.

[57] R. Devreesse, 'L'édition du Commentaire d'Eusèbe de Césarée sur Isaïe: Interpolations et omissions', *RB* 42 (1933), 540–55.

[58] A. Möhle, 'Der Jesaiakommentar des Eusebius von Kaisareia fast vollständig wieder aufgefunden', *ZNW* 33 (1934), 87–9.

[59] Joseph Ziegler (ed.), *Isaias,* xiv of *Septuaginta: Vetus Testamentum Graece* (Göttingen, 1939; 2nd edn., 1967).

[60] See full citation in n. 58.

[61] For what follows see *Jesajakommentar,* pp. xviii ff.

[62] Indicated by dots in the edition at *CI* 56. 33 and 289. 10.

the text of Eusebius is interrupted by intruded fragments: at Isa. 14: 28–32, from Theodoret's *Commentary on Isaiah*, and at Isa. 51: 6 by scholia from the John Catena on Isaiah, taken originally from Theodoret, Cyril of Alexandria, and Severus of Antioch.[63] Ziegler concluded that these interpolations show that F is not the complete commentary of Eusebius but the work as it was reconstituted by an unknown copyist, who inadvertently copied these scholia from other authors along with Eusebius' authentic material.[64] Furthermore, at numerous places in F the scholia are preceded by the lemma *ek tou autou* (sc. *Eusebeiou Kaisareias*), which the copyist often retained from his sources, although Eusebius' actual name is not cited, because he wanted to offer the appearance of a continuous text.[65]

Besides its addition of totally new material, F is valuable because it draws on older and richer sources than the catena tradition which Montfaucon used.[66] According to Ziegler's analysis, based on his own examination of three Roman MSS and the catena catalogue of Michael Faulhaber,[67] the ultimate source of many of the Eusebian scholia edited by Montfaucon is the massive catena on the sixteen prophets compiled by a certain John Drungarios in the second half of the seventh or the eighth century (the 'John' Catena, siglum 'C' in Ziegler's edition). The Isaiah catena of John contains over 4,000 scholia from Cyril of Alexandria, Theodoret, Basil of Caesarea, and Eusebius, who is the source of about one fourth of the scholia. For his edition of F, Ziegler collated the Roman MSS which Faulhaber identified as direct descendants of the John Catena, and marked them with brackets in the printed text. Where C and F agree, the printed text is marked with upper half brackets, and where the C scholia are independent of F they are printed with lower half brackets. Passages unmarked by brackets represent wholly new material from F. Ziegler's introduction may be consulted for detailed discussion of the manuscript evidence.

The manuscript has no title. It begins with a brief but valuable preface on the interpretation of prophetic utterances. The commentary which follows is divided into 158 paragraphs, with no

---

[63] Ibid. 323. 11.
[64] Ibid., p. xxi.
[65] Ibid.
[66] Ibid., p. xix.
[67] M. Faulhaber, *Die Propheten-Catenen nach römischen Handschriften*, iv, pts. 2 and 3 of *Biblische Studien* (Freiburg, 1899).

indication of the book divisions that must have marked the original.
Jerome credits Eusebius with a commentary on Isaiah in ten books,
but in his own commentary on Isaiah he says that the work was
composed of fifteen books.[68] Of the two perhaps the latter figure is
preferable, since Jerome used Eusebius' commentary on Isaiah as a
source when he wrote his own, and was not likely to be wrong with
the book before him. The biblical lemmata which once must have
preceded the scholia have disappeared, although Eusebius' biblical
text can be largely reconstructed thanks to the extensive quotations
which adorn his commentary. It belongs to the hexaplaric recension
of the Septuagint. The biblical text printed in Migne does not belong
to the original commentary but is taken from the official Roman
Sixtine edition.

[68] Jerome, *De viris illustribus* and *In Isaiam* Prologue, cited in Ziegler (ed.),
Jesajakommentar, p. ix.

II

Setting and Character of
the Commentary on Isaiah

This chapter discusses various aspects of the *Commentary on Isaiah* which are preliminary to understanding its significance in Eusebius' works as a whole. It will consider the commentary's date, setting and purpose, relation to previous Christian interpretation of Isaiah, relation to Eusebius' exegesis of Isaiah in his earlier works, and leading theological ideas. Exegetical methods will be treated in the next chapter.

1. The Date of the *Commentary on Isaiah*

Standard authorities set the commentary around the time of the Council of Nicaea (325).[1] Since no precisely datable events are mentioned, estimates must be based on references to Eusebius' other works, on passing allusions to contemporary historical developments, and on general theological and apologetic tenor.

The commentary contains references to the *Chronicle* and the *Onomasticon*, and, indirectly, to the *Martyrs of Palestine*. The first is of little use because the *Chronicle* is one of Eusebius' earliest books.[2] The third consists of a probable allusion to an interrogation which

---

[1] After 323, according to Eduard Schwartz, *RE* vi. 1437; considerably after 324, according to Wallace-Hadrill, *Eusebius of Caesarea*, 57; between 323 and 325, according to J.-M. van Cangh, 'Nouveaux fragments hexaplaires', *RB* 78 (1971), 384–90; 'at work on the commentary around 330', according to Barnes, *Eusebius and Constantine*, 278; 'in der definitiven Friedenszeit', according to Harnack, *Geschichte der altchristlichen Literatur*, ii, pt. 2, 123. J.-R. Laurin, *Orientations maîtresses des apologistes chrétiens de 270 à 361* (Rome, 1954), 97 n. 21, proposed a date during the Great Persecution, between the *Chronicle* and the *Prophetic Selections*, which is implausible in view of the commentary's numerous testimonies to a close association of church and empire.

[2] *CI* 99. 30. The *Chronicle* was certainly finished before 311 because it is cited in another early work, the *Prophetic Eclogues*, cf. *Eclogae propheticae* 1.1.27 ff. (henceforth *EP*), ed. T. Gaisford (Oxford, 1842). On the date of the *Chronicle*, see

Eusebius witnessed during the Great Persecution on 16 February 310, and which he first recounted in the *Martyrs of Palestine*.[3] Since all authorities recognize it as pre-Nicene, it too can do little to specify the date of the *Commentary on Isaiah*.[4]

The second reference may be more helpful. Commenting on Isa. 18: 2, Eusebius says that the 'rivers of the land' (sc. Egypt) must be interpreted allegorically rather than as actual rivers in Egypt, 'about which we have written in the *Topoi*'.[5] As Ziegler noted, this must refer to the *Onomasticon*, whose title in the manuscripts is *Peri tôn topikôn onomatôn tôn en têi theiai graphêi*, and whose preface says that it is provided 'with commentaries on the places'.[6] Wallace-Hadrill proposed a date of composition between 326 and 330, on the basis of Eusebius' silence about Constantine's ecclesiastical foundations in Palestine and the death, about 331, of Paulinus of Tyre, to whom the work is dedicated.[7] This would probably push the date of the *Commentary on Isaiah* into the decade of the 330s. However, Barnes has dated Paulinus' death to 327, thus lowering the *terminus ante quem* of the *Onomasticon* by four years.[8] This would also lower the *terminus post quem* of the commentary and enable a date that much closer to the Council of Nicaea.[9] Like the *Onomasticon*, the commentary says nothing about Constantine's ecclesiastical founda-

Wallace-Hadrill, *Eusebius of Caesarea*, 43; Schwartz, *RE* vi. 1376; Quasten, *Patrology*, iii. 312; and Barnes, *Constantine and Eusebius*, who dates the work at least a decade before 303 (p. 113).

[3] The incident involved Christians who claimed the names of biblical prophets during a trial before the governor of Palestine. Cf. *CI* 283. 28–33 and *Mart. Pal.* 11. 5–13.

[4] See Wallace-Hadrill, *Eusebius of Caesarea*, 39–42; Barnes, *Constantine and Eusebius*, 148–50; Schwartz, *RE* vi. 1407 f.

[5] *CI* 128. 1.

[6] *Meta paratheseôs tôn eis tous topous hypomnêmatôn*, Onomasticon, ed. E. Klostermann, iii, pt. 1 of *Eusebius' Werke* 2. 11–12.

[7] *Eusebius of Caesarea*, 55–6. But see below for Barnes' revisionist dating.

[8] Barnes, building on a case made by Henry Chadwick, 'The Fall of Eustathius of Antioch', *JTS* 49 (1948), 27–35, dates the deposition of Eustathius of Antioch in 327, thus advancing Paulinus' death by about four years, on the authority of Philostorgius (*Historia ecclesiastica*, 3. 15, ed. Bidez), who says Paulinus died six months after the deposition of Eustathius (cf. *Constantine and Eusebius*, 228 and 385 n. 29).

[9] Like the *Onomasticon*, the commentary says nothing about Constantine's ecclesiastical foundations in Palestine, though Eusebius had ample motive and opportunity to introduce them had he wished. This could point to a date not much before 330, on analogy with the same use of the argument from silence as Wallace-Hadrill made regarding the *Onomasticon*.

tions in Palestine.[10] Eusebius' omission is consistent with a date sometime before 330, rather than in the following decade. On the other hand, the value of the *Onomasticon* for dating the *Commentary on Isaiah* depends on whether it is, as most scholars believe, a late work of Eusebius'. That consensus has been challenged by Barnes, who argues that the *Onomasticon* is actually one of Eusebius' earliest works. If he is correct, its usefulness drops considerably.[11]

The commentary reflects a degree of imperial adherence to Christianity which seems unlikely in the East before the defeat of Licinius in 324. Eusebius' discussion of Isa. 60: 3–4 may refer to imperial baptisms, but the reference is too vague to be useful.[12] Isa. 49: 23 ('And kings will be your foster-fathers, and queens your nurse-maids; on the face of the earth they will pay you homage and will lick the dust from your feet') inspired him to draw this vignette of a pious and dutiful Christian magistracy:

Which very thing we have seen fulfilled with our own eyes, literally when in the manner of 'foster fathers' those who hold supreme power bear up the church of God, and their governors, namely the 'principalities and powers' over each nation and province serve the supreme rule in the manner of 'nursemaids', supporting the poor of the church at the imperial command by providing a grain distribution [*sitêresia*] to them. Upon seeing with his own eyes the aforesaid 'rulers and powers' genuflecting in the church of God and resting their brows upon the ground, who would not admit that the prophecy which says, 'on the face of the earth they will pay you homage and will lick the dust from your feet', has not received its fulfilment literally and historically?[13]

This grain ration must refer to the distribution reported by Theodoret, who says in his *Church History* that Constantine issued

---

[10] According to W. Telfer, 'Constantine's Holy Land Plan', *SP* 1 (TU, 63; Berlin, 1957), 697–700, the building programme was an important part of Constantine's vision of a unified Christendom. On the broader development of a Christian 'holy land', see E. D. Hunt, *Holy Land Pilgrimage in the Later Roman Empire, 312–460* (Oxford, 1982). Walker, *Holy City, Holy Places?*, argues that Eusebius had serious theological and church-political reservations about the idea of a Christian 'holy land'.

[11] Barnes, *Constantine and Eusebius*, 110f. See also his 'The Composition of Eusebius' *Onomasticon*', *JTS*, NS, 26 (1975), 412–15. Barnes' re-dating to the 290s is contested in a recent article by Andrew Louth, 'The Date of Eusebius' *Historia Ecclesiastica*', *JTS* 41 (1990), 111–23 (at 118–20).

[12] *CI* 371. 4–8.

[13] Ibid. 316. 9–22. Also see 84. 8–11.

a general instruction to all provincial governors to divide annual grants in each city for the support of virgins, widows, and the clergy.[14] Unfortunately, we have no idea when it began.[15]

The grain ration is mentioned a second time in connection with Isa. 60: 16 ('And you will suck the milk of the nations, and you will eat the wealth of kings . . .'). The wealth of kings is not allegorical. 'Who could look at the grants of grain (*sitodosiai*) given to the church of God by those in power, and gifts to her, and rich dedications offered up, and would not say unambiguously that these very things make credible in a literal sense (*pros lexin*) all that has been said?'[16] The 'gifts and dedications' probably refer not to Constantine's ambitious church construction pro-gramme in Palestine and elsewhere, which Eusebius was to praise in the *Life of Constantine*,[17] but to the emperor's general munificence to the church, such as he had already memorialized in the *Church History* and had experienced personally at the Council of Nicaea.[18]

The prophecy of the destruction of the idols in Isa. 2: 18–21 was fulfilled 'in part' (*ek merous*) by the preaching of the Gospel after the Incarnation, but is especially relevant now (*kath' hēmas*), when the idols' helplessness to protect themselves is revealed by their con-fiscation by imperial agents for the sake of the precious materials from which they are made.[19] This must refer to the commission appointed by Constantine to collect precious metals from pagan shrines and cult objects, which Eusebius mentions twice in his later works on Constantine.[20] Unfortunately, this policy too cannot be dated precisely. Barnes suggested not long after 324, which would be consistent with other indications of an immediately post-Nicene dating of the commentary.[21]

[14] Theodoret calls this subsidy *etēsia sitēresia*: *HE* 1. 11. 2, ed. L. Parmentier and F. Scheidweiler (2nd edn., GCS, no. 44; Berlin, 1954), 47. 2.

[15] Also mentioned by Eusebius in *VC* 4. 28. Probably this is the same subsidy mentioned by Athanasius, *Apol. c. Ar.* 18 (*PG* xxv. 277B), and later by Socrates, *Eccl. hist.* 2. 17 (*PG* lxvii. 217C).

[16] *CI* 376. 36–377. 3.

[17] *VC* 3. 25–51. Also *De laudibus Constantini*, 9. 12–19 (hereafter *LC*, cited accord-ing to the edition of I. A. Heikel, *Tricennatsrede an Constantin*, i of *Eusebius' Werke* (GCS, no. 7; Leipzig, 1902)), 195–295.

[18] Eusebius, *HE* 10. 6; *VC* 1. 42. 2 and 3. 15–16.

[19] *CI* 20. 29–21. 5.

[20] *LC* 8. 1–4, later repeated in *VC* 3. 54.

[21] Barnes, *Constantine and Eusebius*, 247.

Eusebius' exegesis of the messianic peace in Isa. 2: 2–4 also points to a date after 325. He identifies 'the clearest sign' of the time of fulfilment of this prophecy in the establishment of the universal peace of the Pax Romana at the time of the birth of Christ.[22] The correlation of Augustus' subjection of warring cities and nationalities ('polyarchy') with the coming of Christ is a staple feature of Eusebius' political theology.[23] There is no explicit reference to Constantine's repetition and reinforcement of the achievement of Augustus. But the emphasis on personal witness (*ophthalmois horômen*) would seem out of place during the years of tension between Constantine and Licinius preceding the outbreak of war in 324. Also, the reference to 'concord and peace' (*homonoein kai eirêneuein*) seems to echo the Constantinian slogan of peace and harmony so prominent in the emperor's letters, especially at the time of Nicaea and its aftermath.[24] Since Eusebius ardently supported the emperor's campaign for peace and harmony, it is natural to assume that the interpretation of Isa. 2: 2–4 envisaged the Constantinian as well as the Augustan peace.[25]

The general apologetic and theological tenor of the commentary also point to the period right after Nicaea. Eusebius' occasional allusions to persecution do not reveal any sense of urgency or immediacy.[26] A possible exception is Eusebius' interpretation of Isa. 51: 9–16 as a prophecy of consolation in time of persecution. He asks God to intervene 'in our time' (*kath' hêmas oikonomêson*), just as he

---

[22] *CI* 14. 32–15. 13.

[23] Among many passages, see *LC* 16. 7; see further Ch. VI.4.

[24] Examples: *homonoia*, as early as 314, in Constantine's letter of convocation of the council of Arles (*HE* 10. 5. 24); also *homopsychia*, *homopsychos*, and *homophrôn* in the same letter (ibid. 10. 5. 22, 24); several times in the letter to Bishop Alexander and Arius (*VC* 2. 65, 66, 72); and in *LC* 16. 7. Further citations in *A Patristic Greek Lexicon* (hereafter *PGL*), ed. G. W. H. Lampe (Oxford, 1968), s.v.; note esp. *eirênê kai homonoia*, in Constantine's address to the council of Nicaea (*VC* 3. 12) and in his letter to Alexander preserved in Gelasius of Cyzicus, *Hist. eccl.*, 3. 15. 5.

[25] Note how in the *Life of Constantine* Eusebius characterizes Constantine's correspondence to the bishops after Nicaea as expressing the emperor's satisfaction at the re-establishment of peace and harmony (*eirênê kai homonoia*) in the church—obliquely alluding to himself as the one who had restored peace in the troubled church at Antioch after the deposition of Bishop Eustathius of Antioch! (*VC* 3. 59).

[26] Cf. *CI* 181. 23–182. 10; 203. 17–204. 5; 257. 30–258. 4; 277. 12–18; 283. 16–36; 317. 23–7; 333. 26–334. 27; 376. 6–18. One passage appears to refer to Galerius' recantation (*palinôdia*) in the spring of 311 (ibid. 334. 5–8), and follows closely the language of the decree of toleration preserved in *HE* 8. 17. 9.

did against the tyrants of old in the destruction of Pharaoh.[27] The present and future tenses may only be an attempt to make the exegesis more vivid. Besides, Eusebius' counsel of sympathy for the lapsed appears too generalized to refer to immediate events. Commenting on Isa. 51: 12 ('I, I am He that comforts you . . .'), he writes that the prophet's invocation of divine consolation is addressed to those who succumb out of fear and weakness in persecution.

He says these things as though to the more fearful and the weaker ones in the church. For the perfect ones and those who were decorated with the crown of martyrdom obtained a share of his glory. But since 'all are one body', [cf. 1 Cor. 12: 13] and 'when one limb suffers, all the limbs suffer together', he properly offers consolation and healing to the more fearful ones, the weaker, who limp a little in time of persecutions [*tois . . . kata kairon tôn diôgmôn hyposkazousi*], and summons them to repentance.[28]

The summons to unity expresses an important motif, especially Eusebius' conscious binding of the two ranks, the perfect and the weaker ones, in the one body of the church.[29] Eusebius certainly is thinking of the deep tensions in the church during and after the persecution, both in Africa and Egypt.

A second important indication of the date of the commentary is its careful avoidance of subordinationist theological terminology. This is a radical change from Eusebius' language in works written just prior to the Council of Nicaea. *The Proof of the Gospel*, completed some time before Nicaea, spoke frequently of the Logos as a secondary deity.[30] His theological caution in the commentary reflects the ecclesiastical situation immediately after the Council of Nicaea.

Eusebius had attended the council under provisional excommunication at the regional synod convened at Antioch in 324/5.[31] Suppressing his discomfort over the introduction of the terms *homoousios tôi patri* and *ek tês ousias tou patros* into the conciliar

---

[27] Cf. CI 324. 23–4. He was fascinated with the parallel between the Exodus story and the end of persecution; see *HE* 9. 9. 5–8 (= *VC* 1. 38), and my discussion in 'Myth and History in Eusebius' *De vita Constantini: Vit. Const.* 1. 12 in its Contemporary Setting', *HTR* 82 (1989), 421–45.

[28] *CI* 325. 4–9.

[29] Cf. Eusebius *DE* 1. 8 and discussion of this theme in Chs. V and VI.

[30] Eusebius *DE* 4. 5. 3 (159. 7), 4. 7. 2 (160. 32); 5. Proem. 20, 23 (206. 10, 38; 207. 4); 5. 6. 7 (230. 4). Also cf. *HE* 1. 2. 3, 5, 9, and *PE* 11. 14–19, which is devoted to demonstrating the agreement between Hebrew and Greek (middle Platonic) thought on the Second Cause.

[31] For the following I rely on the narrative of Barnes, *Constantine and Eusebius*, chs. 12 and 13.

creed, he assented to the council's decrees and won reinstatement to the episcopacy.[32] The Council of Nicaea sat in June and July of 325. Despite Constantine's fond hopes, it failed to end the Arian controversy. Three months after the council, two supporters of Arius, Eusebius of Nicomedia and Theognis of Nicaea, were excommunicated for refusing to sign the anathemas appended to the Nicene creed. This dissent marked the beginning of bitter strife in the church, as contending parties conspired to advance their candidates in the episcopal sees of the East and to block the careers of their opponents. Those who regarded the Nicene formulations as tending to Sabellianism and hence as a threat to the Eastern theology of the distinct divine hypostases, mounted a counter-offensive which succeeded two years later in deposing Bishop Eustathius of Antioch at a synod in that city. Eusebius, whose theology had been criticized by Eustathius, presided at the synod and was a favourite candidate to become the new bishop of Antioch. For reasons unknown, he refused.[33] At a second session of the council of Nicaea, apparently summoned by Constantine at the end of 327, Arius was readmitted and the excommunications of Eusebius of Nicomedia and Theognis of Nicaea were lifted.[34] By the end of Constantine's reign in 337, the Arian party was in the ascendancy everywhere in the East.

The *Commentary on Isaiah* fits well the period between the first and second sessions of Nicaea (325–7), the most plausible context for Eusebius' reticence on the Arian controversy. To address so divisive an issue in a work designed to celebrate the triumph of the church would have been inept apologetics and, in light of Eusebius' precarious position in 325, perhaps dangerous as well. The *Commentary on Isaiah* completely ignores heresy in the church. It divides the world into those who are members of the godly polity and those who are not—that is, according to belief and unbelief, not orthodoxy and heresy. The only occurrence of *hairesis* in the text is actually an allusion to Acts 28: 21 put into the mouths of Jewish opponents of Christianity.[35] Accusations of heresy, Eusebius implies, are a Jewish

---

[32] See Eusebius' letter to the church of Caesarea, in which he explains his assent (Socrates, *HE* 1. 8), and the discussion in J. N. D. Kelly, *Early Christian Creeds* (2nd edn., London, 1960), 220–6.

[33] See Eusebius' recounting of this with pertinent documentation, in *VC* 3. 59–62.

[34] On the disputed question of whether Constantine reconvened the bishops at Nicaea two years after the original council, see the discussion in R. P. C. Hanson, *The Search for the Christian Doctrine of God* (Edinburgh, 1991), 174–8.

[35] *CI* 119. 6–20.

technique, not a Christian one. A comparison may be made with his willingness to lash out at Marcellus of Ancyra, an extreme advocate of Nicaea, in the years just before Constantine's death, when Eusebius and his party were in a much more secure position (*c.335/6*).

The *Commentary on Isaiah* therefore belongs to the period of Constantine's sole rule in the empire, because the imperial policies it alludes to and reflects only came into being in the East after the defeat of Licinius. A further limitation to 325–8 is probable on the grounds both of Eusebius' avoidance of subordinationist theology and of his silence about the Constantinian foundations in Palestine.

2. The Purposes of the *Commentary on Isaiah*

The New Political Situation: A Christian Emperor

Why did Eusebius choose to write a substantial commentary on the longest book of the Bible soon after the Council of Nicaea? The half decade after Nicaea marked a relative hiatus in his activity as a writer, following the last edition of the *Church History* and preceding the dogmatic tracts and panegyrical literature on Constantine composed in his last years.[36] The best indication of the commentary's purpose is its dominant exegetical theme, what Eusebius calls 'the godly polity' (*to theosebes politeuma*)—its Jewish phase, its transferral to Christianity at the Incarnation, its propagation throughout the world and transition from persecution to patronage, and its final apotheosis in heaven. Eusebius is therefore mainly interested in the historical Christian church and in vindicating its claim to the book of Isaiah, over against the Jews.

The situation of the church after 325 was plainly cause for celebration, at least for someone with Eusebius' view of the relation of religion and culture. His thorough optimism about the compatibility of Christian church and Roman Empire had apparently been justified by the unification of the Roman Empire under an emperor who made no secret of his Christian sympathies.[37] In the West

[36] Excepting the *Onomasticon*, usually dated to this very period; cf. Wallace-Hadrill, *Eusebius of Caesarea*, 55–7, but note Barnes' proposed re-dating of that work to the beginning of Eusebius' career, before the end of the third century (see works cited in n. 11 *supra*).

[37] The most important recent examination of Constantine's policies and Eusebius' attitude to them is Barnes' *Constantine and Eusebius*, to which we have already

Constantine had patronized the church and its interests and values following the defeat of Maxentius in 312, with grants of money to bishops, clerical exemptions from compulsory public liturgies, the empowering of episcopal courts to hear cases on appeal from secular magistrates, legal observance of Sunday as a day of rest, and so on.[38] After the defeat of Licinius in 324, he pursued in the Eastern half of the empire a similar programme of church construction and donations to support the poor. He also took measures against paganism, including a general, if ineffective, proscription of sacrifices, the confiscation of temple treasure mentioned in the previous section,

referred. Barnes rightly emphasizes that Eusebius' basic conviction about the compatibility of church and empire reflects a common Christian opinion at the end of the third century, before the onset of the Diocletianic persecution, and cannot be explained solely as a response, whether sincere or opportunistic, to the career of Constantine (164). Nevertheless, Eusebius' post-persecution works reveal a more concrete and vivid hope for the present and future prospects of the church under a Christian emperor. See J. Sirinelli, *Les vues historiques d'Eusèbe de Césarée durant la période prénicéenne* (Dakar, 1961), ch. 10, esp. 393 f., for the case for an evolution in Eusebius' view of the relation of sacred and secular history. As stated in Ch. VI.4 of this study, scholarship has tended to see this heightened concreteness in relation to the Roman Empire. Hans Eger's 1939 article on Eusebius' theology of history, for example, expressed a widespread judgement that his late works on Constantine reveal a virtual sacralization of the emperor and his reign as the eschatological fulfilment of history; see Hans Eger, 'Kaiser und Kirche in der Geschichtstheologie des Eusebius von Cäsarea', *ZNW* 38 (1939), 97–115. The present study agrees with Barnes in seeing Eusebius' historical optimism as rooted in the peaceful expansion of the church in the late third century, but maintains that the situation after 324 led him to give a special prominence in his exegesis to the visible church (see Ch. VI.1–3).

Surveys of scholarship on Constantine's religious views and policies may be found in N. H. Baynes, *Constantine the Great and the Christian Church* (2nd edn., Oxford, 1972); Joseph Vogt, 'Die Constantinische Frage: Die Bekehrung Constantins', *Relazioni del X. Congresso Internazionale di Scienze Storiche*, 6 (Florence, 1955), 733–79, repr. in *Konstantin der Grosse*, ed. H. Kraft (Wege der Forschung, 131; Darmstadt, 1974), 345–87; and other surveys listed in K. Aland, 'Die religiöse Haltung Kaiser Konstantins', *SP* 1 (TU, 63; Berlin, 1957), 549 f. The present study agrees with the following authorities that Constantine after 312 believed that he was under the patronage of the Christian God: Barnes, *Constantine and Eusebius*; A. H. M. Jones, *Constantine and the Conversion of Europe* (London, 1949); H. Dörries, *Das Selbstzeugnis Kaiser Konstantins* (Göttingen, 1954); Aland, 'Die religiöse Haltung Kaiser Konstantins', 549–600; J. Straub, 'Konstantins Verzicht auf den Gang zum Kapitol', *Historia*, 4 (1957), 297–313, repr. in *Regeneratio Imperii: Aufsätze über Roms Kaisertum und Reich im Spiegel der heidnischen und christlichen Publizistik* (Darmstadt, 1972), 63–9, and id., 'Konstantins christliches Sendungsbewusstsein', *Das neue Bild der Antike*, 2 (Leipzig, 1942), 374–94, repr. in *Regeneratio Imperii*, 70–88. Lane Fox, *Pagans and Christians*, 609–66, also argues for Constantine's explicit Christianity ('the most tireless worker for Christian unity since St. Paul' (658)).

[38] Summary and citation of his policies between 312 and 324 in the West in Barnes, *Constantine and Eusebius*, 48–53.

and selective military action against pagan shrines whose licentious practices offended Christian sensibilities.[39]

From the time of his defeat of Maxentius, Constantine took an active interest in the internal affairs of the church, first in the West by his intervention in the Donatist schism, and then in the East by his summons of the Council of Nicaea, to deal with the Arian controversy.[40] The motives for this interest, so far as they can be determined from Constantine's own words, may be accepted as quite sincere.[41] Constantine shared with his age the conviction that divine powers loomed over the affairs of this world, and that their sponsorship was necessary for military and political success. His Christianity consisted in the first instance in the belief that the supreme god who had guided him to victory at the Milvian Bridge was the God of the Christians.[42] In a manner quite consistent with traditional Roman notions of religion and politics, Constantine believed that the welfare of the empire depended on securing and maintaining God's favourable will.[43] The main function of priesthood was the performance of the rites which expressed the worship

[39] For Constantine's religious policies after 324, see Barnes, *Constantine and Eusebius.* 245–50.

[40] Ibid. 56–61, 208–44.

[41] The priority of Constantine's own words, in his letters and edicts, as evidence of his religious beliefs is defended by Aland, 'Die religiöse Haltung Kaiser Konstantins', 567 f., whose article also reviews and compares the relative value of all the other evidence (coin issues, church construction, pagan and Christian panegyric, etc.). Dörries has carried out this approach through the emperor's own writings most exhaustively, in his monograph *Das Selbstzeugnis Kaiser Konstantins*, as does Heinz Kraft's more limited study *Kaiser Konstantins religiöse Entwicklung* (Beiträge zur historischen Theologie, 20; Tübingen, 1955). Few would now agree with Burckhardt's picture of Constantine as a Napoleonic opportunist in matters of religion, driven only by an insatiable lust for power (*The Age of Constantine the Great* (New York, 1967), 292). Even Eduard Schwartz recognized in the second edition of his study of Constantine that Burckhardt's portrait needed to be amended to account for 'genuinely irrational factors' in Constantine's religious motivation (*Kaiser Konstantin und die christliche Kirche* (2nd edn.; Leipzig, 1936), 66, cited in J. Straub, 'Konstantins christliches Sendungsbewusstsein', *Regeneratio Imperii*, 80.)

[42] Straub, 'Konstantins christliches Sendungsbewusstsein', 70–88, esp. 77–80, and Dörries, *Selbstzeugnis*, 241 ff.

[43] Dörries, *Selbstzeugnis*, 259–65. Compare the exactly similar views of the pagan Galerius in his toleration edict of 311 (Eus., *HE* 8. 17. 6–10) and the Christian Constantine just two years later in a letter to the proconsul of Africa (ibid. 10. 7. 1). For similar pagan testimonies, see Maximin's rescript to the citizens of Tyre (ibid. 9. 7. 3–12) and Celsus (Origen, *C. Cels.* 8. 66). Useful analysis of Roman state religion as a ritual quid pro quo between the gods and men in Hendrik Berkhof, *Kirche und Kaiser: Eine Untersuchung der Entstehung der byzantinischen und der theokratischen Staatsauffassung im vierten Jahrhundert* (Zürich, 1947), 14–27.

mankind owed to divinity. The reason why Constantine exempted Catholic clergy from the onerous duties of the municipal liturgies was to leave them unimpeded for divine services.[44] Among many sources which make this clear, I cite the following passage from his letter to the African vicar Aelafius, because it captures so well the theme of Constantine's divine election as the protector of the peace and cultic worship of the church.

Since I am informed that you too are a worshipper of the Highest God, I will confess to your gravity that I consider it absolutely contrary to the divine law that we should overlook such quarrels and contentions [i.e. the Donatist schism], whereby the Highest Divinity may perhaps be moved to wrath, not only against the human race, but also against me myself, to whose care He has, by His celestial will, committed the government of all earthly things, and that He may be so far moved as to take some untoward step. For I shall really and fully be able to feel secure and always to hope for prosperity and happiness from the ready kindness of the most mighty God, only when I see all venerating the most holy God in the proper cult of the catholic religion with harmonious brotherhood of worship.[45]

So high a view of the emperor's religious mission and of the church's imperial mission, guaranteed that Constantine would take a vigorous interest in the life of the church. He was not all inhibited by being just an unbaptized layman.[46] Constantine regarded his religious calling by God as a consecration for a divinely ordained role in the world analogous to that of the bishops in the church.[47] The much debated *locus classicus* is VC 4. 24, in which Eusebius reports that Constantine said, in the presence of himself and of other bishops, 'Whereas you are (bishops) of those inside the church, I am appointed by God a bishop of those outside (*tôn ektos*).' According to Straub's interpretation, Constantine's reference to *hoi ektos* means to embrace all of his subjects, the Christians as well as the pagans and

[44] Dörries, *Selbstzeugnis*, 289–95.

[45] *Letter to Aelafius*, 8, no. 6 in Kraft's collection of Constantinian documents. See his discussion in *Kaiser Konstantins religiöse Entwicklung*, 172–83, of the textual difficulties in this letter. According to Jones, whose translation I have followed, 'this passage is the key to Constantine's whole religious position'. *Constantine and the Conversion of Europe*, 97.

[46] On the baptism of Constantine, see H. Kraft, 'Zur Taufe Kaiser Konstantins', *SP* 1 (TU, 63; Berlin, 1957), 642–8.

[47] See the convincing articles on this subject by J. Straub, 'Kaiser Konstantin als *episkopos tôn ektos*', *Regeneratio Imperii*, 119–33, and id., 'Konstantin als *koinos episkopos*', *Dumbarton Oaks Papers*, 21 (1967), 37–55, repr. in *Regeneratio Imperii*, 134–58. Cf. also D. de Decker and G. Dupuis-Masay, ' "L'Épiscopat" de l'empereur Constantin', *Byzantion*, 50 (1980), 118–47.

heretics, in so far as their civil and religious well-being falls within his unique competence as the sole possessor of coercive power.[48] The assertion of the emperor's 'episcopal' oversight is fundamental to Eusebius' picture of the pious Christian emperor throughout Book 4 of the *Life of Constantine*.[49]

In view of the conflict between church and Christian emperor which broke out in the reign of Constantine's son Constantius II, one may wonder whether Constantine's Christian contemporaries were sensible of the contradiction of a layman—still unbaptized— performing patently clerical tasks such as convening and attending a council of bishops. Eusebius is commonly given a central respon- sibility for the ease with which the church accommodated itself to a Christian emperor. Nevertheless, it is doubtful that he (or Constantine) recognized all the consequences of investing the em- peror with a quasi-episcopal status. It would take Christians centu- ries to delegate competencies between Christian cleric and Christian magistrate in a legally Christian society. Eusebius' uncritical defer- ence to Constantine must be partially explained by the giddy effect of the turnabout since 312 on a man who by education and outlook naturally regarded the church's new access to power as a wondrous work of Providence.

Because of his role as Constantine's panegyrist and biographer, scholars have carefully studied the political implications and back- ground of his works. Part of the value of the *Commentary on Isaiah* is that it shows Eusebius in a rather different light than do the biography and the speeches, even though it too comes from the period of Constantine's sole rule.[50] The commentary's dominant theme is that the church is the godly polity (*to theosebes politeuma*), a phrase which never means simply 'behaviour' or 'way of life', but which always has a social and corporate meaning. Eusebius does not call the church a polity or, to cite a less common synonym, the city of God, as if he already had a clear vision of the future Byzantine partnership between church and state.[51] Rather he is thinking in the

---

[48] Straub, 'Konstantin als *episkopos tôn ektos*', 123–7.

[49] Ibid. 127–32, and id., 'Konstantin als *koinos episkopos*', 150–7.

[50] Straub's cautionary note that the panegyrical works must be read according to the rules of their literary genre is often overlooked. Cf. 'Kaiser Konstantin als *episkopos tôn ektos*', 125 n. 23. See the study of Gerald Vigna, *The Influence of Epideictic Rhetoric on Eusebius of Caesarea's Political Theology* (Ph.D. diss., North- western University, 1980).

[51] Among many such interpretations, see H.-G. Opitz, 'Eusebius von Caesarea als Theologe', *ZNW* 34 (1935), 19.

first instance as a bishop, as the leader of a visible and concrete ecclesiastical community whose moment has now come and whose historical progress, from its pre-Incarnational existence to its fulfil-ment in the *eschaton*, he believed the Hebrew prophets had foreseen. The focus is more ecclesiastical than imperial—on a church in an empire ruled by Christians, to be sure, but still on a church, not merely the religious arm of a Christian state, in the fashion of the Erastian ecclesiologies of the absolutist states in post-Reformation Europe. The commentary reveals that Eusebius was ready to exploit the opportunities for patronage, for conversions, and for leaving behind old wounds and problems. But it omits the hieratic and quasi-episcopal portrait of Constantine found in the *Life of Constantine*. The godly polity described in the *Commentary on Isaiah* is a community organized under the leadership not of the emperor but of the bishops. The term 'polity' may have been chosen because it could embrace the history of the people of God before the Incarnation, whereas 'church' had exclusively Christian conno-tations. Or it may have been influenced by scriptural passages such as Ps. 86: 3, Phil. 3: 20, or Heb. 12: 22. The political and legal associations of *politeuma* underscored the institutional character of the church.[52] The word appealed to Eusebius as a biblically, apolo-getically, and legally apt designation for the church. Its implications for Eusebius' understanding of the church's relation to the actual political institution of the Roman Empire are problematic. There is at least a suggestion of the church's separate existence from the empire, almost as a state within the state,[53] not in the sense of a rival institution, but more as a token, perhaps not fully conscious, of Eusebius' instinctive allegiance and orientation to the church to which he had devoted his life.[54]

---

[52] See further Ch. IV.

[53] Cf. Eger, 'Kaiser und Kirche in der Geschichtstheologie Eusebs von Cäsarea', 102.

[54] Perhaps this is the place to consider whether Eusebius' use of *politeuma* for the church may have been intended to co-operate with Constantine's agenda for a *Reichskirche*. A. A. T. Ehrhardt has suggested, in an important series of articles on Constantine's legislation, that the emperor adopted the term *corpus Christianorum* as a substitute for the more dangerous religious-political term *populus Christianorum* (A. A. T. Ehrhardt, 'Das Corpus Christi und die Korporationen im spätrömischen Recht', *Zeitschrift der Savigny-Stiftung, Romanistische Abteilung*, 71 (1954), 25–40, esp. 38–40). Ehrhardt believed that Constantine, very alert to the implications of terminology, had on his own initiative identified the Christian church as a *corpus* on the model of the term in Roman law, as an association of persons with a common treasury, under the direction of the bishop and his presbytery as governing council or *curia* of the community. The main evidence for this hypothesis is the use of *corpus*

What Isaiah had predicted was now to be seen 'with our own eyes'.[55] The church which Eusebius celebrated had left behind the threat of persecution.[56] The inner-church tensions created by persecution, such as the Donatist schism in Africa or the Meletian schism in Egypt, should now be magnanimously forgotten. The commentary honours the memory of the martyrs, but suggests that fanaticism and hard feelings are out of place.[57] Of course Eusebius does not name these troubles, nor is there the slightest hint of the Council of Nicaea and the Arian controversy. Heresy is omitted altogether.[58] The church is a well-ordered polity or community, with its presiding bishops, subordinate orders of clergy, baptized laity, and catechumens.[59] The emperors (plural) appear as pious Christians, attending the liturgy, granting poor relief to the church, and repressing the pagan cultus.[60]

Christianorum in the 'edict of Milan', cf. Lactantius, *On the Deaths of the Persecutors*, 48. 9–11, which Ehrhardt says was substituted for the polemically charged *populus Christianorum* (a potential rival of the *populus Romanus*), which Maximin Daia had appropriated from the Christians themselves as an indictment of Christianity's revolutionary pretensions (cf. *ethnos tôn Christianôn* in the translation of Maximin's decrees in *HE* 9. 1. 5 and 9. 9. 14, 17).

Sôma is the literal translation of *corpus*; Eusebius himself had used it in his translation of the Latin text of the 'edict of Milan' (*HE* 10. 5. 10–12). But *sôma* lacks completely the juristic associations of *corpus*. The question arises whether in the *Commentary on Isaiah* Eusebius called the church a corporation (*politeuma*) in order to comply with Constantine's terminology. The answer must be no. Whatever Constantine's intentions were in calling the church a corporation (*corpus*), they do not seem to have influenced Eusebius. If Eusebius intended the church to be understood juristically as a corporation subject to Roman legislative control, he would not have been as free in his use of designations such as *polis* and *laos*, which did not have the same precise connotations. Indeed, *polis* and its derivatives could be interpreted by the state as threatening challenges, as in the response of the judge to the martyrs of Caesarea: when the martyrs said that they were citizens of Jerusalem, the judge had them executed because he suspected that they were engaged in erecting a city hostile to Rome (*Martyrs of Palestine*, 11. 12). Similarly, Eusebius in the commentary often calls the church not only the city of God but also the people of God (*laos tou theou*, *CI* 326. 17–19), the very terms (in Ehrhardt's view) Constantine had sought to eliminate. Therefore it is unlikely that Eusebius had any precise legal refinements in mind when he applied broadly political terminology to the church.

[55] *CI* 15. 10.
[56] Ibid. 325. 23–326. 19.
[57] Ibid. 324. 32–325. 13.
[58] Compare Jerome's frequent allusions to Christian heresies in his commentary on Isaiah, whereas Eusebius does not refer to a single one. See S. Gozzo, 'De Hieronymi commentario in Isaiae librum', *Antonianum*, 35 (1960), 194–203.
[59] *CI* 133. 12–18.
[60] Ibid. 316. 17–25; 316. 10–16; 20. 29–21. 5.

This sketch of the church in the commentary seems pitched at several possible groups: present or future clergy, who were reminded of their eminent roles as archons of the godly polity; the laity, who learned of their secondary place in it; or interested pagans, who might be impressed with the antiquity of the church and its glittering prospects. All of these groups could learn in Eusebius' commentary how the history of the godly polity was revealed in the fulfilment of events (*hê ekbasis tôn pragmatôn*) predicted by the prophet.

In sum, the commentary provided biblical reinforcement of a group identity highly relevant after 325. The corporate body of the church is set forth as the bearer of eschatological meaning in history. In this 'high church' ecclesiology, the church is not a rival to the empire, something that would be unthinkable for Eusebius. Rather it is the primary locus of God's activity in history, compared to which the empire is a secondary phenomenon, a reality of a lesser order, though to be sure also part of God's providential design.

The Status of Judaism

But why choose a work of exegesis as a vehicle for institutional self-celebration? The answer has to do with the second purpose of the commentary.

The *Commentary on Isaiah* is devoted at tiresome length to vindicating Christianity's supplantation of Judaism. Eusebius had already treated the subject massively in *The Proof of the Gospel* and the *Prophetic Selections*. Why a third time? One explanation may be the need to state afresh the boundary between Judaism and Christianity, for the benefit of the new Christian emperor. There is evidence that Constantine was quick to pick up Christianity's animus against Judaism, either on his own initiative or at someone else's suggestion. The evidence is found principally in his letter to the churches after the Council of Nicaea and also in the tone of his legislation on the Jews. Since the letter and pertinent laws date from the same period in which I have dated the commentary (*c.*325–9), the prominence of the Christian–Jewish debate in the commentary may owe something to Eusebius' knowledge of a new attitude to the Jews at the imperial court, compared to the traditional Roman policy of toleration.[61]

[61] This assessment of Constantine's attitude to the Jews departs somewhat from a common opinion that his policy was in fundamental continuity with his pagan

The letter of Constantine to the churches concerning the Nicene Council is preserved by Eusebius in the *Life of Constantine*.[62] Although Eusebius says that the letter was sent to inform bishops who did not attend the council about its proceedings, the contents prove that Constantine was specifically addressing the bishops of the diocese of Oriens on the matter of the date of Easter, since resistance to the Roman and Alexandrian customs accepted at Nicaea was strongest in Syria and Palestine, where many churches still calculated Easter according to the Jewish reckoning of Passover.[63] The letter is too long to quote in full, but a summary will illuminate the emperor's attitude to Judaism and his priorities for Christianity.[64]

Constantine begins by saying that he summoned the bishops to gather together to foster 'unity of faith, sincerity of love, and community of feeling (*agapê homognômôn*) in regard to the worship of Almighty God', since the general prosperity of the empire depends

predecessors. For the latter point of view, see Michael Avi-Yonah, *Geschichte der Juden im Zeitalter des Talmud in den Tagen von Rom und Byzanz* (Studia Judaica, 2; Berlin, 1962), 162–9, and also J. Cohen, 'Roman Imperial Policy toward the Jews from Constantine until the End of the Palestinian Patriarchate (ca. 429)', *Byzantine Studies*, 3 (1976), 1–29. However, Ehrhardt's survey of Constantine's religious legislation reaches a different conclusion. Ehrhardt says that the editing process behind the Theodosian Code, and the complex religious and political realities with which Constantine had to deal, mean that the value of the laws as evidence of Constantine's attitudes must always be balanced by Eusebius' observations in the *Life of Constantine* and by his Constantinian documentation. See 'Constantin der Grosse, Religionspolitik und Gesetzgebung', *Zeitschrift der Savigny-Stiftung, Romanistische Abteilung*, 72 (1955), 185. He illustrates this with reference to the Jews, noting the superior value of the letter on the date of Easter for revealing the emperor's personal views (182). Also relevant is Ehrhardt's article 'Constantine, Rome and the Rabbis', *Bulletin of the John Rylands Library*, 42 (1959–60), 303–7.

[62] *VC* 3. 17. 1.

[63] The issue in Eusebius' day had shifted from the classical 'Quartodeciman' controversy of the second century, when many Christians kept to the practice of ending their fast on Passover (cf. Eusebius, *HE* 5. 23–5). At Nicaea the debate centred on the practice of relying on the Jewish reckoning of Passover to determine Easter Sunday, rather than simply choosing the first Sunday after the first full moon after the vernal equinox. On the Easter issue at Nicaea, see C. J. Hefele and Henri Leclercq, *Histoire des conciles*, 11 vols. in 22 pts. (Paris, 1907–52), i, pt. 1, 450–88. On the subject of Quartodecimanism, see Bernhard Lohse, *Das Passafest der Quartadecimaner* (Gütersloh, 1953), and Wolfgang Huber, *Passa und Ostern: Untersuchungen zur Osterfeier der alten Kirche* (Beihefte zur Zeitschrift für die neutestamentliche Wissenschaft, 35; Berlin, 1969). More recent literature is cited in W. Petersen, 'Eusebius and the Paschal Controversy', in H. Attridge and G. Hata (eds.), *Eusebius, Christianity, and Judaism* (Detroit, 1992), 311–29, an analysis which is hampered by the anachronistic attribution to Eusebius of an 'autocephalous' ecclesiology and an anti-Rome fixation (see esp. 320–1).

[64] See the analysis of the letter in Kraft, *Konstantins Entwicklung*, 223–5.

on God's favour.[65] Unity and concord, familiar Constantinian key-words, were thus the goal of the council.[66] Unlike his dismissal of the 'small and insignificant' theological trifles which set Arius against his bishop,[67] Constantine takes matters of ritual very seriously. Nothing can be more fitting or more honourable 'than that this feast from which we date our hope of immortality, should be observed unfail-ingly by all alike, according to one ascertained order and arrange-ment'.[68] The primary offence of discrepant observances of Easter is that some Christians are relying on the Jews to set the date of Easter. But Constantine objects that the Jews have been afflicted with blind-ness of soul by the defilement of the Crucifixion.[69] Therefore, Chris-tians ought not to have anything in common with such a detestable crowd. The Jews are guilty of parricide; they have lost their reason and gone mad.[70] The proof of their madness is that they sometimes celebrate the feast twice in the same year.[71] Second, Christ has left one feast for our commemoration and has willed that his church be pervaded by one spirit; it is scandalous for members of the church in one place still to be fasting, while elsewhere Easter festivities have begun. Providence wills that there should be one uniform rule. Christians are to have 'nothing in common with that nation of parricides who slew their Lord'.[72] 'For on the one hand a dis-crepancy of opinion on so sacred a question is unbecoming, and on the other it is surely best to act on a decision which is free from strange folly and error.'[73] With the uniform observance of Easter and disaffiliation from the Jews, 'peace and concord' (*eirênê kai homonoia*) will flourish everywhere.[74]

The ideas in this letter show that the emperor was deeply convinced that cultic uniformity was essential to the church's

---

[65] *VC* 3. 17. 1.

[66] *Pros tên tês henotêtos symphônian*, ibid. 3. 17. 2.

[67] Ibid. 2. 71.

[68] Ibid. 3. 18. 1.

[69] Ibid. 3. 18. 2.

[70] Kraft noted the pagan Greek background of this indictment, in which the Jews are guilty of the most heinous crime of parricide, and suffer the divine penalties of blindness and madness (*Konstantins Entwicklung*, 224). But the blindness motif has obvious New Testament associations as well, cf. John 9: 39–41, and Matt 23: 16–17, 19, 24, 26.

[71] That is, their reckoning by the lunar calendar in disregard of the equinox may lead to two Passovers within a twelve-month solar year.

[72] *VC* 3. 19. 1.

[73] Ibid. 3. 19. 2.

[74] Ibid. 3. 20. 2.

integrity, and that religious commerce with the Jews jeopardized that integrity.

Constantine's attitude to the Jews as enshrined in his legislation is at first glance less hostile.[75] Some scholars would emphasize the elements of continuity with Constantine's pagan predecessors.[76] Yet Constantine denied attempts by Jews to confirm their total exemption from serving on municipal councils, and limited the exemptions to selected synagogue officials.[77] He authorized a certain Joseph of Tiberias, a former adviser of the Jewish patriarch and a Christian convert, to build churches in the predominantly Jewish towns of Galilee.[78] The very language of the laws reveals an official contempt for the Jews comparable to the attitude in Constantine's letter on the date of Easter. The Jews are described as 'a feral sect', 'a nefarious sect'.[79] In addition, Barnes' redating of two other laws to Constantine's reign, if correct, weakens the supposed contrast between Constantine's tolerance and his successors' intolerance.[80] One of the laws forbids Jews to own Christian slaves at all.[81] The other prohibits Jews from leading former women employees of the state weaving establishments 'into the association of their turpitude'; Jews who henceforth 'unite Christian women to their villainy' are subject to capital punishment.[82]

In short, Constantine's own words reveal that he was concerned to maintain a clear distance between Jews and Christians. It is likely

[75] The pertinent laws are CT 16. 8. 1–5, 9. 1, and *Sirmondian Constitution*, 4. But see below on CT 16. 8. 6 and 16. 9. 2.

[76] e.g. Avi-Yonah, *The Jews of Palestine*, 164–5; also Amnon Linder, 'The Roman Imperial Government and the Jews under Constantine', *Tarbiz*, 44 (1974), 95–143 (in Hebrew). (I owe this reference to Prof. Robert Wilken.) See now A. Linder's general study, *The Jews in Roman Imperial Legislation* (Detroit, 1987). The position of the Jews in the Theodosian Code is surveyed by Chantal Vogler, 'Les Juifs dans le code théodosien', in Jacques LeBrun (ed.), *Les chrétiens devant le fait Juif: Jalons historiques* (Le point théologique, 33; Paris, 1979), 35–74. See also Cohen, 'Roman Imperial Policy Toward the Jews', 1–29.

[77] CT 16. 8. 2, 3, 4.

[78] Epiphanius, *Panarion* 30. 4. 1 ff., cited in Barnes, *Constantine and Eusebius*, 252.

[79] CT 16. 8. 1 (trans. C. Pharr). Marcel Simon has noted the importance of such polemical language in an official legal pronouncement; see his *Verus Israel* (2nd edn.; Paris, 1964), 267.

[80] The relevant laws are CT 16. 8. 6 and 9. 2, both dated to 339. Barnes believes that the set two laws, along with 16. 8. 1, are fragments of one and the same law, a Constantinian constitution to the praetorian prefect Evagrius in 329—about the time the commentary was written. See Barnes, *Constantine and Eusebius*, 392 f. n. 74.

[81] CT 16. 9. 2, which would confirm Eusebius' otherwise unproven assertion of this fact in VC 4. 27. 1, as noted by Barnes, ibid.

[82] CT 16. 8. 6.

that Eusebius was aware of such an atmosphere at court when he wrote his commentary. This does not mean that he simply trans-ferred official attitudes to Judaism to his contemporary. In fact, he shows a rather open attitude to aspects of Jewish history, based on his interest in literal interpretation and the recovery of the history of the godly polity when it was part of Judaism. But the attitudes of the emperor may have been the immediate occasion for his decision to turn once again to the Jewish–Christian debate over the Old Testament.

The Book of Isaiah

The book of Isaiah was an excellent text for meeting the various elements of Eusebius' agenda. He thought its author was both an apostle and an evangelist, an interpretation encouraged by the Septuagint versions of the calls of both the historical Isaiah and the anonymous prophet who stands behind Deutero-Isaiah:

And I heard the voice of the Lord saying, 'Whom shall I send [*tina aposteilô*], and who will go to this people?' And I said, 'Behold, here I am, send me [*aposteilon me*].' (cf. Isa. 6: 8, LXX)

Go up on a high mountain, you who bring glad tidings [*ho evangeli-zomenos*] to Zion; lift up with strength your voice, you who bring glad tidings to Jerusalem. (Isa. 40: 9, LXX)[83]

From the very beginning Isaiah had occupied a central position in Christian apologetics. In the New Testament, Isaiah is cited or alluded to more often than any Old Testament book except the Psalter.[84] Its popularity never waned. In writers of the first three centuries Isaiah is second only to Genesis in frequency of citations.[85] The reason for this popularity is the ancient Christian conviction that the prophets had foretold the events of Jesus' life and death. Isaiah was especially useful to Christian apologists for defending Jesus' Messianic identity, in texts such Isa. 7: 14 (Matt. 1: 23), 9: 6 (Luke 1: 32–3), 11: 1 (Rom. 15: 12), 28: 16 (Rom. 9: 33), 35: 5 (Matt. 11: 5), 42: 1–4 (Matt. 12: 18–21), 53: 7–8 (Acts 8: 32–3), 53: 4 (Matt. 8: 17), 61: 2 (Luke 4: 18–19), etc. However, Eusebius had already

[83] Cf. ibid. 3. 26–4. 4.
[84] See the index to E. Nestle and K. Aland (eds.), *Novum Testamentum Graece* (25th edn.; London, 1972), 658–721.
[85] *Biblia Patristica*, 6 vols. (Paris, 1975–).

treated Jesus' Messianic identity at length in the *Prophetic Selections* and *The Proof of the Gospel*, and the *Commentary on Isaiah* is rather perfunctory on the subject. Other Isaian themes proved more fruitful.

In common with much of the prophetic tradition, the book of Isaiah repeatedly condemns the hollowness of institutional religion, its cult, its officers, and the society which it legitimates (e.g. Isa. 1: 10–17, 21–6; 3: 1–4: 1; 9: 8–10: 4; 28: 1–29; 43: 22–4; 58: 1–14, etc.). These denunciations were very attractive to Eusebius as a biblical justification for the rejection of the Jews as the claimants to the godly polity. He liked to apply prophecies of military defeat and the fall of Jerusalem to the Roman conquest of Jerusalem under Vespasian and Hadrian, although he also varied the prophetic timetable by foreshortening it to cover events in biblical history, especially Nebuchadnezzar's destruction of the First Temple in 587 BC.

The book of Isaiah is not wholly negative in its evaluation of institutions such as temple, law, holy city, priesthood, and the like. The historical Isaiah possessed a highly developed theology of God's presence in Zion, and eschatological prophecies in Deutero- and Trito-Isaiah speak of a restoration of temple and city.[86] These more positive prophecies could be used to concede a relative validity to Jewish religious institutions so long as Israel was the godly polity. More commonly, Eusebius saw them as fulfilled in the history, life, and institutions of the Christian church, which he regarded as the rebuilt Jerusalem of texts like Isa. 54: 11–14.[87] The historical Isaiah was especially concerned with Zion's political character as the governmental centre of national life, hence his concentration on forms of office appropriate to a society conceived as a polis ruled by God.[88] This feature of the book was directly relevant to Eusebius' concern for the cancellation of the institutions of the godly polity of old and

[86] On the historical Isaiah, see Gerhard von Rad, *Old Testament Theology*, ii: *The Theology of Israel's Prophetic Traditions* (New York and Evanston, 1965), 155–69. For comments on the later parts of the book, see ii. 238–50, 278–97.

[87] This text was already applied to the church by Eusebius in his speech at the dedication of the basilica of Tyre, *HE* 10. 4. 62. Many other Isaian messianic and eschatological prophecies on Jerusalem are developed in this speech in ways that presage their interpretation in the *Commentary on Isaiah*: Isa. 35: 1–4 (*HE* 10. 4. 32), 61: 10–11 (*HE* 10. 4. 48), 54: 4 (*HE* 10. 4. 49), 51: 17–18, 22–3 (*HE* 10. 4. 50), 49: 18–21 (*HE* 10. 4. 51–3), 52: 1 (*HE* 10. 4. 54).

[88] 'All that Isaiah has to say about Israel's deliverance and renewal rests on this *polis* concept'. Von Rad, *Old Testament Theology*, ii. 150. See von Rad's list of key passages and offices, ibid., ii. 150 n. 6.

for a biblical certification of institutional forms of the new godly polity, the church. Another aspect of Isaiah's Zion theology was the impregnability of the city under God's protection.[89] This answered to the contemporary experience of the church, which had survived the attacks of the persecutors in a tremendous test of faith that Eusebius interpreted as a divine deliverance. Finally, Eusebius also applied passages on the new Jerusalem, in light especially of Heb. 12: 22, to the heavenly Jerusalem towards which the church is journeying.

A closely related theme is the universalism of Isaiah's later recensions and additions, from the nations streaming to Mt Zion in Isa. 2: 2–4 to the gathering of the nations prophesied in 66: 18–23.[90] The gathering in of the Gentiles had of course been a staple of Christian preaching since Paul, but it could claim even greater relevance in the years after 325. Eusebius might occasionally regret the nominal Christians brought in by Constantine's conversion,[91] but he had no doubt at all that Christianity was properly the religion of all humanity. This aspect of Isaiah was the most attractive of all.

When the prophet said of God that he was waiting to be sought by those who did not ask for him, and to say 'Here I am' to a nation that did not call upon his name (Isa. 65: 1), Eusebius saw a clear prediction of the calling of the Gentiles to be the new godly polity. Deutero-Isaiah's polemic against idolatry offered rich material for a celebration of Christianity's supersession of pagan polytheism (Isa. 41: 29, 42: 8, 17; 44: 9–20; 45: 20–1; 46: 1–2, 5–7, etc.). The *Commentary on Isaiah* recapitulates this key theme of Eusebian apologetics, but with fresh immediacy and concreteness in light of Constantine's initiatives against the pagan cults. The descriptions of the nations in pilgrimage to Jerusalem were particularly relevant, replete with royalty bearing rich gifts to the priests of the Lord.[92]

A related aspect of Isaiah's universalism is the proclamation of God's solicitude for Israel in terms of world history, not just in terms of Israel's national history.[93] There is a natural affinity between Isaiah's oracles to the nations, not just to Israel, and Eusebius'

[89] Ibid. 156f.
[90] See von Rad, *Old Testament Theology*, ii. 294–7.
[91] *VC* 4. 54 and possibly *CI* 376. 6–13.
[92] Cf. Isa. 49: 23. Other texts from Deutero- and Trito-Isaiah which Eusebius applies to the calling of the Gentiles: Isa. 41: 24–6; 42: 10, 16–17; 43: 5–6, 8–11; 49: 8, 12, 18; 50: 4–5; 52: 11–12; 53: 11–12; 55: 4–6, 12–13; 59: 19–20; 60: 1–2; 65: 11.
[93] Von Rad, *Old Testament Theology*, ii. 162.

orientation to the sweep of universal history.[94] Eusebius shared
Isaiah's confidence that the kings of Assyria, Egypt, Babylonia, and
Persia, not to mention the small fry of Damascus, Moab, Edom, and
Tyre, all served the purposes of God's universal providence, for weal
or woe. The taunt song against the king of Babylon expresses this
confidence in powerful language, as does the great poem on Assyria
in 10: 5–19. The same idea is expanded and developed in Deutero-
Isaiah (cf. Isa. 40: 21–2).

Finally, the Isaian theme of the remnant of Israel. Both Isaian and
post-Isaian prophecies declare that a part of the nation will survive
the divine judgement as a guarantee of the future (cf. Isa. 1: 9; 4: 3; 7:
3; 8: 16–18; 10: 20–3; 11: 11, 16; 14: 32; 28: 5; 30: 17; 45: 5; 48: 17–19;
65: 8–9). It may be true, as von Rad says, that the remnant doctrine
is not a particularly hopeful element of Isaiah's teaching, since it
connotes usually a pitiful rump of the nation.[95] Nevertheless, the
remnant idea was used by Paul in Romans 9–11 to explain the justice
of God's promises, in spite of the unfaithfulness of his people (cf.
Rom. 9: 27, 29, quoting Isa. 10: 22 and 1: 9; also Rom. 11: 5).
Eusebius adopted it from Paul for his own interpretation of the
saints in Israel—the 'friends of God' as he calls them (*hoi theophileis
andres*)—who comprised the godly polity in Israel. His exegesis of
Isa. 65: 8–9 illustrates the theme. Referring back to Isa. 5 and its
parable of the vineyard, as well as to 1: 9, a remnant text, Eusebius
says that the grape which has God's blessing will be an example
(*paradeigma*) for the whole people; it is the elect company of Jesus'
Jewish disciples, the 'seed in Zion' left by the Lord in 1: 9, who will
inherit Mt Zion, the city of the living God, the heavenly Jerusalem
(Heb. 12: 22).[96]

3. Eusebius' Predecessors: Earlier Christian
Interpretation of Isaiah

The Commentary on Isaiah *and traditional apologetic exegesis*

The *Commentary on Isaiah* builds on a traditional core of anti-
Jewish apologetics. Rooted in the New Testament, an exegetical
tradition had developed which was devoted to classical Old Testa-

---

[94] On Eusebius' view of history, see the excellent study of Sirinelli, *Les vues
historiques.*

[95] Von Rad, *Old Testament Theology,* ii. 165.

[96] *CI* 393. 36–394. 19.

ment proof texts and interpretive cruxes. It is preserved most fully in treatises against the Jews, such as Tertullian's *Against the Jews*, in testimonia collections such as Cyprian's *To Quirinus, Three Books of Testimonies*, and in catechetical works such as Irenaeus' *Demonstration of the Apostolic Preaching*. Its exegetical substance has been well studied, especially by those interested in Jewish–Christian relations.[97] Justin Martyr's *Dialogue with Trypho the Jew* has been chosen to demonstrate the exegetical overlap between Eusebius and prior exegetical tradition, though we will also take note of differences. Justin is a good basis for such a comparison. The *Dialogue with Trypho* has long been recognized as a primary source for Jewish–Christian exegetical discussion, and Eusebius knew and respected Justin's work.[98]

Justin's *Dialogue* quotes Isaiah about seventy-seven times. There are four major themes: a critique of Jewish ritualism and an unfavourable comparison with Christian morality of the heart, the rejection of Israel for denying the Messiah, the calling of the Gentiles, and various Christological topics.

Justin took advantage of Isaiah's condemnations of the displacement of covenant ethics by the external cultus, as in his use of the following passages: Isa. 1: 16 (call for true circumcision, *Dial.* 18.2), 1: 23 (evasion of social justice, 27.2), 29: 13 (observance of human commandments instead of heart-felt obedience to God, 27); 58: 1–12 (on true fasting as relieving the misery of the oppressed and the

---

[97] See Simon, *Verus Israel*, 87–123, 165–213; Jean Daniélou, *The Theology of Jewish Christianity* (London, 1964), with lengthy bibliography. For the testimonia tradition, especially the question of a nucleus of traditional proof texts, see C. H. Dodd, *According to the Scriptures* (London, 1952); Jean Daniélou, *The Origins of Latin Christianity* (London, 1977), 263–95; A. von Ungern-Sternberg, *Der traditionelle alttestamentliche Schriftbeweis 'De Christo' und 'De Evangelio' in der alten Kirche bis zur Zeit Eusebs von Caesarea* (Halle, 1913); Per Beskow, *Rex Gloriae. The Kingship of Christ in the Early Church* (Uppsala, 1962), 74–122; Pierre Prigent, *Les testimonia dans le christianisme primitif: L'Épître de Barnabé (I à XVI) et ses sources* (Paris, 1961); J. Rendel Harris, *Testimonies*, 2 vols. (Cambridge, 1916, 1920); Robert Kraft, 'Barnabas' Isaiah Text and the Testimony Book Hypothesis', *Journal of Biblical Literature*, 79 (1960), 336–50; N. Bonwetsch, 'Der Schriftbeweis für die Kirche aus den Heiden als das wahre Israel bis auf Hippolyt', in *Theologische Studien Theodor Zahn dargebracht* (Leipzig, 1890), 1–22 (unavailable to me).

[98] Eus., *HE* 4. 18. On Justin's exegesis of the Old Testament, see Willis A. Shotwell, *The Biblical Exegesis of Justin Martyr* (London, 1965); Pierre Prigent, *Justin et l'ancien Testament* (Paris, 1964); von Ungern-Sternberg, *Traditionelle Schriftbeweis*, 6–27; Adolf von Harnack, *Judentum und Judenchristentum in Justins Dialog mit Tryphon* (TU, 39; Leipzig, 1913), 47–98; Jean Daniélou, *Gospel Message and Hellenistic Culture* (London, 1973), 199–220; Oskar Skarsaune, *The Proof from Prophecy* (Leiden, 1987).

lowly, 15 and 40), 58: 13–14 (denial that Sabbath observance was mandated, except for hardness of heart, 28), and 66: 1 (God's presence in the Temple only provisional, 22). Eusebius' treatment of these verses is quite similar, though he is more dispassionate on the subject of Sabbath observance, noting the Jewish requirement of rest without a polemically charged judgement.[99] An original feature of Eusebius' criticism is the geographical restrictiveness of the Mosaic law because of its location in Jerusalem.[100] The explanation may be that Justin was more keenly devoted to the place of the historical city of Jerusalem in the Christian dispensation because of his sympathy for the millenarian doctrine of Revelation.

The second and third themes are closely related, and some passages in the *Dialogue* speak of them together. For Justin the rejection of Israel is evident principally in the fall of Jerusalem to the Romans and Judaism's loss of its privileged offices of priesthood, prophecy, and kingship. These are also prominent themes in the *Commentary on Isaiah*. The relevant texts are Isa. 1: 7 (Hadrianic prohibition of Jewish entry into Jerusalem, *Dial.* 16. 2); 1. 8 (the fall of Jerusalem and the loss of kingship, prophecy, and priesthood, 52. 4); 2: 5–6 (calling of the Gentiles, 24); 5: 21 (the gifts of prudence and wisdom really belong to the Christians, 39); 11: 1–3 (the spiritual gifts, especially prophecy, now given to the Christians, 87. 2); 29: 14 (rejection of chosen people, cancellation of the gifts, 32 and 78); 39: 8–40: 17 (prophecy has disappeared among the Jews, 50); 62: 10–12, 63: 1–7, 42: 6–7 (calling of the Gentiles, 26); 63: 15–19, 64: 1–12 (rejection of Israel, calling of the Gentiles, 25); 65: 1 (calling of the Gentiles, 24); 65: 5–12 (the old people and the new people, 136); 66: 24 (eschatological punishment waiting for the Jews for the rejection of Christ, 44).

In a large number of passages Justin asserts flatly that Isaiah's references to Israel actually mean Christians, who are the true Israel, as in his treatment of Isa. 42: 1–4 (*Dial.* 12. 3, 125, and 130); 29: 14, 42: 6–7, 16, 19–20, 43: 10, 49: 6 (*Dial.* 122–4).

Eusebius' exegesis of these texts agrees substantially with Justin's, though there are differences of emphasis. Eusebius has an even keener interest in the fall of Jerusalem, to which he alludes time and again. Besides the passages already found in Justin, the following texts are applied to the Roman conquest: Isa. 1: 20, 31; 2: 6–9; 5: 11–

---

[99] *CI* 360. 33–361. 8.   [100] Ibid. 322. 37–323. 3.

17, 25–30; 6: 3–4, 11–13; 17: 9–11; 29: 3, 5–8; 34: 9–10; and 51: 17–19. An important difference between them is Justin's commitment to the physical rebuilding of Jerusalem in the millenial reign of the saints, as in his interpretation of Isa. 65: 17–25 and 66: 5–13 (*Dial.* 81, 85). Eusebius sees their fulfilment in the present life of the Christian church, the city of God on earth.[101] Finally, Eusebius is less interested in the Christian appropriation of the gift of prophecy, because of his opposition to Montanism, although in the *Church History* he had acknowledged Justin's claim that the spirit of prophecy was still alive in the church of the second century.[102]

Lastly, Christological and messianic topics, to which according to von Ungern-Sternberg the burden of the *Dialogue*'s scriptural demonstration is devoted:[103] Justin gives a Christological/messianic interpretation to Isa. 3: 9–15 (Jews' rejection of Christ, *Dial.* 133); 7: 14 (the virgin birth, 43, 66, 84); 8: 4 (Christ conquers Damascus and Samaria in the homage paid by the Magi, 77–8); 9: 6 (Christ gives spiritual gifts to Christians, 87); 33: 13–19 (birth of Christ; the Eucharist; the Parousia, 70); 35: 1–7 (Christ's public life, especially the healing miracles, 69); 42: 1–4 (Jacob is Christ, 123, 125, 130); 42: 5–13 (God addresses his Christ, not himself, 65); 50: 4 (Passion prophecy, 102); 51: 4–5 (Christ as the new Law); 52: 15 (Jewish rejection of Jesus, 118); 52: 10–15, 53: 1–12, 54: 1–6 (Christ's vicarious death, 13, 42–3, 102, 114); 54: 8–9 (Noah as a type of Christ, 138); 57: 1 (Jews' rejection of Christ, the just man; prophecy of the Resurrection, 16, 97); 60: 1 (Christ is the light who will shine in Jerusalem, 113); 65: 2 (Passion prophecy, 97).

Once again, Eusebius gives similar or identical interpretations, with a few exceptions. In Isa. 8: 4 he assumes that Samaria and Damascus refer to the historical nations of which they were capitals, and sees the fulfilment of the prophecy in their capture by the Assyrians.[104] By comparison, Justin has no interest in the actual history of Israel; he is content to see Damascus and Samaria as references to the Magi and to equate the king of Assyria with Herod. Eusebius, with the godly polity firmly in mind, sees the new law of Isa. 51: 4–5 not as Christ himself but as the law of the Christian

---

[101] Ibid. 391. 19–398. 4; 404. 13–31.
[102] *HE* 4. 18. 8, citing *Dial.* 82. See Ch. V.3.2 on Eusebius' notion of prophetic inspiration.
[103] *Der traditionelle Schriftbeweis*, 15–20.
[104] *CI* 56. 1–6.

church, and the ratification of the Noachic covenant of 54: 8–9 as a promise made to the godly polity.[105]

Thus both Eusebius and Justin tend to read Isaiah in the same way when mining the text as Christian apologists, though their apologetic purposes are not exactly the same. The difference in their exegetical methods shows this more clearly. Although both of them rely heavily on the fulfilment of prophecy, they have different ideas of how prophecy should be interpreted. For Justin the prophet speaks unambiguously, without the complexity (*amphibolia*) that invites allegorization.[106] Eusebius is more aware of the importance of interpretation in understanding prophetic metaphor.[107] Furthermore, Eusebius blends traditional prophetic interpretation with a more austerely historical and literal interpretation that marks his (and of course Origen's) exegesis as a new departure in Christian biblical studies.

A good illustration of the advances made by the Alexandrians over their predecessors is Eusebius' discussion of Isa. 43: 15. The Septuagint version of this reads, 'I, the Lord God, your Holy One, who has made known Israel as your king' (*egô kyrios ho theos ho hagios hymôn ho katedeixas Israêl basilea hymôn*). For Justin this text is one of many Jacob passages exploited for Christological and apologetic purposes. Jacob was never a king, he reasons, so the prophecy must be speaking of Christ, the eternal king.[108] Eusebius is normally just as ready to give a Christological meaning to Jacob/Israel. But in this verse he knows that the Septuagint is probably an erroneous translation, and that the version of Symmachus has preserved the actual meaning of the Hebrew: 'I the Lord your God, your Holy One, the creator of Israel [*ktistês Israêl*], your king.' Therefore, he quietly eschews the Christological interpretation in favour of a historical one.[109]

Another example of Justin's more exuberant liberties with the biblical text is his treatment of Isa. 3: 10, 'Let us bind the just man, because he is distasteful to us' (LXX). Justin attempts to score a debating point with his Jewish interlocutors by observing that there

[105] *CI.* 322. 37–323. 6; 341. 21–6.

[106] *Dial.*, 51. I owe this observation about Justin's view of *amphibolia* to R. M. Grant, *The Letter and the Spirit* (London, 1957), 124.

[107] *CI* 3. 1–17.

[108] *Dial.*, 135.

[109] *CI* 280. 11–34. The Septuagint translators perhaps misread Hebrew *bôre'* (creator) as *mar'eh* (manifesting, showing), because they construed 'king' in apposition to 'Israel' rather than to 'I'.

is a discrepancy between the Septuagint and the Hebrew, and quoting once the alleged Septuagint version, 'Let us take away (*arômen*) the just man', and once the alleged Hebrew version, 'Let us bind [*dêsômen*] the just man'.[110] Justin's motive seems to be to disarm some of the Jewish objections that Christians were unfamiliar with the Hebrew, a charge certainly evident in the debate over Isa. 7: 14. The MT of Isa. 3: 10 does present a problem, but not in the way Justin insinuated.[111] It is the Septuagint, perhaps based on an originally correct Hebrew reading, which has *dêsômen*, not *arômen*. The latter word appears to be a conflated reading of Isa. 3: 10 and 57: 1 ('See how the just one has perished, and none takes it to heart; and just men are taken away [*airontai*] and no one notices', LXX), perhaps further influenced by John 19: 15 (*aron, aron, staurôson auton*). Such modified biblical citations are typical of an age of free spiritual exegesis, as in the famous instance of Justin's citation of Ps. 95: 10 as 'The Lord reigned *from the tree* (*apo tou xylou*)', in which the addition of 'from the tree' represents a Christian targumic adaptation.[112] Justin saw the absence of the phrase from the biblical text as the result of Jewish censorship of the manuscripts. Eusebius, on the other hand, was protected from such errors by Origen's Tetrapla. In his discussion of Isa. 3: 10 he uses the Septuagint's version because it was congenial for his apologetic purposes, even though he must have known that the non-Septuagintal versions differed considerably from the Septuagint, since Origen had obelized *dêsômen*, as well as other parts of the verse.[113]

A last instance of the distance separating the free exegesis of the testimonial tradition from the more scholarly approach of Eusebius is Justin's interpretation of Isa. 7: 14. He returns to this verse repeatedly in the *Dialogue*, because of its primacy among Old Testament messianic proof texts, and because it was hotly controverted among Jews and Christians.[114] Justin is the first Christian writer to demonstrate awareness of the Jewish critique of the Septuagint translation

---

[110] *Dial.*, 133, 136–37. Hegesippus also quotes this verse as *arômen*, in Eusebius, *HE* 2. 23. 15.

[111] See the critical apparatus in K. Elliger and W. Rudolph (eds.), *Biblia Hebraica Stuttgartensia* (Stuttgart, 1967–77), 680.

[112] *Dial.*, 73; cf. the brief discussion in Daniélou, *Theology of Jewish Christianity*, 96 f.

[113] *CI* 23. 1–28. For Origen's reading see J. Ziegler (ed.), *Isaias*, xiv of *Septuaginta: Vetus Testamentum Graecum* (2nd rev. edn.; Göttingen, 1967), 132.

[114] *Dial.*, 43, 66–8, 71, 84. On Jewish messianic interpretations of Hezekiah, see H. L. Strack and P. Billerbeck, *Kommentar zum Neuen Testament aus Talmud and Midrasch*, 6 vols. (Munich, 1922–61), i. 31, 75.

of Hebrew *'almah* as *parthenos*. But his solution is once again to accuse the Jews of having mutilated or misinterpreted the Hebrew original.[115] He clings to the Septuagint as the book of the church and reproaches the Jews for abandoning it.[116] Eusebius, on the other hand, tries to integrate rather than repress the evidence of the other Greek versions, although he tacitly abandons Origen's untenable philological defence of the Septuagint.[117] He too knows, probably from Justin himself, of Jewish claims that the prophecy referred to the birth of Hezekiah. But he responds with the chronological objection that Hezekiah was already 9 years old when Ahaz became king, and thus could not have been the person spoken of by the prophet.[118] This philological and chronological discussion is quite different from Justin's bald assertion of Jewish bad faith.

Biblical Scholarship: Origen as Exemplar

The *Commentary on Isaiah* makes frequent direct and indirect allusions to Origen's *Commentary on Isaiah*.[119] This is to be expected, considering Eusebius' profound veneration of Origen. As Pamphilus' co-worker at Caesarea in the restoration of Origen's library, Eusebius had collaborated with him in a defence of the master, composing the sixth book of the *Defence of Origen* to go with the earlier five written by Pamphilus.[120] He had also devoted much of Book 6 of the *Church History* to a biography of Origen.[121] To Eusebius, Origen was *ho thaumasios anêr, ho hieros anêr*.[122] Nevertheless, critical examination will show that he was anything but slavish in his use of Origen's exegesis of Isaiah.

[115] *Dial.*, 71, 84.

[116] Ibid.

[117] Origen had argued (wrongly) that the usage of Deut. 22: 23–6 (MT) justified the LXX reading of *'almah* as *parthenos* (*C. Cels.* 1. 34). For Eusebius' earlier position, see *EP* 4. 4–5.

[118] *EP* 4. 4 (178. 16–29), based on data taken from 2 Kings 16: 2, 18: 2.

[119] On the tradition of learned exegesis of Isaiah which Origen inaugurated, see Roger Gryson and Dominique Szmatula, 'Les commentaires patristiques sur Isaïe d'Origène à Jérôme', *Revue des Études Augustiniennes*, 35 (1990), 3–41.

[120] Only the first book is extant, in the Latin translation of Rufinus. Text in *PG* xvii. 521–616. On the apology for Origen, see Pierre Nautin, *Origène: Sa vie et son œuvre* (Christianisme antique, 1; Paris, 1977), 99–153.

[121] See R. M. Grant, 'Early Alexandrian Christianity', *Church History* 40 (1971), 133–44, and 'Eusebius and His Lives of Origen', in *Forma Futuri: Studi in onore del Cardinale M. Pellegrino* (Turin, 1975), 635–49; Nautin, *Origène*, chs. 1–3, a comprehensive examination; Patricia Cox, *Biography in Late Antiquity* (Berkeley, 1983).

[122] *EP* 4. 4 (179. 2), 4. 5 (181. 30).

Origen wrote the first Christian commentary on the book of Isaiah. Except for two short fragments preserved in Book 1 of Rufinus' translation of the *Defence of Origen*, it is completely lost. According to Eusebius, Origen composed the work at Caesarea during the reign of Gordian (238–44).[123] He also reports that the commentary, in thirty books, was complete only up to the vision of the beasts in the desert (Isa. 30: 6, LXX).[124] Jerome had both it and Eusebius' commentary at his disposal when he wrote his own commentary about 408–10, although the twenty-sixth book had disappeared in the meantime.[125] In the *Prophetic Selections* Eusebius had already made reference to Origen's *Commentary on Isaiah* as a resource for the more zealous student of the prophetic testimonies.[126]

The Florentine manuscript of the nearly complete *Commentary on Isaiah* of Eusebius provides proof, if any were needed, that Eusebius worked with Origen's commentary beside him. At seven different points the manuscript indicates the verse at which Origen finished a book of his commentary.[127] A nearly complete table of its thirty books can be reconstructed with these and similar notes in the margins of several biblical MSS.[128] On the basis of the notations, Ziegler asserted that Eusebius borrowed extensively from Origen.[129] But all they prove is that he consulted Origen as an acknowledged authority. Eusebius was quite capable of writing in genres such as apologetics and history without resorting to mere borrowing from Origen. Why should it be any different with his exegesis?

---

[123] *HE* 6. 32. 1; Nautin, *Origène*, 411.

[124] *HE* 6. 32. 1.

[125] Jerome, *Commentariorum in Esaiam libri I–XVIII*, in S. Hieronymi Presbyteri, *Opera*, pt. 1: *Opera Exegetica*, 2 and 2A, ed. M. Adriaen (*Corpus Christianorum, Series Latina* (hereafter *CCL*), lxxiii–lxxiiiA; Turnholti, 1963), lxxiii. 3. 86, 91. A letter of Jerome's containing a catalogue of Origen's works speaks of thirty-six books on Isaiah (*Ep.* 33. 4).

[126] *EP* 4. 4, 5 (179. 2, 181. 30).

[127] *Isteon d' hôs mechri toutôn Origenei proêlthen ho—katos tôn eis tên prophêtên exegêtikôn tomos.* The following verses of Isaiah bear such annotations: Isa. 10: 11 (eleventh book of Origen's commentary, *CI* 73. 29 f.), 10: 23 (twelfth book, 77. 34 f.), 13: 16 (fifteenth book, 99. 25 f.), 14: 5 (sixteenth book, 101. 35 f.), 14: 19 (seventeenth book, 103. 5 f.), 16: 8a (nineteenth book, 111. 14–16), and 30: 5 (thirtieth book, 195. 20 f.). See *Jesajakommentar*, pp. xxxii–xxxiii.

[128] In Rahlfs' listing they are MSS 393, Q (Codex Marchalianus), and the Syro-Hexapla. The first two also contain marginal scholia drawn from Eusebius' *Commentary on Isaiah*. See *Jesajakommentar*, pp. xxvii–xxxi.

[129] Ibid., p. xxxi.

Furthermore, unlike Origen, Eusebius commented on the entire sixty-six chapters of Isaiah. If his exegesis were wholly or largely derivative, we would expect him either to cease writing altogether or for there to be some clear difference in method and content between what comes after Isa. 30: 5 and what came before. But no such difference exists.

Let us now consider the two fragments of Origen's commentary preserved in Pamphilus' apology for Origen. The first is taken from the first book of the commentary.

Since the Apostle says, 'Because you are eager for manifestations of the Spirit'; and since, the Spirit being one, as many of those who are called individually 'holy spirits', the same number have the Holy Spirit in them; therefore in the same manner it must be said of Christ. For from one Christ many 'christs' come, of whom scripture says, 'Touch not my anointed ones, and do not revile my prophets' [Ps. 104: 15]. And thus from one God there are said to be many gods, all namely in whom God dwells. But to us one is God the Father from whom are all things, one is therefore true God who, if I may say so, is the head [*praestator = proestôs*?] of divinity, and one is Christ the maker of 'christs', and one is the Holy Spirit who makes the holy spirit in the individual souls of the saints. Since Christ, through that which Christ is, makes 'christs' [anointed ones], so too by virtue of what he is, Son of God and proper and only-begotten Son, he makes sons of God all those who receive the spirit of adoption from him.[130]

Pamphilus had excerpted this passage in order to refute the charge that Origen had impaired the unity of Christ and had denied his uniqueness. Unfortunately, he does not tell us which verse of Isaiah Origen was expounding. We may tentatively identify the lemma as Isa. 1: 2, for Eusebius uses it to interject a brief discussion of prophetic inspiration.[131] Perhaps Origen was advancing his favourite theme of the birth of the Word in the souls of Christians, for Isa. 1: 2 reads, 'I have begotten sons and exalted them, but they have disobeyed me'.

If the conjecture is correct, Eusebius may have omitted all of the theological speculation and pastoral application because it held little interest for him. Nevertheless, Origen's influence is evident in one place. Speaking of Isa. 1: 2, which addresses heaven and earth as personified beings, Eusebius says that they stand respectively for the dwelling places of the heavenly powers and of mortals. But he also

---

[130] In Pamphilus, *Defence of Origen* (hereafter *Apol. Or.*) 1. 5 (*PG* xiii. 218).
[131] *CI* 4. 24–31. Cf. Ch. V.3. 2.

introduces an anonymous speculation (*phasin tines*) that the prophet
spoke to heaven and earth because they had an animating soul.[132]
Eusebius often uses anonymous attributions when he wants to separate himself from one of Origen's provocative interpretations.

The second fragment, from Book 28 of Origen's commentary, is a
gloss on Isa. 26: 19, 'The dead will rise, and those in the tombs will
be raised, and those in the earth will rejoice'. Pamphilus quoted this
and other passages from Origen to prove that he accepted the biblical and ecclesiastical doctrine of the resurrection of the body.[133] It
seems clear from the excerpt, which is too lengthy to repeat here,
that Origen used Isa. 26: 19 to defend the traditional doctrine of the
resurrection of the dead against the naïve literalism of the simple and
the rationalist criticism of the more sophisticated. A reference to
Rev. 20: 6 shows that he wanted to avoid a literal interpretation of
the thousand-year reign of the saints with Christ by explaining the
two resurrections as those of the righteous and the wicked, with no
importance attached to the thousand-year interlude. The resurrection of the dead would be truly universal, including not only those
buried in tombs and graves, but even those whose bodies had been
dismembered or had never been buried at all. The resurrection of the
dead would properly be a resurrection of the body, although in a
transfigured state, since Paul could not possibly have been speaking
of the soul in his discussion of the Resurrection in 1 Cor. 15. It is
likely that Pamphilus emphasized these aspects of Origen's doctrine
of resurrection because of attacks during the Great Persecution on
Origen's Platonist eschatology.[134]

The *Commentary on Isaiah* shows no evidence of Origen's discussion of Isa. 26: 19 or of the Christian opposition to Origen which
inspired Pamphilus' and Eusebius' defence of Origen.[135] Instead,

---

[132] *CI* 4. 34–9. For Origen's views on the animate nature of the heavenly bodies, cf.
De princ. 1. 7. 2–5, and the recent study of Alan Scott, *Origen and the Stars: A History
of an Idea* (Oxford, 1991).

[133] In Pamphilus, *Apol. Or.* 1. 7 (*PG* xiii. 218–20).

[134] For Origen's doctrine of resurrection, cf. *De princ.* 2. 10, 3. 6. 2–6, and *C. Cels.*
5. 17–19, 7. 32, 8. 49–50. See H. Chadwick, 'Origen, Celsus, and the Resurrection of
the Body', *HTR* 41 (1948), 83–102. For the anti-Origenist position we have the
fragment of Methodius of Olympus' *Aglaophon or On the Resurrection* preserved in
Epiphanius, *Panarion*, 64. 12–62. Origen's alleged denial of the resurrection of the
body was eighth on the list of fifteen articles circulated against Origen (Nautin,
Origène, 127 f.). See Barnes, *Constantine and Eusebius*, 198–201, and Nautin,
Origène, 134–44, for the anti-Origenist movement that provoked the writing of the
Apology for Origen.

[135] *CI* 170. 22–171. 12.

Eusebius' interpretation compares the Greek versions of the text and resolves various minor difficulties. The contradiction of 26: 19 ('For the dead will rise') and 26: 14 ('The dead shall not see life') is removed by applying the latter to those who sinned unto death and will not enjoy eternal life and salvation, and the former to those who endured unto death and who will sleep until the resurrection. On the other hand, Eusebius' interpretation of the second part of 26: 19 is probably derived from Origen, because he equates the dew of 26: 19b (in the LXX, 'Your dew is a healing for them') with the forgiveness of sins wrought by the Logos. In his *Commentary on the Song of Songs* Origen had interpreted the rain of Songs 2: 11 as the Word of God.[136]

A more extensive comparison is possible on the basis of Origen's nine homilies on Isaiah, all that have survived from an original twenty-five, in the Latin translation of Jerome.[137] The homilies deal with the following texts:

Hom. 1 6: 1 ff.	Hom. 4 6: 1 ff	Hom. 7 8: 18–21
Hom. 2 7: 14	Hom. 5 41: 2; ch. 6	Hom. 8 10: 10–14
Hom. 3 4: 1	Hom. 6 6: 8–9	Hom. 9 6: 8–9[138]

The most important difference in the homilies is Origen's preference for the practical application of the biblical text in the contemporary spiritual life of his congregation, as compared with Eusebius' interest in the salvation history of the godly polity. For Eusebius the chronological datum of the temple theophany ('In the year that King Uzziah died') places Isaiah's vision in the broader history of the people of God. Scripture says elsewhere (2 Chr. 26: 16–21) that Uzziah had contracted leprosy as a punishment for his attempted usurpation of the cultic prerogatives of the priests. The correlation of illness and vision meant for Eusebius that the glory of the Lord

---

[136] Origen, *Commentary on the Song of Songs* (hereafter *Comm. Songs*), 3. 13. In the eighth homily on Jeremiah (*Hom. Jer.* 8. 3) Origen extended the imagery to include the prophets and saints as rain clouds watered by the Logos.

[137] *PG* xiii. 219–53. In the prologue to his *Commentary on Isaiah*, Jerome listed these homilies as among his Christian antecedents in the exposition of Isaiah, as well as Origen's 'semeiôseis', which he translated as *excerpta* (*Comm. Is.* Prol. (*CCL* lxxiii. 3. 90–1)). On the homilies see most recently Gryson and Szmatula, 'Les commentaires patristiques sur Isaïe', 124–31. On the literary character of the scholia, see Nautin, *Origène*, 372–5. Of the scholia (*semeiôseis*) on Isaiah, only two tiny fragments may be traced to them; see J. B. Pitra (ed.), *Analecta Sacra*, 8 vols. (Paris, 1876–91), iii on Isa. 39: 7 and 66: 1.

[138] Rejected as an anonymous forgery by Baehrens, 'Die neunte fragmentarische Jesaja-homilie des Origenes, eine Fälschung', *Theologische Literaturzeitung*, 49 (1925), 263 f. But see the current state of the question in Gryson and Szmatula, 'Les commentaires patristiques', 27–31.

could not return to the temple until the polluted king was gone.[139] He shared the Chronicler's interest in demonstrating the justice of God's ways with men in the historical experiences of the godly polity.

But as far as Origen was concerned, the date of Uzziah's death was in itself meaningless. Of the dating of Jeremiah's prophetic ministry in Jer. 1: 2–3, he wrote, 'What do I care about this history?' if some useful teaching cannot be derived from it.[140] In the homilies on Isaiah he observes that Isaiah couldn't see God until his vision because he was a sinner; the dating of the vision in the last year of King Uzziah was only an external indication of the time in his life when Isaiah passed from being a sinner to the vision of God. Says Origen: 'Nor is it written in vain that "And it happened in the year that King Uzziah died, I saw the Lord . . ." Uzziah or Pharaoh live in each one of us, and we do not really live when we do the works of Egypt . . .'[141]

The identity of the Seraphim also drew different interpretations.[142] In the *Homilies on Isaiah* Origen twice repeats an earlier statement in *On First Principles* that the two Seraphim were the Lord Jesus, the Son of God, and the Holy Spirit.[143] *On First Principles* had attributed this exegesis to a Hebrew teacher, although this detail is omitted in the *Homilies*.[144] The whole theophany is a vision of the Trinity. Eusebius reads it differently. For him all the Old Testament theophanies are self-manifestations of the Logos, since the unbegotten Father of the universe remains forever unseen by mortal eyes.[145] In his discussion he refers to John 1: 18, which is basic to his theology of divine transcendence and revelation.[146]

---

[139] *CI* 37. 19–29.

[140] Origen, *Hom. Jer.* 1. 2–3, P. Nautin and P. Husson (eds.), *Origène: Homilies sur Jérémie*, 2 vols. (SC, nos. 232, 238; Paris, 1976–7).

[141] *Hom. Is.* 1. 1 (*PG* xiii. 219). The allegorization of Uzziah's leprosy as our sin is repeated in *Hom. Is.* 4. 3 (*PG* xiii. 232C–233C) and 5. 5 (*PG* xiii. 237B–238A). In the latter homily Origen mentions the biblical tradition of Uzziah's leprosy, though he is silent about the extra-biblical traditions known to Josephus and Eusebius; cf. *Hom. Is.* 5. 3 (*PG* xiii. 236C–237A).

[142] On Origen's interpretation of the Seraphim, see most recently Joseph Trigg, 'The Angel of Great Counsel: Christ and the Angelic Hierarchy in Origen's Theology', *JTS* 42 (1991), 35–51, and M. Hollerich, 'Origen's Exegetical Heritage in the Early Fourth Century: The Evidence of Eusebius', in R. Daly (ed.), *Origeniana Quinta* (Leuven, 1992), 592–8, for its controversial status in the fourth century.

[143] *Hom. Is.* 1. 2 (*PG* xiii. 221C); *Hom. Is.* 4. 1 (*PG* xiii. 230D–231D).

[144] *De Princ.* 1. 3. 4; 4. 3. 14.

[145] Cf. A. Weber, *ARXH. Ein Beitrag zur Christologie des Eusebius von Caesarea* (Rome, 1964), 29–31, 93–5.

[146] *CI* 36. 2–11.

Origen accommodated his interpretation of the vision to the biblical prohibition against seeing God and living (cf. Exod. 33: 20) by noting that the wings of the Seraphim prevented Isaiah from looking upon the actual face of God.[147] Eusebius seems to refer circumspectly to Origen's trinitarian interpretation:

> Some think there are two Seraphim, but I, based on the idea expounded by the sacred scriptures which says, 'the Seraphim stood round about him', think they are many, and that they are bodyguards, as it were, like a crown from all sides, surrounding his throne with light and enlivened by him . . .[148]

The subordinationism of Origen's interpretation, which might suggest that the second and third members of the Trinity were creatures, would have been highly suspect in the wake of the Council of Nicaea, when Eusebius had successfully negotiated the lifting of the provisional excommunication imposed upon him only half a year before the council. Judging from Origen's fondness for the trinitarian interpretation, it probably appeared in his *Commentary on Isaiah* and therefore represents a distinctive feature of Origenist exegesis which Eusebius discreetly passed over.

In interpreting Isa. 7: 14, Eusebius borrowed from Origen's second homily on Isaiah, or from the actual commentary, to explain the discrepancy between the Emmanuel prophecy as uttered by Isaiah and as quoted by Matt. 1: 23.[149] The quotation in Matthew says 'they will call' (*kalesousi*) rather than 'you will call' (*kaleseis*), a discrepancy which Origen attributed to the emendation of some unintelligent scribe who sought to avoid crediting Ahaz with recognizing Jesus as Emmanuel. Eusebius also refers to misguided copyists (*mê noêsantes tines = non intellegente, sed ad faciliora currente*), but cares more about the contemporary focus of the prophecy in the time of Ahaz, as well as its fulfilment to come in the distant future. If the prophet had actually said, 'they will call his name Emmanuel', he reasoned, then the whole prophecy would have been projected exclusively into the future, whereas it was also intended to give present consolation and exhortation to Ahaz and his people. For Origen the prophecy is really addressed to us, since the house of David is the church, and David himself is a type of Christ. Eusebius takes the reference literally to mean the present descendant

---

[147] *Hom. Is.* 1. 5 (*PG* xiii. 223C–D).
[148] *CI* 38. 12–16.
[149] Ibid. 49. 5–28. Cf. Origen, *Hom. Is.* 2. 1 (*PG* xiii. 225B–226A).

of David, King Ahaz, for whom Emmanuel is grounds for hope in actual, historical freedom from Judah's enemies.

From the third homily Eusebius apparently gleaned an allegorical interpretation of Isa. 4: 1, although he only mentions it as a possibility.[150] He prefers to see the prophecy that seven women will take hold of one man fulfilled historically in the desperate circumstances of the Jews at the time of the Roman invasion and the destruction of the temple.[151] He says that he knows another interpretation according to which the seven women are the seven powers of the Holy Spirit (cf. Isa. 11: 2–3), who take up their home with Christ, the first man, because he alone is able to receive (*chôrein*) them. This is very close to Origen's opinion that the seven women are the seven spirits of the one spirit of God. Their shame is the opprobrium which they suffer at the hand of false spirits who pervert their true natures. Jesus takes away their shame by sponsoring their growth in men through the production of perfect spiritual fruit.[152] He is distinguished from Moses, Joshua, Isaiah, and the like, because the spirits take up a permanent rather than a merely temporary abode with him.

A puzzling feature of the interpretation alluded to by Eusebius is that he speaks of Christ as the first man (*ton prôton . . . anthrôpon*),[153] whereas the biblical text and Origen's homily both use the cardinal number (*heis, unus*) rather than the ordinal. If this is not merely a verbal slip, a speculation about Christ as the first man may underlie the anonymous exegesis reported by Eusebius. Does his wording reflect a doctrine akin to that which Origen's enemies accused him of teaching? According to a summary preserved by Photius, number six in a list of fifteen charges made against Origen held that he taught that the soul of Adam was identical with the soul of Christ.[154] The truth of this cannot be determined. In any case, the point remains that Eusebius reads the

---

[150] *CI* 25. 37–26. 11.

[151] Probably on the basis of the gruesome account of Josephus, *The Jewish War*, 5. 424–38, 412–19, 566, and 6. 193–213, quoted by Eusebius already in the *Church History* (*HE* 3. 6).

[152] *Hom. Is.* 3. 1 (*PG* xiii. 228B).

[153] *CI* 26. 9.

[154] Photius, *Bibliotheca* 117 (*PG* ciii. 396), discussed by Nautin, *Origène*, 114–44. It may have originated in Origen's allegorizing of Adam as a type of Christ and Eve as a type of the church; Socrates (*HE* 3. 7) says that such an allegory is found in Book 9 of Origen's *Commentary on Genesis*, according to a lost part of Pamphilus' *Defence of Origen*. Nautin denies that Origen ever held such a doctrine (*Origène*, 126).

text prophetically in terms of the fate of the Jews rather than as a Christological allegory.[155]

The eighth homily deals with Isa. 10: 10–14, part of the taunt song against the king of Assyria. Once again Eusebius offers a historical interpretation of a text which Origen allegorizes. A good indication of his distance from Origen is his discussion of whether the king of Assyria stands for the devil. Origen thought so,[156] an identification which Eusebius cites (anonymously) as an alternative to his historical reading.[157] Elsewhere in the commentary the king of the Assyrians is regularly interpreted literally,[158] another indication of the commentary's historical orientation, since Eusebius himself had followed Origen's allegorization in *The Proof of the Gospel*.[159]

Origen's *Homilies on Isaiah* are thus important though fragmentary evidence of Eusebius' independence as an exegete. The literary difference between a homily and a commentary does not weaken the value of the evidence. Origen frequently introduced technical considerations and literal interpretation into his homilies, the pastoral nature of which did not necessarily bind him to a spiritual interpretation.[160]

To the direct evidence of Origen's writings we add the indirect testimony of Jerome, who used both Eusebius' and Origen's commentaries in composing his own. In the preface Jerome lists his predecessors in the study of Isaiah and mentions that Eusebius'

---

[155] Though he shares the view that Christ possessed the seven spirits of Isa. 11: 2–3 in a way different from inspired human beings like the prophets and apostles, because in him the fullness of divinity dwelt (Col. 2: 9). Cf. Eusebius' comments on 11: 2–3 (*CI* 81. 26–82. 18). Origen's exegesis of Isa. 4: 1 is paralleled in the Christian literature to the first three centuries only by Victorinus of Pettau in his commentary on Revelation, *In Apocalypsim* 1. 7, ed. J. Hausleiter (*CSEL* xlix; Vienna, 1916), 28, 30; also in his *Tractatus de Fabrica Mundi* 7–8 (*CSEL* xlix. 6–8). Since Jerome says Victorinus, the first Latin exegete of Isaiah, owed much to Greek exegesis, he probably borrowed his interpretation from Origen. See the remarks of Victorinus' editor, *CSEL* xlix. pp. viii–xii.

[156] *Hom. Is.* 8. 1 (*PG* xiii. 251D).

[157] *CI* 74. 17–21.

[158] Ibid. 46. 6, 13; 52. 16, 21; 56. 3, 29, etc.

[159] *DE* 4. 9.

[160] See Erich Klostermann's remarks on this subject in his 'Formen der exegetischen Arbeiten des Origenes', *Theologische Literaturzeitung*, 72 (1947), 203–8. See also the comments of P. Nautin on Origen's use of the tools of ancient grammar to elucidate the literal meaning of the text in his homilies on Jeremiah, *Origène: Homilies sur Jérémie* (SC, no. 232; Paris, 1976), 132–6.

commentary was written *iuxta historicam explanationem.*[161] In Book 5 of the commentary Jerome twice refers to Eusebius' promise to give a historical interpretation of Isaiah, which Jerome acknowledges was not at all Origen's intention. But he criticizes Eusebius for inconsistently falling back upon Origen's clever allegorizations whenever the literal sense failed him.[162] Jerome thus testifies that Eusebius' intention differed from Origen's precisely on the point of allegorical interpretation, a difference we have seen borne out in practice in discussing the homilies. He does not accuse Eusebius of lack of learning or originality, but only of resorting to Origen and to allegory when the historical approach seemed inadequate.[163]

Jerome twice refers explicitly to Origen's commentary.[164] Both Jerome and Origen interpret Isa. 2: 22 as Christological prophecy, whereas Eusebius construes it in its historical context.[165] The Septuagint omitted this verse, which was known to exegetes only from the version of Aquila. Considering Jerome's rebuke, it is noteworthy that he gratefully adopts Origen's Christological reading, while it is Eusebius who keeps to *historica explanatio*. The other passage in question is Isa. 6: 9–10, an ancient Christian proof text (cf. Matt. 13: 15 and parallels). Jerome says that Origen discouraged the Christian practice of explaining away its deterministic implications by accusing the Jews of having falsified the original Hebrew.[166] Eusebius makes no such accusation, although he does prefer the more voluntaristic reading of the Septuagint as the basis for interpretation.[167] Origen's Tetrapla must have shown him the textual discrepancy between the Septuagint and the Hebrew, but in this case

---

[161] Jerome, *Comm. Is.* Prol. (*CCL* lxxiii. 3. 91–2). On this work see now the detailed study of Pierre Jay, *L'Exégèse de Saint Jérôme, d'après son 'Commentaire sur Isaïe'* (Paris, 1985).

[162] Ibid. 5. Pref. (*CCL* lxxiii. 160. 25–30), and 5. 18. 2 (*CCL* lxxiii. 190. 29–35).

[163] Even the specific example that Jerome cites as a lapse into allegory is really a fulfilment of prophecy (cf. *CI* 119. 6–36).

[164] Besides these two direct references, note Jerome's allusion to Eusebius' interpretation (though not by name) in a discussion of Isa. 19: 18 (*Comm. Is.* 5. 19. 18 (*CCL* lxxiii. 198. 17–21)) and his almost certain use of Origen in a later discussion of the same verse (ibid. 5. 19. 18 (*CCL* lxxiii. 283. 6–285. 59)). Eusebius read the text as a prophecy of church life and institutions (*CI* 132. 33–133. 26); Origen read it as moralistic allegory.

[165] Compare Jerome, *Comm. Is.* 1. 2. 22 (*CCL* lxxiii. 39–41. 51) and *CI* 21. 15–18.

[166] Jerome, *Comm. Is.* 3. 6. 9–10 (*CCL* lxxiii. 92. 50–4).

[167] *CI* 42. 1–29.

Eusebius ignores the testimony of philology for the sake of a more apologetically congenial text.

A final observation about Jerome's commentary is that he seems to have drawn on Eusebius much more than on Origen.[168] His affinity for Eusebius is probably based on their shared commitment to literal interpretation, however much he believed Eusebius fell short of it in practice.[169] One could hypothesize that the preponderance of Eusebian material in Jerome's commentary is just an accident of historical preservation, which has given us Eusebius' *Commentary on Isaiah* but not Origen's, and that Origen was actually a common source of both.[170] However, Jerome's frequent use of Eusebius even for Isa. 30: 6–66: 24 suggests that he relied on him for

---

[168] For Jerome's citations and borrowings from Eusebius, see the index to the *CCL* edition of Jerome's commentary. The list of references to Eusebius can be expanded on the basis of the new material published by Ziegler. Anonymous references which can now be identified as Eusebian include, for example, Jerome's allusion to the identification of Sennacherib in Isa. 36: 1: 'I read in a certain commentary that this is the same Sennacherib who captured Samaria, which is completely wrong . . .', Jer., *Comm. Is.* 11. 36. 1–10 (*CCL* lxxiii. 431. 119–21), a criticism of Eus., *CI* 231. 7–12. Cf. also Jer., *Comm. Is.* 5. 10. 11 (*CCL* lxxiii. 163. 3–8) and Eus., *CI* 98. 4–9 on Isa. 13: 11. Jerome also borrowed from Eusebius without acknowledgement, as in his identification of Isaiah as not just a prophet but an evangelist and an apostle, cf. Jer., *Comm. Is.* Prol. (*CCL* lxxiii. 1. 18–30) and Eus., *CI* 3. 26–4. 4. Also compare Jer., *Comm. Is.* 5. 14. 8–10 (*CCL* lxxiii. 168. 1–8) and Eus., *CI* 102. 7–24. Ziegler draws attention to Jerome's habit of adopting biblical citations from Eusebius' commentary, often translating Eusebius' Septuagintal text directly into Latin, without consulting his own Latin translation (*Jesajakommentar*, pp. xlviii–xlvix). As Ziegler notes, previous research on Jerome's use of his sources will have to be corrected in light of the new material; cf. Gozzo, 'De S. Hieronymi commentario in Isaiae librum', 58–63.

An article of Simonetti, as summarized by Gryson and Szmatula ('Les commentaires patristiques', 7–8), has drawn similar conclusions as to the relative dependence of Jerome on Eusebius and Origen: from Eusebius he took the themes of the victory of the church over paganism and the church's replacement of Israel as the heir of the divine promises, but from Origen he took his concerns with heresy and orthodoxy and with the spiritual life of the individual soul, neither of which interest Eusebius. See M. Simonetti, 'Sulle fonti del *Commento a Isaia* di Girolamo', *Augustinianum*, 24 (1984), 451–69.

[169] Although, as we have seen, Jerome himself readily resorted to allegory. On Jerome's exegesis, see Jay, *L'exégèse de Saint Jérôme*; H. F. D. Sparks, 'Jerome as Biblical Scholar', in *The Cambridge History of the Bible*, i. 535–41; J. N. D. Kelly, *Jerome: His Life, Writings and Controversies* (New York, 1975).

[170] This was the opinion of Eusebius' first editor, Bernard Montfaucon: 'Nec abs re forte dicas Eusebium et Hieronymum eadem ipsa ex Origenis Commentariis hausisse', cited by Ziegler, *Jesajakommentar*, p. xlviii. Even without the benefit of the new material published by Ziegler, Gozzo, 'De S. Hieronymi commentario in Isaiae librum', 60, had pointed out that this was purely conjectural. See now the above-cited articles of Simonetti and Gryson-Szmatula (nn. 119, 168).

the whole book. Most of the unidentified references in Jerome's discussion of 30–66 have now turned up in the new edition of Eusebius' commentary.[171]

4. Eusebius' Interpretation of Isaiah in His Other Works

The book of Isaiah had already figured prominently in the *Prophetic Selections* and *The Proof of the Gospel*. The fourth book of the *Selections* gives separate glosses of varying length to the following verses of Isaiah: Isa. 2: 1–4, 3: 1–10, 3: 12, 7: 10–16, 8: 1–4, 8: 18–20, 9: 5–7, 10: 33–11: 10, 16: 5*, 19: 1–4, 19: 19–21, 26: 16–19*, 28: 14–17a, 30: 27*, 31: 9b*, 35: 1–7, 40: 3–5, 40: 9–11, 41: 2–7*, 42: 1–7, 43: 10, 45: 12–16, 48: 12–16, 49: 1–11, 50: 1–11, 52: 5–7, 52: 10–53: 12, 55: 2–5, 57: 1–4*, 59: 19–21, 61: 1–3, 61: 10–11*, 62: 10–63: 3a*, 63: 11*, 64: 10–65: 2*. The scriptural index to Heikel's edition of the *Proof of the Gospel* lists six full columns of references to Isaiah, many of which contain substantial discussions of the biblical text. But only fifteen of the thirty-five Isaian texts glossed in the *Prophetic Selections* are discussed at length in the *Proof* (those marked with an underline) and ten of them (those marked with an asterisk) are not even cited.

Comparison of Eusebius' approach to Isaiah in these three books is inviting because they were written during three distinct periods: the *Selections* sometime during the Great Persecution, the *Proof* sometime after the Edict of Milan but before the period of Constantine's sole rule, and the *Commentary on Isaiah* not long after the defeat of Licinius.[172] On the other hand, the usefulness of such a comparison is somewhat limited by the different genres of the works. The *Selections* is a catechetical work written to provide a basic introduction to Christian doctrine.[173] The *Proof* is an apologetic treatise designed to prove Christian doctrine from Old Testament prophecies.[174] Both of these works use the ancient technique of glossing biblical proof texts, but the *Proof* is conceived on a far more massive scale and arranges the

---

[171] References from Jerome's commentary on Isa. 30–66 which are now identifiable as Eusebian in origin are found on the following pages of the *CCL* edition: 397. 29, 405. 65, 431. 119, 571. 78.

[172] Dates for all three works can only be approximate; cf. Wallace-Hadrill, *Eusebius of Caesarea*, 57 f., and Barnes, *Constantine and Eusebius*, 277–9.

[173] Ibid. 169. Cf. *EP* 4. Pref. (168. 16–27).

[174] *DE* 1. Prol. 1.

texts thematically rather than according to the sequence of the biblical books from which they are excerpted. The *Commentary on Isaiah*
is a technical work of exegesis that uses the method of the line-by-line
scholarly commentary as practised by Origen.

Nevertheless, the difference in the genres cannot obscure strong
similarities. The four extant books of the *Selections* were originally
the second part of a longer work called *The General Elementary
Introduction*, the first five books of which (now lost) vindicated
the Judaeo-Christian tradition over paganism, while the remainder
vindicated Christianity's version of that tradition over against
Judaism's. This is also the apologetic design underlying *The Proof of
the Gospel* and *The Preparation for the Gospel*, which Eusebius
planned as complementary works covering the same subjects as parts
two and one, respectively, of the *General Elementary Introduction*.[175] Both the *Selections* and the *Proof* are outstanding examples of
the traditional method of scriptural proof-texting, and, as one of the
authorities on the *Schriftbeweis* has written, in these works the proof
from scripture was allied with Alexandrian theology and achieved a
form which insured its further existence in Christian theology.[176] As
for the commentary, we have already demonstrated that it incorporates much traditional Christian anti-Jewish apologetic along with
its purely literal interpretation. Similarly, the catechetical and apologetic purposes of the *Selections* and the *Proof* did not keep Eusebius
from making the kind of scholarly observations, such as the textual
evidence of the various Greek versions, that take up so much of the
Commentary on Isaiah.[177]

Modern authorities like Schwartz and Wallace-Hadrill disagree
on whether the exegesis of Isaiah in the *Selections* and the *Proof* is
consistent with the exegesis of the commentary. Schwartz asserted
that there was very considerable agreement, while Wallace-Hadrill
denied this and stated flatly that there was 'strikingly little similarity'
between the commentary and the earlier works.[178] The lack of a

---

[175] *PE* 1. 1; cf. Barnes, *Constantine and Eusebius*, 178.

[176] Von Ungern-Sternberg, *Der traditionelle Schriftbeweis*, 297.

[177] E.g. *EP* 4. 7, where the versions of Aquila and Symmachus are cited along with
the LXX of Isa. 9: 5–6, and many such citations in *DE*, see the register of names, s.v.,
Akulas, Symmachus, and Theodotion.

[178] Schwartz, *RE* 6. 1436–7; Wallace-Hadrill, *Eusebius of Caesarea*, 82. In fairness
to Schwartz it should be pointed out that he has a list of passages where the commentary diverges from the other works.

reliable text of the commentary hampered comparisons.[179] With the aid of Ziegler's new edition, E. des Places devoted a chapter of his study of Eusebius' textual interpretation to the comparison of five sections of Isaiah in various of Eusebius' works: Isa. 19: 1–4, 35: 1–7, 7: 14, 53: 7–8, and 61: 1–2(–3a).[180] His results were inconclusive. He found a good deal of overlap in the way in which Eusebius approaches these verses of Isaiah in the *Selections*, the *Proof*, and the *Commentary on Isaiah*, especially in terms of the anti-Jewish apologetic. What differences he identified do not seem significant. The degree of similarity is not surprising, since with the exception of Isa. 19: 1–4 all of the Isaian passages des Places chose to analyse were firmly rooted in the church's catechesis and apologetics, and are therefore passages in which Eusebius is most likely to advance conventional interpretations.

The present study has reached the following general conclusions, which are treated elsewhere in more detail.

1. While eschatological interpretations of Isaiah are found in all three books, the *Prophetic Selections* gives the most attention to the return of Christ in glory, presumably because it was composed during the persecution of Diocletian.[181] The rapid ascendancy of Constantine and the changed fortunes of the church account for the diminished eschatological emphasis of the later works.[182]

2. The *Commentary on Isaiah* shows a much stronger interest in Old Testament history and in the present history of the church than either of the other two books, as demonstrated most vividly in texts where the institutional church displaces the person of Christ.[183] The stronger historical orientation is partly due to the commentary's character as a work of exegesis rather than apologetics or catechesis, and partly to its contemporary setting.

Contemporary secular history receives veiled allusions in the *Commentary on Isaiah*. If des Places had examined Eusebius' exegesis of the great peace prophecy in Isa. 2: 2–4, he would have discovered that the commentary notes the contemporary peace of

---

[179] As noted by J. Moreau, 'Eusebius von Caesarea', *RAC* vi. 1078.
[180] Des Places, *Eusèbe de Césarée, commentateur*, 157–88.
[181] *EP* 4. 8, 9, 18, 19, 24, 33. Cf. Barnes, *Constantine and Eusebius*, 168.
[182] See Ch. VI.5 of the present study for a discussion of the *CI*'s eschatology.
[183] See Ch. VI. 2.

the Roman Empire, 'which we have seen with our own eyes', a reference to the unification of the empire under Constantine after the battle of Chrysopolis. In the *Prophetic Selections* the peace prophesied by Isaiah means both the Pax Romana inaugurated by Augustus as a providential preparation for the Incarnation, and the spiritual and psychological peace of converts to the church.[184] No mention is made of contemporary political peace. The *Selections* also declares that the second coming of Christ will be a more perfect fulfilment of Isa. 2: 2–4, but the gloss in the *Commentary on Isaiah* ignores the second coming altogether.[185]

3. Both the *Selections* and the *Proof* are more exclusively devoted to a Christological and messianic interpretation of Isaiah than the commentary. Though the *Commentary on Isaiah* incorporates much of this traditional exegesis, it serves other purposes as well.[186]

4. The three books share common theological presuppositions, but the commentary scrupulously avoids overtly subordinationist expressions of the relationship between the Word of God and the uncreated God of the universe.[187]

These works seem to have had little direct influence on one another, although frequent statements in the earlier works show that the idea of writing a commentary had been in Eusebius' mind for a long time.[188] In a long section in Book 7 of the *The Proof of the Gospel*, Eusebius offers the reader a running commentary on selected verses from chapters 6–9 of the book of Isaiah: Isa. 6: 1–3, 8–11; 7: 10–16; 7: 18–25; 8: 1–4; 8: 5–8; and 9: 1–7.[189] The interpretation is Christological and messianic, since he regards them as a composite testimony to the circumstances of the Word's incarnation.[190] As he will do in the *Commentary on Isaiah*, he sometimes offers both a literal and a figurative fulfilment of the prophecies, but only within the New Testament and the apostolic age.[191] The *Commentary on Isaiah*, on the other hand, also looks to fulfilment

---

[184] *EP* 4. 1, especially p. 170, ll. 16–22 of the Gaisford edition.
[185] Ibid. 4. 1 (173. 25–9).
[186] On the relation of the *CI* to traditional Christological and messianic exegesis, see Section 3 in the present chapter, and Section 2 on the purpose of the commentary.
[187] See Section 5 in the present chapter.
[188] E.g. *EP* 4. 23 (206. 125–7); *DE* 3. 2. 75 (108. 2–4).
[189] *DE* 7. 1. 2–154.
[190] Ibid. 7. Prol. 1.
[191] E.g. ibid. 7. 1. 51.

in Isaiah's own time, later Old Testament history, and contemporary history as well.[192] Even close parallels in topic selection and treatment fall short of direct borrowing.[193]

5. The Theological Ideas of the *Commentary on Isaiah*

The theological yield of the *Commentary on Isaiah* is rather slight, especially if one seeks fresh insight into Eusebius' mind in the aftermath of Nicaea.[194] The commentary is silent about the Arian controversy and the council. Their only reflection is the negative evidence of Eusebius' avoidance of calling the Logos a second God (*deuteros theos*), though the term was common in the Eastern tradition of subordinationist theology and prominent in Eusebius' works written only a decade before Nicaea.[195] The forays into the divinity of the Logos that play an important role in Books 4 and 5 of *The Proof of the Gospel* are reduced to brief assertions in the *Commentary on Isaiah*. The book of Isaiah did not lack stimulus for theological reflection, but Eusebius seems to have decided against it for two reasons. Ecclesiastical infighting after Nicaea discouraged ambitious theologizing that might expose one to the attacks of rivals—better to wait for stabler circumstances when one could be surer of protection

---

[192] See, for example, the commentary's exegesis of Isa. 6: 1; 7: 1–3, 5–9, 10–13 (cf. *CI* 47. 1–48. 12 with *DE* 1. 39), 14 (the *CI* applies the prophecy of the Virgin Birth as a contemporary consolation to Ahaz and his generation, as well as to the future), 18–19, 20, etc.

[193] E.g. on Isa. 9: 6, cf. *DE* 7. 1. 135–9 and *CI* 65. 21–66. 16.

[194] On Eusebius' theology see Wallace-Hadrill, *Eusebius of Caesarea*, 100–38; Weber, *ARXH. Ein Beitrag zur Christologie des Eusebius von Caesarea*; Berkhof, *Die Theologie des Eusebius von Caesarea*; Colm Luibheid, *Eusebius of Caesarea and the Arian Crisis* (Dublin, 1978); Gustave Bardy, 'La théologie d'Eusèbe de Césarée d'après l'Histoire Ecclésiastique', *Revue d'histoire ecclésiastique*, 50 (1935), 5–20; Opitz, 'Eusebius von Caesarea als Theologe'; H. D. Saffrey, 'Un lecteur antique des œuvres de Numénius', in *Forma Futuri* (Turin, 1975), 145–53; F. Ricken, 'Die Logoslehre des Eusebius von Caesarea und der Mittelplatonismus', *Theologie und Philosophie*, 42 (1967), 341–58; Hanson, *The Search for the Christian Doctrine of God*, 46–59; Walker, *Holy City, Holy Places?*, 51–116.

[195] See Justin, *1 Apology* 13. 3, ed. Krüger (10. 6): the Logos has a second place after God; id. *Dial.* 56. 4: the Logos is 'distinct in number' compared to the Father. Origen, *C. Cels.* 5. 39 (SC 147: 118. 21), 6. 61 (SC 147: 332. 27): the Logos a second God; ibid. 7. 57 (SC 150: 146. 10–12): the Logos receives a second rank after the God of the universe. See the discussion of the secondary status of the Logos in Eusebius in G. L. Prestige, *God in Patristic Thought* (London, 1952), 141–6, and Hanson, *The Search for the Christian Doctrine of God*, 48–52.

from attack.[196] Second, doctrinal theology was less important to Eusebius than the desire to glorify the triumph of the church as the fulfilment of prophecy.

In this section we will summarize the theological doctrine of the commentary. Nothing Eusebius says departs from the normal assessment of him as a traditional exponent of the Origenist theological heritage, in which the Logos serves as a mediating agency between the one and the many, between God in the strict sense and the intelligible and sensible created orders.[197] The hierarchical ontology is middle-platonic, of the type represented by the second-century pagan philosopher Numenius, whom Eusebius had excerpted in *The Preparation for the Gospel*.[198] However, Eusebius lacked Origen's subtlety and speculative brilliance. His interpretation of the divine hypostases in the spiritual world appears to have exaggerated the master's distinction and subordination of the Logos in relation to the unbegotten God.[199] Nevertheless, he was not strictly speaking an Arian. His association with the Arian party arose from the fear that Nicaea would be construed as a repudiation of the Origenist theology of the distinct hypostases.[200]

Theological speculation plays very little role in the *Commentary on Isaiah*. Eusebius talks frequently about the Logos, but largely in terms of the economy of salvation. The Logos is the inspirer of prophecy.[201] He is the subject of the temple theophany in Isa. 6, as of

---

[196] Soc. *HE* 1. 23.

[197] See the recent sketch in Young, *From Nicaea to Chalcedon*, 16–21, and Adolf Harnack, *History of Dogma*, 7 vols. (New York, 1961), iii. 136 f.

[198] Esp. *PE* 11. 18. See Ricken, 'Die Logoslehre des Eusebius von Caesarea'; E. des Places, 'Numénius et Eusèbe de Césarée', *SP* 13 (TU, 116; Berlin, 1975), 19–28; id., *Eusèbe de Césarée, commentateur*, 48–51; Saffrey, 'Un lecteur antique de Numénius'.

[199] Hanson, *The Search for the Christian Doctrine of God*, 52; Wallace-Hadrill, *Eusebius of Caesarea*, 124–33; J. N. D. Kelly, *Early Christian Doctrines* (London, 1958), 255 f. Wallace-Hadrill suggests that the link between Eusebius and Origen was Dionysius of Alexandria, who may have been responsible for Eusebius' abandonment of Origen's doctrine that the divine hypostases were *homoousios* (127, 131).

[200] Cf. the recent defence of Eusebius' independence of strict Arianism by Luibheid, *Eusebius of Caesarea and the Arian Crisis*. Weber's study of Eusebius' Christology also emphasizes the traditional character of his thought, cf. *ARXH. Ein Beitrag zur Christologie des Eusebius von Caesarea*. Hanson, too, recognizes that he was not an Arian in the formal sense, but judges that '. . . undoubtedly he approached it nearly' (p. 59).

[201] *CI* 4. 29–31.

all the Old Testament theophanies, since the unbegotten God has never been seen by man (cf. John 1: 18).[202] When scripture speaks of the Holy One of Israel, it means the only-begotten Word of God, also metaphorically called 'the arm of the Lord'.[203] The Logos watches over the history of Israel, a protective custody which Eusebius sees symbolized in the prophetic allusion to the silently flowing waters of Siloam (Isa. 8: 5–6). The Logos irrigates the souls of the people, even when unacknowledged; he is the Emmanuel prophesied in Isa. 7: 14, 'God with us'.[204]

The Logos' decisive intervention in Israel's history was his Incarnation. His rejection by his people precipitated the historical disaster of AD 70 and the opening of the godly polity to the Gentiles. The smoke in the temple theophany is a grim prediction of the Roman destruction of the Second Temple.[205] The birth of the incarnate Word is a miraculous virgin birth, predicted in Isa. 7: 14 and 53: 2.[206] Isa. 11: 1 ff. predicted the Saviour's interweaving (*symplokê*) of humanity and divinity. The branch of 11: 1 is 'the man according to the flesh of our saviour', assumed by the only-begotten Son of God for his sojourn among men. The several spirits of 11: 2–3 stand compositely for the fullness of divinity (Col. 2: 9), 'God the Word, who dwells in him'. The manner of this divine indwelling is different from prophetic or apostolic inspiration. The language of the assumption of humanity by the Word of God and of the divine indwelling in the temple of Jesus' humanity, complete with citation of Col. 2: 9, a future Antiochene proof text, is noteworthy, since Eusebius is normally classified as an adherent of the Logos-sarx Christological framework.[207] His incarnational theology is stated most succinctly in a gloss on Isa. 61: 1–3, which he attributes directly to the incarnate Logos:

---

[202] Ibid. 36. 3–38. 9. Also mentioned here are the appearances to Abraham, Isaac, Jacob, Moses, and Ezekiel.

[203] Ibid. 32. 38, 334. 35–6.

[204] Ibid. 56. 7–25. See also Eusebius' comments on Isa. 7: 14 and 8: 1–4.

[205] Ibid. 40. 14–17.

[206] Sometimes literally *enanthrôpêsis*, more commonly *parodos, parousia,* and *epiphaneia.* See *Jesajakommentar,* ed. Ziegler, Index, s.v.

[207] Divine indwelling of the Logos is also mentioned at *CI* 294. 18–19. Cf. A. Grillmeier, *Christ in Christian Tradition: From the Apostolic Age to Chalcedon (451)* (New York, 1965), 180–2. On Col. 2: 9 and Antiochene Christology, see ibid. 397, 424, 449, and Jaroslav Pelikan, *The Emergence of the Catholic Tradition (100–600),* i of *The Christian Tradition: A History of the Development of Doctrine* (Chicago, 1971), 253.

This [i.e. that 61: 1–3 is spoken by the Logos with regard to himself] should be clear to those who think that the Christ of God is neither a mere man [*psilos anthrôpos*] nor an incorporeal and fleshless Word without any share of a mortal nature. They say that he is at the same time God and man, God in so far as 'the only-begotten' is 'God who is in the bosom of the Father' [John 1: 18], but man in so far as he is understood to be 'from the seed of David according to the flesh' [Rom. 1: 3].[208]

The chief features of his Christology thus include: opposition to the view that Christ was a mere man (*psilos anthrôpos*), long notorious in the region of Syria and Palestine because of its association with Paul of Samosata;[209] apparent adoption of the Logos-sarx framework, that is, the assumption that the Logos was substituted for a human soul in Christ;[210] and close dependence on classical New Testament passages such as Rom. 1: 3 and John 1: 18.

Eusebius' Christology is sometimes criticized for emphasizing the didactic function of the Incarnation at the expense of the Atonement.[211] In the *Commentary on Isaiah* Christ's Incarnation is often interpreted didactically, as in this passage on Isa. 43: 8–11:

The cause of the coming of Christ and the witness of the apostles to all nations is none other than to preach the knowledge of the God of the universe, and faith in him, and understanding about him, to those who before were uncomprehending, without understanding and unbelieving and in ignorance of him, and therefore the eyes of the mind were blind, and they were caught by the error of godless idolatry.[212]

But there are also instances where Eusebius expounds an understanding of Christ's death as expiatory sacrifice and redemption from the power of Satan.[213] Such language was deeply rooted in catechesis, the liturgy, and the New Testament itself, all of which treated Isaiah as a central inspiration for reflecting on Christ's Passion, death, and Resurrection. Eusebius could hardly escape its in-

---

[208] *CI* 378. 36–379. 1.

[209] See Eusebius' hostile account of Paul in *HE* 7. 27–8.

[210] Also evident in phrases like 'the fleshly instrument assumed by me for the sake of men' (*to di'anthrôpous analêphthen moi organon sômatikon, CI* 318. 27), and 'my corporeal humanity' (*ton emautou sômatikon anthrôpon,* ibid. 319. 17–29).

[211] Wallace-Hadrill, *Eusebius of Caesarea,* 100 ff., and Kelly, *Early Christian Doctrines,* 225. This is a major feature of the analysis of Eusebius' theology in Walker, *Holy City, Holy Places?,* 80–92.

[212] *CI* 279. 4–9. See also 269. 15–19. The didactic function of the Incarnation is a Eusebian commonplace, e.g. *HE* 1. 2. 23.

[213] See his comments on Isa. 43: 1, 50: 4–7, 52: 13–53: 12, and 63: 5–6.

fluence. Where the *Commentary on Isaiah* is concerned, there is scant evidence for an imbalance between a didactic-revelatory theology of the Incarnation and a redemptive, atoning theology of the Cross.

The Logos' intervention in history did not end with the Incarnation. For Eusebius, the Logos is the rock of Matt. 16: 18, upon which the church is founded.[214] This church is the instrument of evangelization to carry the Gospel-preaching to all men; the bishops, as the successors of the apostles of Christ, exercise rule (*archê*) over the godly polity in its Christian dimension.[215] And at the end of time the Logos will return with his avenging angels for the final judgement.[216]

Deutero-Isaiah, with its vigorous monotheism, yields most of the texts which coax statements from Eusebius on the sensitive subject of the relation of the Logos and the unbegotten God.[217] Sometimes, as with Isa. 45: 21, he will simply refer the text to the Logos without further comment.[218] When he chooses to confront the implicit challenge to Christian belief and piety of Isaiah's insistence that there is none besides the Lord, he will work in some kind of distinction between God and his Word, so that the text can be given a dual reference. One of his techniques is to adopt the Servant texts, which were traditionally interpreted Christologically, and to emphasize the Father-Son relation implied by the ambiguity of *pais* in Greek, and then to use these texts to force open the radical monotheism of other texts. He interpreted Isa. 43: 10b ('I, the Lord, and the servant [or son, *pais*] whom I have chosen') as referring to Father and Son, so that Isa. 44: 6b ('I am the first and I am the last, besides me none is God') may be understood in light of the earlier verse. As he says of Isa. 44: 6b: 'For the statement having been once made through the above verse (sc. 43: 10b), it is incumbent on us to invoke the same statement in relation to every theological assertion. For what was declared correctly once, is grasped everywhere as true.'[219] By definition there is only one unbegotten principle (*agennêton*) and one monarchical power over the universe. But his Word is revealed to be

---

[214] *CI* 293. 17–19.
[215] Ibid. 12. 22–8.
[216] His ecclesiastical and eschatological functions are discussed in more detail in the first three sections of Ch. VI.
[217] Examples: Isa. 42: 6–8, 43: 10–13, 44: 6–7, 44: 24.
[218] *CI* 297. 2–13.
[219] Ibid. 284. 14–18.

divine as well, on the basis of John 1: 1. The prophet spoke ambiguously in 44: 6b for the sake of his listeners who might confuse belief in the Father and his Word with polytheism.[220]

One other verse should be mentioned in this discussion, because Eusebius cited—for the only time—the speech of pre-existent Wisdom in Prov. 8: 22–31, which was so central as an exegetical crux in the Arian controversy.[221] Isa. 44: 24 reads, 'Thus says the Lord who redeems you and who forms you from the womb, "I the Lord, who accomplished all things, stretched out the heaven alone and hollowed out the earth."' In expounding the Logos' creative function, Eusebius quotes John 1: 1 to establish that the *kyrios* of Isa. 44: 24 is the Logos of the Johannine prologue. A further biblical support which he invokes is Prov. 8: 27a, 'When he made ready the heavens, I was there with him.' The Logos, says Eusebius, ministered (*diêkoneito*) to the Father, performed the Father's ordinances by his own will and order.[222] But he quotes no more than Prov. 8: 27a, so that he is not forced to address the Son's generation by the Father. Since he will deal at length with Prov. 8: 22–31 in the controversial treatises against Marcellus of Ancyra,[223] his very brief allusion is another indication of his reluctance to venture into issues which at that time could only provoke trouble.

---

[220] *CI.* 284. 19–33.

[221] On Prov. 8: 22–31 in the Arian controversy, see Pelikan, *Emergence of the Catholic Tradition*, 191–7.

[222] *CI* 287. 14–288. 2.

[223] Cf. *On the Ecclesiastical Theology* 3. 2. 3, discussed by Weber, *Christologie des Eusebius*, 127–31.

III

Eusebius as Exegete: Interpretive Method in the Commentary on Isaiah

The last chapter charged Jerome with misrepresenting Eusebius when he accused him of lapsing into Origenist allegory. To justify the charge we need to examine Eusebius' intentions and his performance as a biblical interpreter in the *Commentary on Isaiah*.[1] We will see that for Eusebius the difference between 'literal' (historical) and 'spiritual' interpretation meant something like the difference between fact and interpretation. His blend of literal and spiritual interpretation was marked by a dedication to grammatical analysis of the text, an acceptance of the church's traditional apologetic exegesis, a belief in the supernatural inspiration of biblical prophecy, a moderate and cautious exploitation of figurative interpretation, and a vivid sense of the hand of God in the events of his own day.

[1] Among earlier investigations, see Wallace-Hadrill, *Eusebius of Caesarea*, 72–99; Carmel Sant, 'Interpretatio veteris Testamenti in Eusebio Caesariensi', *Verbum Domini*, 45 (1967), 79–90; and des Places, *Eusèbe de Césarée commentateur*, 87–142. Wallace-Hadrill agrees with the present study in emphasizing the literal fulfilment of prophecy in Eusebius' exegesis, but ignores the importance of Old Testament fulfilments in Isaiah's lifetime and afterwards: 'Eusebius appears, indeed, to have been uneasy about historical reference to contemporary events embedded in the narrative of Isaiah' (p. 82). Nothing could be further from the truth. Sant recognizes that Eusebius' apologetic exegesis is distinguished by its foundation in the events of salvation history (p. 80), and rightly stresses that figurative or allegorical interpretation plays only a subordinate role in his exegesis. However, he doesn't appreciate how important it was to Eusebius to believe that the prophet possessed a direct vision of the whole of salvation history. As a result he fails to see that Eusebius thought prophecy was fulfilled literally (not just spiritually, *kata dianoian*) in events and institutions of Christian history. For Eusebius it was crucial that the redemptive work of Christ, the new people of God, the priesthood and the church—treated by Sant as realities accessible only to spiritual interpretation—were *visible* facts, verifiable by all. Otherwise, Sant's study of his interpretive method is clear and persuasive. Des Places's study, unlike the previous works, was able to take advantage of the new edition of the nearly complete *Commentary on Isaiah*. His rather cursory analysis of Eusebius' use of literal and spiritual interpretation in exegeting Isaiah concludes that Eusebius saw the two approaches as complementary methods (111 n. 8 and 125).

The opening section of this chapter analyses Eusebius' prefatory statement of purpose and his interpretive vocabulary. The second section describes him at work as a practitioner of the various tasks ancient grammar prescribed for understanding the literal meaning of a text. The third section explains his distinction between literal and spiritual interpretation. And the last section places Eusebius in the broader exegetical development of the third to fifth centuries.

1. The Preface to the *Commentary on Isaiah*

Eusebius was keenly interested in arguments about how to interpret the Bible, as we see for example in his polemic in the *Church History* against millenarian literalism and his attention to Origen's exegesis in Book 6 of the same work.[2] His technical vocabulary on the subject consists mostly of stock expressions and phrases rather than strictly defined terms.[3] The *Commentary on Isaiah* actually ignores much of the conventional allegorical terminology.[4] *Allêgoria* and its derivatives are used only about half a dozen times, three of which occur in the same passage; *tropos* and its derivatives only slightly more common; *theôria* in a technical hermeneutical sense but twice; and *anagôgê*, one of Origen's favourite terms, not at all.[5] *Ainigma* and *ainittomai* occur more often. The most common term for a more than literal meaning is *dianoia*, often in contrast with *lexis* or *historia*.

Ziegler's new edition commentary preserves a one-paragraph preface missing in Montfaucon's edition of the catena fragments.

---

[2] *HE* 3. 39. 10–13 (against the millenarianism of Papias); ibid. 6. 18–19, 22–5, 31–2 (on Origen); ibid. 7. 24–5 (on Dionysius of Alexandria's critique of millenarianism).

[3] As much as possible we will keep to Eusebius' actual exegetical vocabulary. Modern discussions of terminology often run the risk of over-systematizing patristic practice. Henri Crouzel has observed, for example, that Origen shows no awareness of the terminological distinction between 'typology' and 'allegory' that has been so prominent in the scholarly literature. In fact Origen never used the word 'typology', and 'allegory' could mean any kind of non-literal interpretation. H. Crouzel, 'La distinction de la "typologie" et "d'allégorie" ', *Bulletin de littérature ecclésiastique*, 65 (1964), 172. Grant, *The Letter and the Spirit*, 142, reminds us of the fluidity of ancient exegetical terminology.

[4] For ancient exegetical terminology, see Grant's valuable appendix to *The Letter and the Spirit*, 120–4; H. N. Bate, 'Some Technical Terms of Greek Exegesis', *JTS* 24 (1922–3), 59–66; J. Pepin, *Mythe et Allégorie* (2nd rev. edn.; Paris, 1976), 87–92, 559–63.

[5] Index, *Jesajakommentar*, s.v.

Since there is no title and the text begins rather abruptly, Ziegler concluded that it must originally have been longer.[6] The complete preface must have contained the statement reported by Jerome in which Eusebius promised to offer a literal interpretation of Isaiah. Though truncated, the new material is a useful statement of his intentions.

At times the Spirit showed the prophet his revelations plainly, so that there is no need for the techniques of allegory [*tropôn allêgorias*] to interpret the words, but (it is sufficient) to use the simple meanings alone [*psilais tais lexesin*]. But at other times (he showed them) through symbols of other realities [*pragmatôn*], which suggest another meaning [*dianoian*] by expressive [*emphantikois*] words and names—as in the case of dreams, 'eleven stars in number appeared to offer Joseph homage' [cf. Gen. 37: 5–10], in this way his brothers being represented; and in another example, he saw his brothers collecting ears of corn, a famine being thus symbolized [*êinigmenês*] [cf. Gen. 41: 1–36]. It is similar with the present prophet. Many of the things which he prophesied were seen through symbols, and many things were said in complex fashion, with those meant literally [*pros lexin*] woven together in the same passage with those meant spiritually [*pros dianoian*], as are found in the teachings of our Saviour, in which he is described as having said: 'Do you not say that there are four months and harvest is coming? Lift up your eyes and see the fields, that they are already white for the harvest' [John 4: 35]. Of these words, part is literal, but you would find much else that is spiritual [*dianoiai*], just as is the case with the present prophet, with whom you will find words that are immediately [*autolexei*] comprehensible, such as: ' "What is your abundance of sacrifices to me?" says the Lord; "I have had enough of burnt offerings", etc.' [Isa. 1: 11a]. But this is understandable by spiritual meaning [*pros dianoian*] alone: 'My beloved had a vineyard on a hill in a very fertile place, etc.' [Isa. 5: 1b].[7]

Revelations which are delivered plainly can be understood in the normally accepted meanings of the words and are therefore immediately comprehensible (*autolexei*).[8] But expressive and vivid words indicate that a deeper meaning (*dianoia*) is intended, the character of which is metaphorical rather than strictly allegorical; of Eusebius' three examples, only the Joseph material is genuinely allegorical, since the number 'eleven' possesses an intended but hidden meaning that the colour 'white' does not have in Jesus' harvest metaphor.

---

[6] Ibid., p. x.

[7] *CI* 3. 1–17.

[8] The same word Justin had used to describe prophetic utterance, cf. *First Apology* 32. 1, ed. Krüger (25. 16).

The examples presume that the distinction between literal and spiritual (or allegorical) interpretation depends on whether words are used in their normal meaning or in a special meaning intended by the author. Context and literary form (dream interpretation, parable, allegory, plain speech, etc.) determine which applies. Esotericism is not the issue. Rather, spiritual meaning has to do with salvation history, the continuous involvement of God in the historical life of Israel, culminating in Jesus' public ministry. The appropriate exegetical milieu is therefore the traditional catechesis of the church. There is no indication that spiritual interpretation should advance a private speculation, as Origen tended to do with the allegorical exposition of his own philosophical theology.[9] The opening paragraph of the commentary thus makes very limited claims for the occasion, the method, and the content of spiritual interpretation.

2. The Search for the Literal Meaning

When Eusebius speaks of the literal or historical meaning of the biblical text, he most often uses the phrase *kata* (or *pros*) *lexin*, less often *kata* (*pros*) *historian*.[10] Occasionally *lexis* and *historia* occur together as synonyms.[11] In the commentary *historia* means narrative history,[12] so *kata* (*pros*) *historian* refers to the fulfilment of prophecy in actual historical events, such as Nebuchadnezzar's campaign against Judah, or in other episodes of Old Testament history.[13] But it also can refer to the fulfilment of prophecy in the Christian era, even a miraculous event such as the virginal conception of the Logos in Mary's womb.[14] The phrase *kata* (*pros*) *lexin* means the literal sense, the plain, normal, customary meaning of a word. *Kata lexin* also refers to historical events and to the historical fulfilment of prophecy, and in fact is more common in this sense than *kata historian*.

To establish the literal sense of the biblical text, Eusebius drew on his thorough acquaintance with ancient grammar. He uses technical

---

[9] Cf. Grant, *The Letter and the Spirit*, 90–6.
[10] *Jesajakommentar*, ed. Ziegler, Index, s.v. More rarely he uses phrases like *hê procheiros lexis* (63. 27) or *psilê lexis* (3. 3; 84. 25; 369. 8).
[11] Ibid. 51. 13; 107. 13, 23; 108. 4–17.
[12] Ibid. 142. 76; 147. 25; 184. 26; 231. 1 (here *historia* is a synonym of *diêgêsis*).
[13] Ibid. 57. 2 (Isa. 8: 7–8); 249. 13 (40: 1–2).
[14] Ibid. 124. 15 (Isa. 19: 1).

terminology like *ekdosis*, an authoritative edition of a text (applied even to the sacred text of the church), and *antigraphos*, an actual manuscript copy.[15] He indicates the proper speaker in a biblical passage if there is confusion about it.[16] He marks transitions from indirect to direct speech, distinguishes singular from plural forms, and establishes important transitional points to a new subject matter (*hypothesis*).[17]

Specialized secular disciplines which aided him as a historian also helped him as an exegete. Chronology, ethnography, mythology, and geography all provided valuable information.[18] Etymology was another useful tool. Because etymology is often associated with allegorical interpretation, it may seem out of place to include it in a discussion of Eusebius' literal interpretation. And yet the etymological study of words was an accepted part of classical literary and linguistic scholarship.[19] Christian lexica differed from pagan collections only in that they were intended not for pure philological scholarship but as exegetical aids, consisting mostly of lists of biblical Hebrew and Aramaic place- and personal names.[20] Because Christians regarded the scriptures as inspired oracles, there was a natural tendency to exploit etymological meaning to uncover a deeper spiritual meaning in the text. Nevertheless, it was the existence of the lexica which gave rise to their allegorical exploitation, not the other way around. Franz Wutz, the foremost student of this Christian literature, noted long ago that the lexica were compiled in a sincere attempt to recover the actual, root meaning of the words, and only then put to use to discover hidden spiritual meanings.[21]

This seems to be the case with Eusebius' use of etymology. Although he applies the etymological meaning in ways that combine if

---

[15] Ibid. 205. 28.

[16] Ibid. 47. 23–4 (7: 13); 365. 32–4 (59: 12).

[17] Ibid. 15. 14; 153. 31 (to mark the beginning of the little apocalypse of Isa. 24–7); 174. 18–21 (to mark end of apocalypse); 275. 19–32; 283. 1–2.

[18] Chronology: ibid. 46. 8–36 (on Isa. 7: 8, an obscure verse for which he consulted Jewish expertise). Mythology: 298. 26–9 (Bel), 298. 29–30 (Dagon), 165. 13–19 (Baal of Pe'or). Ethnography: 246. 1–2 (Chaldean science, cf. also the comments on Isa. 47: 12–13), 100. 1–18 (Arabs/Saracens pitching tents in abandoned Babylon). Geography: 142. 4–21 (Seir), 195. 22–196. 5 (Leontopolis, Cynopolis), 150. 20–1 (Kittim), 45. 30 (Samaria), 177. 34 (Rhinocoroura), 194. 35–6 (Tanis).

[19] Cf. *RAC* vi. 819–31 on both pagan and Christian etymology.

[20] Ibid. 826.

[21] Franz Wutz, *Onomastica sacra: Untersuchungen zum Liber Interpretationis Hebraicorum Nominum des Hl. Hieronymus* (TU, no. 41, pts. 1 and 2; Leipzig, 1914), 351.

not confuse literal and spiritual interpretation, he takes it for granted
that the indispensable first step is to establish the root meaning of the
Hebrew original. Some examples will demonstrate this. Some of the
instances were part of an already established exegetical patrimony;
others were probably drawn from an etymological handbook called
The Interpretation of Hebrew Names, which has been preserved in
a Latin translation of Jerome.[22]

The etymology of Emmanuel, 'God with us', had obvious Christian connotations sanctioned by the New Testament itself (Matt. 1:
23). But Eusebius, with his interest in the history of Israel, was able
to give it a contemporary application in the reign of Ahaz as well.[23]
Christian exegetical tradition had also appropriated the root meaning of *Iêsous* as saviour, as Eusebius was fond of noting wherever
derivatives of *sôtêr* appeared in the text of Isaiah.[24] A more original
example of his use of etymology is his explanation of the enigmatic
word *Ariêl* as 'lion of God', which he probably derived from *The
Interpretation of Hebrew Names*.[25] At Isa. 15: 9, in the oracle against
Moab, he identified Ariel as the largest of the villages in the region of
Areopolis.[26] At 21: 8 the LXX rendered the obscure 'And a lion
called out . . .' of the Massoretic text with the even more obscure
'And call Uriah . . .', presumably because the translators confused
Hebrew *'aryeh* with *'ûrîyah*.

Eusebius wisely ignored the LXX in favour of the version of
Theodotion, which has 'Ariel' in Greek transcription.[27] With the
help of his etymology of Ariel as lion of God, he saw here a reference
to the roaring lion of Satan (1 Pet. 5: 8) and interpreted it as the

[22] The original title was probably *Hermêneia tôn hebraikôn onomatôn*. Eusebius
says in the *Church History* that this work was attributed to Philo (*HE* 2. 18. 7).
Jerome credited Origen with an addition to the original book that treated New
Testament names (*PL* 23: 771), cited in Nautin, *Origène*, 237 n. 50. The entire work
was actually anonymous, neither part having been written by Philo or Origen, though
Origen knew and used it (see Nautin, ibid., with citations). Modern critical edition of
Paul de Lagarde reprinted in S. Hieronymi, *Opera Exegetica* (*CCL*, lxxii; Turnholti,
1969), 59–161. All references are to the page and line of de Lagarde's edition, listed in
the margins of the *CCL* edition. Wutz, *Onomastica sacra*, is the fundamental modern
study of its origins and content.
[23] *CI* 48. 22–49. 4.
[24] E.g. ibid. 117. 19–20 (from Isa. 17: 10, 'God your saviour'); 134. 23 (Isa. 19: 20,
'The Word will send a man to save them . . .'); 166. 18–22 (26: 1, 'Behold, a strong city,
and he will set a wall and perimeter around it as a salvation . . .').
[25] *Liber interpretationis Hebraicorum nominum* (hereafter abbreviated as *Int. Heb.
nom.*), ed. de Lagarde 37. 19, 44. 17, 56. 27.
[26] *CI* 108. 14, 24–5; cf. 188. 31–3.
[27] Aquila and Symmachus follow the MT and read 'lion' and 'lioness'.

avenging angel who will work the overthrow of Babylon prophesied in the next verse (21: 9).[28] Finally, at Isa. 29: 1 Eusebius states that he has learned from Jewish interpreters that the altar of sacrifice in Jerusalem was named Ariel, lion of God, because it consumed the burnt offerings at the sacrificial rites.[29] These three instances show how Eusebius exploited the etymology of an enigmatic Hebrew word—as well as geography, Jewish exegetical lore, and the non-Septuagintal versions—to arrive at a literal and historical interpretation of the text. In none of the three does etymology lead to a merely allegorical interpretation.

Other sample etymologies in the *Commentary on Isaiah*: Israel, 'man who sees God'; Idumean, 'earthly'; Edom, 'earthly'; Kedar, 'darkness'; and Karmel, 'circumcision'.[30] Some of these were common coin in the Alexandrian tradition, being found in Origen and previously in Philo, and also in *The Interpretation of Hebrew Names*.[31] Given the philosophical concerns of Alexandrian exegesis, these etymologies are highly susceptible to allegorization in the service of platonic anthropology and metaphysics. Eusebius is quite ready to exploit them in this fashion, as a check of the relevant passages will show. Nevertheless, the allegorical meaning is rarely the main point of his interpretation, and is usually subordinated to the historical fulfilment of prophecy.

Consider, for example, how fulfilment of prophecy is the main motif of Eusebius' etymology of Kedar in Isa. 42: 11 ('Let the desert and its villages rejoice, the hamlets and those who dwell in Kedar; those who dwell in Petra shall rejoice . . .'):

Then he again preaches good tidings to the desert, about which so much has been said already, 'the desert and its villages', or according to the other versions: 'and its cities'; for there are many cities represented in the various constituencies [*politeias*] of the church, as indicated in the vision of Egypt, in which it was prophesied that there would be 'five cities in Egypt speaking

---

[28] *CI* 141. 1–13.
[29] Ibid. 187. 25–35, probably in part based on Jewish lore preserved in Caesarea, cf. Ch. V.3.1.
[30] Ibid. 349. 24; 222. 29–30; 223. 6; 273. 15–16; 211. 23–4.
[31] Israel: *mens videns Deum*, Origen, *Homilies on Numbers* 11 (*PG* xii. 648); *Int. Heb. nom.* 13. 21. Idumaean: *Gêinos*, Origen, *Fragments on Lamentations*, frag. 116 (ed. E. Klostermann, *Origenes' Werke*, iii. 227. 26); *Int. Heb. nom.* 63. 22. Edom: *terrenus*, Origen, *Homilies on Exodus*, 6 (*PG* xii. 336); *Int. Heb. nom.* 5. 24. Kedar: darkness, *Int. Heb. nom.* 4. 6–7. Karmel: knowledge of circumcision, *Int. Heb. nom.* 26. 7–8. Philonic instances are noted in Wutz's tabulation of Philo's etymologies, *Onomastica sacra*, 733–9.

in the tongue of Canaan and swearing by the name of the Lord of hosts' [Isa. 19: 1]. And it is stated that the 'hamlets and those who inhabit Kedar' and even beyond these 'those who dwell in Petra shall rejoice'. Kedar is beyond Arabia at the edge of the desert, which they say is held by the Saracen people, by whom the Word wished to indicate all those who inhabit the deserts and ends of the earth, because of the spiritual joy of God that is going to visit us by the grace of Christ. And Petra is a city of Palestine composed of superstitious men and saturated with demonic error; the prophet says that the dwellers of this same city shall have a share of grace: 'Those who dwell in Petra shall rejoice'. The course of events [*hê dia tôn pragmatôn ekbasis*] has confirmed the truth of these words, since in our day [*kath' hêmas*] the churches of Christ are established even in that very city of the Petrans, and throughout its countryside, and in the desert places of the Saracens. And besides, Kedar is translated 'darkness', because of those who have converted from darkness to the light which was prophesied to the nations. The Word says 'And those who inhabit Petra will rejoice' similarly; 'And the rock was Christ [*petra*] . . .'.[32]

This passage mixes together the historical fulfilment of prophecy ('the course of events', a stereotyped formula), geography, association of related passages by keyword (rock, cities), etymologically grounded allegorization, ethnography, etc. But the unifying theme is Eusebius' conviction that he was witnessing in his own time the actual fulfilment of what Isaiah had prophesied long ago. The exegetical focus is his confidence that even massively pagan communities will prove powerless to resist the Gospel in the new era.

But Eusebius' most valuable resource for the literal meaning of the text was Origen's Hexapla. Origen's training in grammar had acquainted him with the techniques developed by scholars in Alexandria to determine interpolations and scribal errors in recovering the authentic texts of the Greek literary classics. He put his knowledge of textual criticism to work in preparing a massive synopsis of the extant Greek versions of the Hebrew Bible, together with a Greek transliteration of the Hebrew text.[33] The purpose of this project, on which he laboured for many years, has been variously suggested as the fixing of the true text of the Septuagint, of which Origen had found divergent manuscripts; the preparation of a Septuagint corrected with reference to the Hebrew, for the sake of discussion with

[32] CI 272. 34–273. 18.
[33] For the following, I rely on the discussion of the Hexapla in Nautin, *Origène*, 303–61.

the Jews; and the attainment of the original Hebrew text of the Bible,
just as Alexandrian philologists sought to attain the original text of
Homer in their preparation of a critical edition.[34] Although the work
is commonly referred to as the Hexapla, Origen seems at first to
have been satisfied with a synopsis of four versions, preceded by
the Greek transliteration of the Hebrew, which Eusebius calls
'Tetrassa,' 'fourfold',[35] for the four versions of Aquila, Symmachus,
Theodotion, and the LXX. After discovering the existence of two
more versions, one in Nicopolis near Actium during a trip to
Greece, and the other reportedly found in a jar in the neighbour-
hood of Jericho, Origen prepared a six-fold synopsis, with transliterated Hebrew, that Eusebius calls 'Hexapla'.[36]

If Pierre Nautin's analysis is correct, neither synopsis contained a
Hebrew text in Hebrew characters. Rather, Origen adapted a synopsis in use in the Alexandrian synagogue, which originated as a reading aid for Jews who had lost the knowledge of Hebrew but were
still bound to pronounce the sacred text in the original words. At the
stage of its evolution when Origen obtained it, the synopsis had
already added the versions of Aquila and Symmachus, hence
Origen's otherwise puzzling placement of the Septuagint, the
church's authoritative text, in the fourth column, followed by the
version of Theodotion.[37] He discarded the Hebrew text in Hebrew
letters because of the difficulties it posed for Greek copyists and
because of his inability to use it.[38] In the column reserved for the
Septuagint, he entered a revised version corrected on the basis of
various LXX manuscripts and his other Greek versions. Passages
absent in the Septuagint were marked with an asterisk, and passages
in the Septuagint not contained in the other versions with an ob-
elus.[39]

Eusebius used the Tetrapla, not the Hexapla, in the composition
of the *Commentary on Isaiah*.[40] Because the new edition of the

---

[34] Ibid. 344–53, esp. 353.

[35] *HE* 6. 16. 4. Elsewhere, 'Tetrapla', see *Origène*, 451 f.

[36] Origen's own statements on these versions, which he calls the 'fifth' and 'sixth',
are preserved in several psalm catenae and reprinted by Nautin, *Origène*, 310.

[37] Ibid. 333–42.

[38] For an estimate of Origen's very limited knowledge of Hebrew, see Hanson,
Allegory and Event, 167–73, and Nautin, *Origène*, 339.

[39] Nautin, *Origène*, 342 f.

[40] As did Origen himself, according to Jerome (*Comm. Is.* Prol.). Eusebius
never cites the fifth or sixth versions which Origen added to create the Hexapla
(*Jesajakommentar*, p. xxxix).

Commentary makes available a great number of new Tetraplaric
citations lost in the catenae collections used by Montfaucon, it permits a closer assessment of Eusebius' exegesis than has hitherto been
possible. Since the establishment of a proper text is the first priority
for the commentator, let us examine his use of the Tetrapla, especially of the first column, the Greek transliteration of the Hebrew. It
will tell us much about the limits and the strengths of Eusebius'
exegetical method. Another reason for studying Eusebius' use of the
synopsis is that it represents an area of scholarship where he was
obliged to do original work for the last thirty-six chapters of Isaiah.
The fact that his tetraplaric citations do not diminish in the part of
Isaiah on which Origen did not comment (Isa. 30: 6 ff.) is convincing
proof of his facility with it. Nor should we forget that his training in
the school of Pamphilus had consisted first in the correction and
copying of manuscripts of the Hexapla.[41]

Eusebius' attitude to the Septuagint resembles Origen's.[42] In the
Church History he had approved of Irenaeus' assertion of the divine
inspiration of the Septuagint as a defence of its version of Isa. 7: 14
against the versions of Aquila and Theodotion.[43] However, the prologue to Book 5 of the *Proof of the Gospel* offers a somewhat
different perspective.

It is our present task, therefore, to collect these same expressions from the
prophetic writings of the Hebrews, so that by their agreement in each
separate part the demonstration of the truth may be established. And we
must recognize that the sacred oracles include in the Hebrew much that is
obscure both in expression and meaning, and are capable of various translations in Greek because of their difficulty. The Seventy Hebrews in concert
have translated them together, and I shall pay the greatest attention to them,
because it is the custom of the Christian Church to use their work. But
whenever necessary, I shall call in the help of the editions of the later
translators, which the Jews are accustomed to use today, so that my proof
may have stronger support from all sources.[44]

Thus Eusebius recognizes the Septuagint as the default text because
of its traditional place in the life of the church. But for philological
and apologetic reasons it may be supplemented with other sources.

---

[41] Reprinted in Nautin, *Origène*, 322 ff.

[42] Cf. Hanson, *Allegory and Event*, 163 f.

[43] *HE* 6. 8. 10–15, quoting Irenaeus, *Against Heresies* 3. 21. 1,2. Of course Eusebius
was also familiar with Jewish traditions about the inspiration of the Septuagint. See his
excerpts of the *Letter of Aristeas* in *PE* 8. 2–6.

[44] *DE* 5. Prol. (trans. Ferrar).

In purely literary terms the Septuagint is only a work of translation. Often the obscurities of the original Hebrew may be rendered more than one way in Greek, hence the value of the other versions. Second, the currency of the non-Septuagintal versions among contemporary Jews makes them useful for controversial discussion. As the index to the *Proof of the Gospel* shows, Eusebius uses them liberally.

In the *Commentary on Isaiah* roughly the same philological and apologetic principles are operative. The versions are often invoked when the Septuagint is obscure. Thus in one of the longest non-LXX citations, Eusebius makes Symmachus the basis for the whole of his commentary on Isa. 16: 5–14, because the traditional translation was too obscure to understand clearly.[45] The same is true of the Septuagint translation of texts such as Isa. 3: 25, 8: 16, 23: 2, 27: 12, 33: 7, and 45: 9 (where he admits that the Septuagint expresses the original *asaphôs*).[46] Another literary relativization of the Septuagint arises from his practice of commenting on passages which Origen had added to the corrected text, indicating them with an asterisk.[47] Although Eusebius recognizes such passages are additions to the church's traditional text, he treats them on the same terms as the ecclesiastical text, especially if they advance his apologetic programme. Thus Origen added the clause, 'A holy seed is its pillar', derived from a corrupt Hebrew text, to Isa. 6: 13. Eusebius acknowledges its absence in the church's manuscripts, but insists it is not superfluous (*peritton*) because the other versions bear testimony to it. The clause happens to support his exegesis of 6: 9–13 as a prediction of the Jews' rejection of Jesus and of the remnant, the holy seed, which accepted him.

The Septuagint is sometimes supplemented or displaced by the other versions if it seems to present an interpretive crux of some sort, such as an apparent contradiction between prophecy and history. At Isa. 11: 14 the LXX says that Ephraim and Judah will first (*prôton*) gather booty from Moab, and that the Ammonites will be the first (*prôtoi*) to obey them. The passage as a whole (11: 10–16) is a prophecy of the conversion of the nations and the ingathering of the dispersion, the kind of text Eusebius likes to apply to the Christian evangelization of the Gentiles. To avoid the historical error of saying

---

[45] *CI* 110. 12–112. 33.
[46] Ibid. 25. 29–35; 59. 12–17; 150. 24–5; 177. 26–30; 214. 28–215. 4; 290. 32–291. 6.
[47] For example, ibid. 21. 15–19 (Isa. 2: 22); 43. 15–44. 11 (6: 13); 221. 11–13 (34: 4).

that Moab and Ammon were the first non-Jewish peoples to accept Christianity, Eusebius notes that *prôton* and *prôtoi* are Septuagintal additions not found in the Hebrew or the other versions, and therefore are not the basis of his interpretation.[48] He treats the LXX as an inferior witness and grants precedence to the versions as expressions of the original Hebrew.

The other versions may also be preferred if they offer a translation which serves favourite apologetic themes. In the messianic prophecy of 11: 1, he adopts *kormos* (trunk) from the versions rather than LXX *rizê* (root), because the trunk with its branches lopped off is a more convincing image of the cessation of the Davidic line after the Exile, an important motif in Eusebius' anti-Jewish apologetic.[49] At 53: 2, another traditional Christian messianic proof text, Eusebius singles out the version of Aquila for the phrase 'like a root from untrodden ground' (*apo gês abatou*), whereas all other versions have 'thirsty ground' (*gê dipsôsê*), because he saw it as a prophecy of the virgin birth.[50] The Hebrew original of Isa. 9: 5 is defended because in his view it asserts more clearly the divinity of the Messiah.[51]

These examples illustrate Eusebius' willingness to subordinate the LXX to the other translations and to the original Hebrew.[52] As a rule, however, he rarely scuttles the traditional text. Instead, he tries to preserve the Septuagint reading along with the other versions, either by a harmonization of two or more readings, or by offering separate interpretations. The effect of either strategy is to undercut naïve confidence in the verbal fidelity and authority of a text that was the basis of liturgy, devotional life, preaching, and doctrine. In practice he substitutes Origen's Tetrapla as the most reliable avenue to the authoritative Hebrew original.

How does he justify such a substitution? As we have seen, his rationale is both scholarly and apologetic, a dual motivation which marks so much of his exegetical and historical writing. We will return to this rationale once we have looked more carefully at his view of the other versions and especially at his use of the 'Hebrew' column of the Tetrapla.

[48] For example, *CI* 89. 21–4; also 113. 21–114. 6.
[49] Ibid. 81. 8–16.
[50] Ibid. 335. 2–13.
[51] Ibid. 65. 18–67. 14.
[52] They may be supplemented by examples from other works by Eusebius in the analysis of D. Barthélemy, 'Eusèbe, la septante, et "les autres" ', in André Benoit (ed.), *La Bible et les Pères* (Paris, 1971), 53–5.

Of the other three Greek versions, Eusebius most often cites Symmachus, about twice as often as Aquila and three times as often as Theodotion.[53] Symmachus' version was known in antiquity for its clarity and smoothness, based on a desire to express the sense rather than the literal character of the original.[54] Eusebius shared this view of Symmachus' version, which he frequently qualifies as clearer (*saphesteron*).[55] The version of Theodotion is not described in the commentary in any special way, and is usually quoted in conjunction with one or both of the other versions. The peculiar quality of Aquila, also widely recognized in antiquity, was his scrupulous and even pedantic fidelity to the most literal aspects of the Hebrew text, a judgement echoed by Eusebius.[56] Given his incapacity with Hebrew, to which we will turn in a moment, he found Aquila's literalism most valuable. Aquila, he says in discussing Isa. 59: 11, has rendered the Hebrew wording in its proper literal meaning (*kalôs kyriolektôn tên Hebraikên lexin*), compared with the Septuagint.[57]

Eusebius' interpretation of Isa. 23: 18 deserves close study because of its demonstration of how he exploits Aquila. The LXX reads:

And it will happen that the commerce of it [i.e. of the city of Tyre] and the wages [*hê emporia autês kai ho misthos*] shall be holy to the Lord; it will not be gathered for them but for those who dwell before the Lord will be the whole of its commerce, to eat and drink and to be filled as a memorial symbol before the Lord.

Observes Eusebius:

To seek out the exact form of the reading, I gave my attention to the translation of Aquila, which says, 'And it will happen that its commerce and wages [*emporion autês kai misthôma*] are consecrated to the Lord'. Thus the Hebrew has, precisely [*akribôs*], 'commerce and wages' [*emporion kai misthôma*] without the articles, not according to the Septuagint, 'the commerce and the wages', by which it appears to mean *all* the commerce and *all*

---

[53] *Jesajakommentar*, ed. Ziegler, Index, 443 f. Wallace-Hadrill's assertion of Aquila's dominance (*Eusebius of Caesarea*, 62) in Eusebius' Old Testament exegesis must now be corrected, at least for the *Commentary on Isaiah*.

[54] So Jerome, *Commentary on Amos* 3. 1, cited in H. B. Swete, *An Introduction to the Old Testament in Greek* (Cambridge, 1900), 51.

[55] *CI* 82. 23–4; 110. 12; 215. 15; 290. 33–4. Barthélemy noted that Eusebius owed these characterizations of the non-Septuagintal versions to Origen, cf. 'Eusèbe, la septante, et "les autres"', 52.

[56] On Origen's judgement of Aquila's literal accuracy, cf. the citations assembled by Nautin, *Origène*, 335 n. 72.

[57] *CI* 365. 16–24. At Isa. 1: 25 Aquila is *leukôteron* (ibid. 12. 11).

the wages [emphases added], but according to Aquila 'its commerce and wages are consecrated to the Lord'. For not its whole commerce nor its whole wages but a part of the commerce and a part of the wages are consecrated to the Lord.

And this is what has been fulfilled in our day [*kath' hêmas autous*]. For the church of God is established in the city of Tyre, as indeed in the rest of the nations, and many of the wages in it and what is stored up for business are offered to the church and consecrated to the Lord. The things that people bring they offer in piety, not for themselves in order to enjoy the gifts offered to God, but 'for those who dwell before the Lord', namely, for those who serve at the altar, 'for the Lord had enjoined that those who preach the gospel should live by the gospel' and 'those who serve at the altar share in the sacrificial offerings'. [1 Cor. 9: 13][58]

Eusebius goes on to say that it is possible to harmonize the rest of the Septuagint's version with the Hebrew reading and with the other versions, except for the phrase 'the whole of its commerce' (*pasa hê emporia*), which is not attested outside the Septuagint.

This wordy quibbling over definite articles illustrates several points. First, it shows how Eusebius used Aquila as a strict equivalent of the Hebrew. He says, 'To seek out the exact form of the reading, I gave my attention to the translation of Aquila...' and concludes that the Hebrew must have precisely what he found in Aquila. Second, his grammatical scrupulosity serves apologetic motives as much as pure philology. He wants to round off the oracle on Tyre, tenth and last of the oracles on the nations, with a prophecy of the city's contemporary renewal and return to prosperity after persecution, because he was a good friend of Paulinus, bishop of Tyre, for whom he composed the long oration preserved in *HE* 10. 4 and delivered at the dedication of the rebuilt basilica of Tyre. He stresses the prophecy's contemporary fulfilment with emphatic language: '*ho dê kai plêroutai kath' hêmas autous; to apotelesma ... ergois autois kath' hêmas plêroumenon*'.[59] Finally, this interpretation is one of many examples in the *Commentary on Isaiah* of the application of a prophecy to the concrete life of the institutional church: Eusebius is giving his readers a biblical exhortation for dedications and contributions of their business profits to the welfare of the church and its clergy. He cares about the absence of the definite article in the Hebrew perhaps because he does not wish converts to

[58] *CI* 152. 23–153. 2.
[59] Ibid. 152. 31; 153. 9–10.

think they must contribute the whole of their wealth to the church; a part (*meros ti*) will be sufficient.

Eusebius' reliance on Aquila for the exact form of the Hebrew does not suggest he had confidence in his facility with the language. The evidence of the *Commentary on Isaiah* shows his ability to use even the transliterated Hebrew text of the Tetrapla was severely limited.[60] When he refers to the Hebrew text, he does so normally only because he has a uniform reading among the non-Septuagintal versions. This is true of the vast majority of instances where 'the Hebrew word' or 'the Hebrew reading' is mentioned. A check of the index shows that with few exceptions Eusebius customarily appeals to the Hebrew only when he is able to find a uniform attestation for it in Aquila, Symmachus, and Theodotion, referred to collectively as *hoi loipoi hermêneutai*.[61] Even then he avoids a direct quotation of the content of the transliteration, satisfying himself with the bare statement that it agrees with *hoi loipoi hermêneutai*. The inference is unavoidable that his main evidence for the Hebrew is not his comprehension of the transliteration but the harmony of the Greek versions. When they agree, they must be reliable indications of the Hebrew. That he could read the Hebrew text in Hebrew script seems on the evidence of the commentary out of the question, quite apart from Nautin's thesis that Origen's Tetrapla and the Hexapla never contained a Hebrew Bible.

There are indeed some instances where Eusebius quotes directly from the transliterated Hebrew text. These mostly involve well-known biblical proper nouns that Eusebius could have recognized visually if the transliterated Hebrew resembled the Greek spelling of the word, a conjecture which could be easily checked by consulting

---

[60] On Eusebius' knowledge of Hebrew, cf. E. Nestle, 'Alttestamentliches aus Eusebius', *Zeitschrift für die alttestamentliche Wissenschaft*, 29 (1909), 57–62. Barnes is not convincing in his statement that Eusebius had 'some genuine knowledge of the language and its grammar'. Other than the many citations of 'the Hebrew' listed in Ziegler's index to the commentary, which I dismiss as really based on the Greek versions, the only evidence Barnes offers is Eusebius' explanation of Hebrew *Basan* as 'shame'. However, Eusebius could have learned this simply by consulting *The Interpretation of Hebrew Names*, where the etymology given in the second entry for Basan is *confusio sive pinguedo vel siccitas* (45. 3 ed. de Lagarde), although Jerome did emend the first entry so that in the extant form it reads: *Basan bruchus sive pinguedo. Nam quod interpretari solet ignominia vel confusio, busa dicitur* (16. 18–19, ed. de Lagarde).

[61] This can be easily confirmed by comparing the valuable lists of references on p. 444 of Ziegler's edition, where entries under *das Hebräische* are matched by entries on the same page and line under *die übrigen Übersetzer*.

Aquila. Examples: Eusebius could have known that the Hebrew of Isa. 25: 10 had 'Moab' rather than 'the region of Moab' (in the LXX *hê Moabitis*, sc. *chôra*) both from the transliteration and from the version of Aquila, which he quotes in the discussion of this passage.[62] Similarly, when Eusebius comments that the dragon or serpent (*drakôn*) of Isa. 27: 1 (LXX) is called *leviathan* in Hebrew, he could have inferred this from the version of Aquila, whose translation *epi leviathan ophin* parallels the Septuagint's *epi drakonta ophin*, and confirmed his inference by finding *leviathan* spelled out in the transliteration.[63]

In Isa. 21: 2 the Septuagint translators substituted Persians for Medes, but Eusebius knew from the unanimous testimony of the other versions that the Hebrew had to have 'Medes', rather than 'Persians'. A quick check of the transliteration would confirm the presence of a Hebrew word, *Madaî* that looked much like the Greek form *Mêdoi*.[64] In this case Eusebius had occasion to consult the Hebrew because of a contradiction between the LXX of 21: 2 and Isa. 13: 17. If the LXX version of 21: 2 were accepted, the prophecy that the Elamites and the Persians would overthrow Babylon appeared to contradict Isa. 13: 17, where the prophet identified the Medes as the captors of Babylon. The correct prophetic and historical sequence could be preserved by accepting the evidence of the other Greek versions. The Septuagint translation could be harmonized with them if one recalled that historically the Persians succeeded the Medes not long after the destruction of Babylon; the LXX may have hinted at the Medes when it spoke of 'the ambassadors of the Persians' in 21: 2. 'In this way', he concludes with satisfaction, 'the integrity of the passage could be maintained.'[65]

Sometimes Eusebius reveals by his allusion to the spelling of names that he is feeling his way rather than reading with real comprehension. He observes that the Hebrew name translated by the LXX in Isa. 21: 8 cannot be 'Uriah' because the letters spelling the name in the transliteration are not the same as the letters spelling 'Uriah' in Isa. 8: 2. This is true, since as noted in our earlier reference to Isa. 21: 8 the Hebrew has *'aryeh* (lion), in Greek transcription perhaps *arie*, whereas Uriah (*'ûrîyah*) may have looked like *ouria*,

---

[62] *CI* 165. 6–9.
[63] Ibid. 173. 28–174. 1. Origen had already given this interpretation (C. Cels. 6. 25).
[64] *CI* 138. 27–139. 13.
[65] Ibid. 139. 13.

neither *aleph* nor *he* being represented. However, one gets the impression that Eusebius has been forced to make a painstaking letter-by-letter comparison of the words in the transliteration in order to reassure himself the LXX has no basis in the original. Frustrated by the obscurity of the LXX, he ignores it entirely rather than mount a harmonizing salvage operation.[66]

Isa. 28: 1, an oracle against Samaria, contains a Hebrew phrase which the RSV translates as 'of the rich valley', in Hebrew *geî'-shemanîm*, literally, 'valley of oils'.[67] All four versions reflect this meaning: *tou orous pacheôs* (LXX, though 'mountain' is obscure here), *pharangos liparôn* (Aquila), *pharangos piotêtôn* (Symmachus), and *pharangos pionôn* (Theodotion).[68] With this sort of unanimity Eusebius would not as a rule bother to cite the transliteration, but in this case he has a strongly apologetic reason for appealing to the authority of the Hebrew original. 'One of the brethren', perhaps Pamphilus, had told him of a Christian tradition that the Hebrew of Isa. 28: 1 contained the name 'Gethsemani' and was therefore a prophecy of Judas' betrayal of Jesus in the garden. The tradition fits the heavily apologetic flavour of his exegesis of this passage, so he adopts it. Although Gethsemani is not actually in the Hebrew, Eusebius is not far off the mark. *The Interpretation of Hebrew Names* defined Gethsemani as *vallis pinguedinum*, the Latin equivalent of the Greek translation of *geî'-shemanîm*,[69] and Gethsemani appears to derive from Aramaic for 'oil vat'.[70] Nevertheless, the transliteration does not seem to have been of much use if his chief source is someone's oral report.

Other evidence that he could make but feeble use of it is his interpretation of the Hebrew phrase *'êl gibbôr* in Isa. 9: 5 as 'mighty God' (*dynatos theos*). Although all the non-Septuagintal versions

---

[66] Ibid. 140. 23–141. 31.

[67] Francis Brown, S. R. Driver, and C. A. Briggs (eds.), *A Hebrew and English Lexicon of the Old Testament* (Boston, New York and Chicago, 1906), 161. The NRSV has changed this to 'rich food'.

[68] *Isaias*, ed. Ziegler, 215. In the hexaplaric apparatus of his critical edition of Isaiah for the Göttingen series, Ziegler reports the version of Aquila as *pharangos liparôn*, which I have adopted in my analysis. However, his edition of the *Commentary on Isaiah* gives the version of Aquila as *pharangos rypariôn* (*CI* 179. 7). Is the latter a copyist's error?

[69] *Int. Heb. nom.* 61. 22.

[70] *Interpreter's Dictionary of the Bible*, 4 vols. (New York and Nashville, 1962), ii. 387. According to the new *Anchor Bible Dictionary*, ed. D. N. Freedman, 6 vols. (New York, 1992), ii. 997, from Hebrew and Aramaic words for oil-press.

render *'êl* as *ischyros* rather than *theos*, Eusebius knew that *'êl* meant
God in Hebrew, and he apparently guessed from the parallelism of
the phrase in Aquila, Symmachus, and Theodotion that *gibbôr*
meant mighty: *ischyros dynatos* in Aquila and Symmachus, *ischyros
dynastês* in Theodotion.[71] There is also the possibility that he borrowed the etymology from Origen. In any case, here too an apologetic motive prompted the venture into the Hebrew original. The
Septuagint's phrase 'angel of great counsel' did not credit Christ
with a properly divine dignity, an inadequacy that Origen had also
felt in answering the criticisms of Celsus.[72] Eusebius declared that
the Hebrew original endowed Christ with a greater honour by
explicitly recognizing him as God. He protected the Septuagint
version by admitting that he might also be called appropriately the
angel of great counsel, in the sense that by virtue of his divinity the
Saviour had exclusive access to the ineffable will of the Father.[73]

    The last example, Isa. 19: 18, is the most problematic in that it
suggests more originality on Eusebius' part than we have seen thus
far. The LXX reads: 'On that day there will be five cities in Egypt
speaking in the Canaanite language and swearing by the name of the
Lord; one city will be called *polis-asedek*.' The Massoretic text has
'îr ha-heres, 'city of destruction', probably a pun for *'îr ha-heres*,
'city of the sun', i.e. Heliopolis,[74] a reading attested in the Qumran
Isaiah scroll and in other early versions.[75] Eusebius only gives the
version of Symmachus, *polis hêliou*. From other sources we know
that both Aquila and Theodotion simply transliterated the Hebrew
into Greek characters as *polis-ares*.[76] His interpretation of Isa. 19: 18
is based on a composite of the Septuagint and Symmachan versions.
Understanding *polis-asedek* as 'city of righteousness', he combines
the Septuagint with Symmachus' 'city of the sun' and interprets
the passage ecclesiologically as a prophecy of the coming of the
Christian church to Egypt, since Mal. 4: 2 calls Christ 'sun of

---

[71] See his extensive commentary on this passage in *CI* 65. 18–67. 14. There is no
etymology for *gibbôr* in *The Interpretation of Hebrew Names*.

[72] *C. Cels.* 5. 53. On Origen's interpretation of this passage, see now Joseph Trigg.
'The Angel of Great Counsel: Christ and the Angelic Hierarchy in Origen's Theology', *JTS* 42 (1991), 35–51.

[73] *CI* 66. 2–16. Cf. also 77. 3–8.

[74] *Hebrew and English Lexicon of the Old Testament*, 249.

[75] *Biblia Hebraica Stuttgartensia*, ed. K. Elliger and W. Rudolph (Stuttgart, 1977),
703.

[76] For Aquila and Theodotion, cf. Codex Marchalianus and the Syro-Hexapla of
this verse, cited in *Isaias*, ed. Ziegler, 191.

righteousness' and the church may therefore be considered as the city of the sun of righteousness. This is a typical example of how he harmonizes the versions to produce the apologetically most useful interpretation.

But Eusebius also draws attention to 'the exact wording of the Hebrew', which he says is 'Areopolis'. We have seen that when Eusebius appeals to the precise wording of the Hebrew text, without referring to the unanimous testimony of Aquila, Symmachus, and Theodotion, he is really making an inference based on the Greek transliteration or is following the version of Aquila as equivalent to the Hebrew. He apparently derived the ostensible Hebrew reading of 'Areopolis' from Aquila's Greek transliteration of Hebrew *'îr ha-heres* as *polis-ares*, hence Areopolis, a Moabite urban name with which he was familiar.[77] In the *Onomasticon* he reported that some consider the Greek etymology of Areopolis to be 'city of Ares'.[78] Furthermore, the *Interpretation of Hebrew Names* says that Ares means 'sun', so that Areopolis might have suggested to him 'city of the sun', consistent with the interpretation he has espoused on the basis of the version of Symmachus.[79] Instead, however, he makes the curious claim that Areopolis actually means 'city of the *land*'. This reading too supports an ecclesiological interpretation: the universal and catholic nature of the church, which is the city of God established throughout the whole land or world. How did Eusebius come by this peculiar etymology? Perhaps he conjectured that Aquila's and Theodotion's *ares* stood for Hebrew *'ereṣ*, which does not how-ever appear in his Hebrew glossary. It is also possible that he guessed that it came from Aramaic *'ar'â*, which he may have known from the local Palestinian dialect of Aramaic or from Syriac.[80] Here, then, is an instance where Eusebius may be drawing on his own knowledge, but perhaps of Aramaic rather than Hebrew.

To summarize the conclusions of this section: we have been examin-ing Eusebius' use of the various tools ancient grammar provided for deriving the literal meaning of a text, with major attention to his use

[77] Cf. the Moabite city mentioned in the *CI* 108. 16, 110. 8–9.

[78] Eus., *Onomasticon*, ed. Klostermann, 36. 25–7. On the actual etymology of Moabite Areopolis, see Glen Bowersock, 'The Arabian Ares', in *Tria Corda*, 142–5.

[79] For Ares = 'sun', cf. *Int. Heb. nom.* 31. 16.

[80] A knowledge of Syriac is implied by his claim to have translated the correspond-ence of Jesus and King Abgar of Edessa, taken from the Edessene royal archives, for inclusion in the *Church History* (*HE* 1. 13. 5, 22).

of Origen's biblical synopsis. As we have abundantly documented, Eusebius' scholarship was inspired both by literary-critical and by apologetic goals. We can admire his energy in pursuing these goals while criticizing his inability to keep them distinct. From his point of view, the criticism would probably lack force. His main project was to open the intended meaning of a *prophetic* text, which he took for granted was oriented towards Christian claims. For this purpose he used the best tools at his disposal. The present section has sought only to illustrate how he exploited his education and his scholarly resources to unpack what he saw as the literal meaning of the prophetic oracles.

Perhaps we can say that the most positive achievement of this level of his exegesis was his use of the Tetrapla to relativize the status of the Septuagint and to recognize the *de facto* authority of the Hebrew original. The recognition did not result in a formal dethronement of the traditional text of the church. That was certainly never Eusebius' intention. But it is at least an implicit consequence of the critical method he employed in his commentary. The scripture that he actually interpreted was Origen's synopsis, which he treated as a virtual diatessaron of the Old Testament. The apologetic overlay of his exegesis should not conceal the fact that he elevated the versions to a status equal to the Septuagint. They claimed their authority as comparable and sometimes superior expressions of a text prior in time and authority to all of them, the Hebrew original. This was a prerequisite step towards Jerome's decision to jettison the ecclesiastical text altogether in favour of a fresh approach to the original. Eusebius never took the step, but his persistent appeals to 'the Hebrew', however limited in scope and execution, show that he would not have disapproved of it.[81]

---

[81] Barthélemy has also credited Eusebius for this achievement in the above cited article, 'Eusèbe, la septante, et "les autres"', 64 f. We should draw attention to his thesis in this article that Eusebius saw the non-LXX versions as providential unveilings of the true meaning of the Hebrew Bible, concealed in the pre-Christian era by the obscurity of the Septuagint. If correct, this interesting speculation suggests that Eusebius sought to co-opt a similar invidious comparison of LXX and non-LXX versions being made by rabbinic commentators, who were seeking to discredit a translation now thoroughly identified with Christianity. So far as the *Commentary on Isaiah* is concerned, however, I can find no evidence of such a theory, except perhaps for Eusebius' explanation that the LXX ignored the MT's 'mighty God' in the messianic prophecy of Isa. 9: 6 (LXX 9: 5), because it preferred to be silent about the transcendent greatness of such a title, indicating the saviour by a phrase ('angel of great counsel') with a special meaning (*CI* 66. 32–5). But this passage is only partially supportive, since for Eusebius the other versions are even less useful than the LXX, and Eusebius ends by appealing to the Hebrew itself.

3. Prophecy Fulfilled: Biblical Interpretation
kata lexin and *kata dianoian*

This chapter began with a discussion of Eusebius' opening statement on the exegesis of a prophetic text. In the first section we saw that Eusebius seemed to limit spiritual interpretation to passages where the literary form of the text (metaphor, parable, allegory) required it. At that point we left the subject of the relation of literal and spiritual interpretation in the commentary in order to study Eusebius' methods of identifying the literal meaning of the text. The present section returns to the initial question and argues that spiritual interpretation aims to uncover the inner, religious, and supernatural dimension of historical events. This is the dominant though not the only meaning of Eusebius' spiritual interpretation. Historical events were not mere ciphers or codes for ineffable realities to which they had only a symbolic or arbitrary relation.[82] The spiritual interpretation of a prophetic text revealed the meaning of a historical event in the overall design of God's salvific plan.[83] The history of Israel during its tenure as the godly polity was the medium in which God worked out his plan to bring the city of God to its final goal in heaven at the end of human history. From this perspective no aspect of Israel's history was merely secular, since the Logos was directing and governing its whole history at every step of the way. The prophet's mission was to interpret the meaning of the nation's history by

---

[82] There is a contrast here with the approach of Origen, at least as some of his critics have read him. Cf., e.g. R. P. C. Hanson's study of Origen's biblical exegesis, *Allegory and Event*, especially ch. 10. Hanson criticized the 'revisionist' interpretation of Origen's exegesis associated especially with Henri de Lubac and Jean Daniélou, who are more enthusiastic about Origen's use of allegorical interpretation. For de Lubac's view of Origen, see *Histoire et esprit: L'Intelligence de l'Écriture d'après Origène* (Paris, 1950), and *Exégèse médiévale: Les Quatre sens de l'Écriture*, 2 vols. in 4 pts. (Paris, 1959–64), i, pt. 1, 198–304 explicitly on Origen. De Lubac and Daniélou themselves differ on the precise evaluation of Origen's allegory, with Daniélou holding that only part of Origen's spiritual interpretation is authentically Christian. De Lubac's rejoinder may be found in ' "Typologie" et "allégorisme" ' *RSR*, 34 (1947), 181–226. On Daniélou's research in Origen's exegesis, see the works cited on p. 190 n. 2. A convenient summary of the discussion of allegory and typology is found in the study of Jo Tigcheler, *Didyme l'Aveugle et l'exégèse allégorique* (Nijmegen, 1977), 44–51. Henri Crouzel, *Origen: The Life and Thought of the First Great Theologian* (San Francisco, 1989), 61–84, also defends Origen's spiritual interpretation. Much of the French ecclesiastical school's defence of Origen's exegesis may be granted without negating the basic point of this study, which has to do with the religious significance of history as a process. On that point there is an essential difference between Origen and Eusebius; Hanson's critique is right.

[83] For more on this subject, see Ch. V.3.

declaring the divine will and predicting the consequences of the nation's deeds and policies. In a sense spiritual interpretation really amounted to repeating, from the hindsight of historically fulfilled prophecy, what Isaiah had proclaimed long ago.

There may be an analogy here with the modern historian's distinction between fact and interpretation, or event and meaning. In Eusebius' approach to prophecy and history, the literal fulfilment of prophecy referred to historical events in their bare facticity, which could be verified by any external observer. The spiritual fulfilment of the prophecy referred to the religious meaning that was embodied in and realized by the events. Because questions of meaning concern intellectual and spiritual objects that only the mind is capable of grasping, spiritual interpretation is properly described as *kata dianoian*. Philo and pagan authors used *dianoia* to mean both an instrument for knowing divine and heavenly realities, and the hidden meaning discerned by the allegorist.[84] In Eusebius, too, *dianoia* means the mental faculty by which we understand and the conceptual object that is understood, but in his usage the word has been brought down to earth and historicized. Spiritual interpretation tells us about the divine dispensation and enactments that according to the Bible actually guide human history and of which the human events are a ratification and realization. It also tells us about the subjective spiritual condition of the human actors in history, their moral well-being and their relation to God, as revealed in their historical destiny. Underlying both is a view of divine and human causality and co-responsibility that Eusebius presumes throughout his commentary and that informs his historical writing as a whole.[85]

This seems the most helpful way to understand Eusebius' habitual contrast of prophecy fulfilled *kata lexin* and *kata dianoian*. Let us now examine passages where he invokes both modes of interpretation. The first set has to do with prophecies fulfilled within the history of the Old Testament. A second set will have to do with prophecies fulfilled in the Christian era.

A large part of the *Commentary on Isaiah* is devoted to historical interpretation rooted in the history of Israel. Inner-biblical

---

[84] On *dianoia* in allegorical terminology, see Grant, *The Letter and the Spirit*, 125 f.
[85] Well analysed by Glenn Chesnut, *The First Christian Histories*, ch. 3, esp. 86 f. Chesnut explores the development of Eusebius' philosophy of history in terms of the classical historiographical tradition, but it has biblical antecedents as well.

fulfilments of prophecy are especially evident in comments on the first third of the book of Isaiah, through ch. 23, which concludes the ten oracles against the nations (13–23). This part of Isaiah is most explicitly defined in time and place, as compared to the eschatological tone of sections such as chs. 24–7, ch. 34, or Trito-Isaiah. The historical narrative of Isa. 36–9 receives an almost exclusively literal interpretation. And sections of Deutero-Isaiah which refer directly to exilic and post-exilic history are interpreted literally. In general Eusebius was quite ready to situate prophecy within the horizon of Israelite history if references to persons, places, or events showed this was appropriate. But various cues, such as a classic Christian proof text, an explicitly eschatological prophecy, rare or obscure diction, traditional keywords, or an 'open' text that lacked historical specificity, could be invitations to move to a Christian frame of reference.

Consider his reading of the oracles against the nations in Isa. 13–16, to which should be added the song against Assyria in 10: 5–19. A regular theme here is that literal interpretation of the prophecy has to do with the nations' political and military defeats, and its spiritual meaning with the overthrow of their gods. Isa. 10: 16–19 predicts that Assyria will suffer the divine wrath for arrogantly exceeding its commission to chastise Israel. The prophecy is fulfilled literally (*pros men lexin*) in Nebuchadnezzar's destruction of Assyria and spiritually (*pros de dianoian*) in the eclipse of the tutelary demon of Assyria, which presides over the nation's destiny.[86] Similarly, the oracle against Moab (15: 1–16: 14) is fulfilled literally (*kata tên historian*, 108.4; *pros lexin*, 108.17) in the invasion of Assyrians and Babylonians and in the subsequent Arab domination of Moab (cf. Isa. 15: 7, LXX).[87] Because the text is wholly comprehensible in its obvious and direct sense, Eusebius disavows allegorical interpretation (*tên tropikên . . . theôrian*) as forced and unnecessary.[88]

These ideas are developed at greater length in the treatment of the taunt song against the king of Babylon (Isa. 14: 3–21), much of which is given a strictly literal interpretation.[89] But at 14: 20 a discrepancy between the versions provokes a digression. The

---

[86] *CI* 76. 10–15.

[87] Ibid. 108. 3–8.

[88] What we find is the same sort of spiritual interpretation as in the foregoing passage; see the interpretation of the demon Dibon, ibid. 108. 19–38.

[89] Ibid. 102. 11–103. 5.

Septuagint of 14: 20 reads, 'You destroyed my land and slew my people', an assertion which Eusebius says accords plainly with the historical fact of the Babylonian campaigns against Judah in the sixth century. Therefore nothing further need be sought to explain the text (104. 3–5). But the Hebrew and the other versions read, 'You destroyed your own land and slew your own people', a literal crux which conceals a deeper meaning (*bathyteron hypoballei noun*, 103. 34). Since the king of Babylon did not actually destroy his kingdom, the invisible power which presides over the Babylonian nation is being hinted at (*ainittetai*, 104. 10). This power co-operated (*synepratten*, 104. 20) in Babylon's imperial hegemony, and was considered by the people to be their god. Therefore he was responsible for their destruction, since they exhibited the same pride as he when he sought glory equal to that of the true God (14: 14), and both nation and demonic patron fell together.[90] By way of further explanation, Eusebius refers the reader to the Danielic doctrine of national archons (Dan. 10: 13, 20–1, and 8: 20–1), and to the LXX version of Deut. 32: 8, which patristic writers understood as expounding the same idea of angelic watchers over the nations of the earth. Eusebius himself discussed this doctrine at length in the *Proof of the Gospel*.[91]

Thus Isa. 14 tells how the historic fate of Babylon is implicated with the fate of their patron archon. Historical destiny is a working out or reflection of a struggle waged on a higher, spiritual plane. An instructive comparison can be made here with Origen's exegesis of Isa. 14. In *On First Principles* Origen denied that a verse such as 14: 12 could apply to the historical king Nebuchadnezzar. A worthier interpretation applied the text, and indeed the whole chapter, to the primeval fall of Lucifer.[92] In the *Homilies on Jeremiah* he saw Nebuchadnezzar as a symbol of the devil's striving to subdue human souls.[93] Eusebius ignored both the pastoral application and the primeval myth, because they were marginal to his fundamental interest in Isaiah's prophecies about Jewish and Christian history.

Eusebius believed that Isaiah's prophecies were fulfilled in the Christian era as well. He found abundant prophecies predicting the events of Christ's life, death, and resurrection, the fate of the Jews,

---

[90] *CI.* 104. 18–36.
[91] *DE* 4. 7–8.
[92] *De Princ.* 1. 5. 5 and 4. 3. 9.
[93] *Hom. in Jer.* 1. 4 (SC 232, 200. 22–9), 19. 4 (SC 238, 230. 13–232. 18).

the calling of the Gentiles and the evangelization of the Roman Empire, the persecutions, the present prosperity and life of the church, and the return of Christ as judge at the end of time.[94] Prophecies of these events were capable of the same dual interpretation of external event and inner spiritual meaning as were prophecies fulfilled in the Old Testament. So were eschatological prophecies as yet unfulfilled.[95] Numerous examples can be found of the literal fulfilment of prophecy in Christian times, sometimes highly specific in nature, as in the reading of Isa. 27: 11b as literally and historically fulfilled (*pros lexin kai pros historian*) in the women who reported Jesus' resurrection.[96] Eusebius was especially impressed by prophecies fulfilled in his own time, which he encouraged his contemporary readers to verify.[97] Often, however, it is unclear whether a particular prophecy should be construed literally or spiritually.

Our stress on Eusebius' historical focus is not meant to suggest that he repudiated his Origenist heritage. He never ceased to think of himself as a protégé of Origen. As an exegete he depended constantly on ways of reading scripture that he owed above all to Origen. We saw this in our discussion of his use of techniques of literal interpretation derived from Alexandrian philology and grammar. He is equally indebted to his great predecessor when he seeks a deeper than literal meaning. He takes it for granted, for instance, that figurative interpretation is necessary to explain anthropomorphic descriptions of God.[98] Standard symbolic equivalents of certain key words are also adopted from Origen and the Alexandrian

---

[94] These apologetic themes are discussed elsewhere in the present study. Messianic prophecies are reviewed in the comparison of Eusebius and Justin in Ch. II.3.1, as are texts applied to the fall of Jerusalem in AD 70. Prophecies applied to the institutional church, to contemporary history, and to final eschatology are discussed in Ch. VI. On the calling of the Gentiles, to texts listed in Ch. II.3.1, add Isa. 4: 2–3, 8: 9–10, 18: 1–2, 41: 17–18, 42: 16, 43: 5–6, 8–11, 45: 22–3, 49: 5, 12, 18, 55: 4–6, and 59: 20. On world evangelization: Isa. 11: 14, 19: 1, 34: 16–17, 42: 10, 45: 18–19, 50: 4–5, 52: 11–12, 53: 11–12.

[95] Cf. interpretations of Isa. 2: 1–4 (15. 21–16. 3), 9: 3 (63. 19–64. 17), 19: 1 (124. 4–125. 21), and 46: 1–2 (298. 22–299. 11).

[96] *CI* 177. 13–24.

[97] Ibid. 371. 4–27 (Isa. 60: 3–4 applied to Christian kings), 316. 10–25 (49: 23 fulfilled *kata lexin* in the attendance of the emperor and his entourage at the liturgy and in imperial patronage of the church), 20. 29–21. 5 (2: 20–1 fulfilled in official repression of paganism), 14: 32–15. 14 (2: 1–4 fulfilled visibly in universal peace), 152. 20–153. 3 (23: 18 fulfilled in the church in Tyre after the persecution).

[98] Ibid. 70. 10–12 (Isa. 9: 11–13), 268. 20–2 (42: 1). Of course the figurative interpretation of biblical anthropomorphism was known to him from Hellenistic Judaism as well, cf. *PE* 8. 10 (Aristobulus).

tradition. Hills and high mountains often stand for haughty souls
uplifted against God. Cedars, cypresses, and oaks are metaphors for
foreign kings. Deserts represent nations who did not know God,
especially when Eusebius is expounding the calling of the Gentiles.
Forest (*drymos*) is given the same interpretation. Animals are invari-
ably allegorized, especially to serve the interpretation that Isaiah is
prophesying that the preaching of the Gospel brings men from a
beastly to a civilized way of life.[99]

Water and streams stand for the Word of God or the inspiration of
the Holy Spirit.[100] Water symbolism is especially important because
of the association of Pss. 86: 3 and 45: 5 (LXX) with the city of God,
a conjunction of symbolic meanings (Logos/Holy Spirit + church/
city of God) which is discussed in Ch. VI, Sect. 1. But the chaotic
waters of the sea are construed as the sea of unbelievers.[101] Place
names also are liable to symbolic interpretation, often on the basis of
etymologization, as seen above in Section 2.

Eusebius' use of symbolic interpretation is generally restrained.
Most of the keyword allegorizations, for example, are treated as
expressive metaphors of the type mentioned in the preface. The
Septuagint of Isa. 11: 5 reads, 'The Lord will lay waste the sea of
Egypt, and will lift his hand against the river with a mighty wind,
and will strike seven channels, so that one may cross on foot.'
Eusebius begins by recalling his prefatory remarks on the need to
distinguish literal and spiritual meaning, using the example of the
root of Jesse and the flower and stump of Isa. 11: 1. Such language,
he says, even those who do not wish to are constrained to interpret
figuratively (*tropikôs hermêneuein*). Jesse is the actual person, the
father of David, but the object of the prophecy, a descendant of
Jesse, has been represented symbolically. A similar mix of literal and
figurative expression is found in 11: 15. 'Egypt' is the actual country,

---

[99] For hills, cf. *CI* 199. 8–201. 12 (Isa. 30: 25–6); 20. 6–16 (2: 14); 274. 12–20 (42:
15). Trees as kings: 101. 31–102. 10 (14: 8); 20. 6–16 (2: 13); 238. 11–14 (37: 24). Deserts
as gentile nations: 227. 9–228. 14 (35: 1–2); 229. 16–30 (35: 6–8); 281. 1–5 (43: 19).
Forests as same: 211. 1–212. 2 (32: 15); 394. 20–3 (65: 10). Animal allegorization: 5. 3–
13 (1: 3); 90. 17 (11: 15); 100. 19–32 (13: 21–2); 224. 27–226. 6 (34: 11–15), especially
curious because of the interpretation that the deer of 34: 15 (LXX) must be the
apostles, since the deer is a ritually clean animal (Deut. 14: 5) and scripture says many
fine things about deer (cf. Pss. 41: 2, 28: 9; Prov. 5: 19; Job 39: 1, 3; S. of S. 2: 9); 226.
34–227. 3 (34: 17).
[100] Ibid. 93. 1–10 (12: 3); 229. 16–22 (35: 6); 281. 5–6 (43: 19); 283. 6–15 (44: 1–4);
344. 27–9 (55: 1), etc.
[101] Ibid. 89. 27–9 (11: 15).

but the events predicted happened only once, during the time of the Exodus. The lack of a subsequent realization means that 'sea' and 'river' must be taken allegorically (*allegorikôs*). Eusebius builds a detailed parallel between the Exodus events and similar (*homoiotropa*) events in Egyptian history since the spread of Christianity, creating a religious and political portrait of Egypt between Augustus and Constantine. The interpretation is more typological than allegorical, being based on a congruence of Old Testament and Christian history. Its content is as much secular as religious, reflecting Eusebius' belief that the prophetic vision encompassed both the sacred and secular realms.[102]

When Eusebius feels compelled to seek a more than literal meaning, the *dianoia* which he discovers will usually have to do with the working out of God's salvific plan in history. The main locus of God's activity in the world is the corporate entity called the godly polity. His non-literal interpretation usually relates the biblical text to some aspect of the godly polity's history. This explains why even what he calls allegorical interpretation has a historical bearing. What pastoral flavour the *Commentary on Isaiah* possesses comes from his reliance on traditional catechesis and apologetics aimed at showing how Christianity replaced Judaism as the historical embodiment of the godly polity. It is rarely pastoral in the sense of Origen's *Homilies on Jeremiah*, which try to relate the scriptures to the spiritual life of individual believers.[103]

W. den Boer has noted that allegory originated in pagan culture in order to salvage the Homeric poems, by showing that the poems really taught that the gods and heroes were: (1) representations of the elements of the universe (physical allegory); (2) the parts of the soul (psychological allegory); or (3) personifications of virtues and vices (moral allegory).[104] Allegorical interpretation tended to be intellectualist and individualist, to serve metaphysical and ethical didactic ends. Alexandrian Christian adaptation of pagan allegory to

---

[102] Another oracle on Egypt, Isa. 19: 5–7, inspired Eusebius to a similar use of figurative interpretation in the service of understanding the historical fulfilment of prophecy. Ibid. 127. 17–128. 36.

[103] For moral and spiritual interpretation of this sort, see *CI* 84. 18–26 (Isa. 11: 7— here Eusebius introduces as an alternative an Origenist interpretation that the spiritual man is the one who feeds on the nourishing Word, the hidden *nous* of the scriptures); 146. 31–147. 18 (22: 12–14); 170. 5–21 (26: 17–18); 195. 27–196. 12 (30: 6–7); 217. 14–21 (33: 16); 269. 24–270. 23 (42: 5); 312. 23–9 (49: 10); 358. 11–34 (58: 5–6).

[104] W. den Boer, 'Allegory and History', in W. den Boer *et al.* (eds.), *Romanitas et Christianitas* (Amsterdam and London, 1973), 17.

some degree shares the same ends, though scholars differ about precisely how far such ends shaped Origen's exegesis.[105] In the *Commentary on Isaiah* of Eusebius they have left little mark. The techniques of Alexandrian spiritual interpretation are useful to him, but within an interpretive framework that is his own: the history of the godly polity in the light of prophecy.

4. Between Antioch and Alexandria

Before concluding the chapter we should place Eusebius in the broader exegetical development of the early church. Discussion about how to understand the Bible figured in many of the critical developments in early Christianity, going back to Jesus' interpretations of the law and the prophets and to Paul's reconsideration of the Mosaic law. In the sub-apostolic period the Montanist movement and the engagement with Gnosticism both involved the problem of the proper way to read the Bible.[106] In the late second and third centuries educated Christians began to consider how to present the Bible—both the Jewish scriptures and its Christian supplement—plausibly and convincingly to the Graeco-Roman élite, a development closely associated with the catechetical school at Alexandria. Alexandrian allegory, which came into being for frankly intellectualist purposes, represented a significant departure from the mixture of typology and cautious, largely Jewish allegory on which traditional exegesis depended.[107] Resistance came from various quarters, at first from Christians still devoted to millenarian eschatology.[108] In

---

[105] See, e.g. the works mentioned above in n. 82.

[106] The effect of both on scripture formation and interpretation is considered in Hans von Campenhausen, *The Formation of the Christian Bible* (Philadelphia, 1972), 75–88 (gnosticism), 147–67 (Marcion), and 221–30 (Montanism).

[107] R. P. C. Hanson, 'Biblical Exegesis in the Early Church', *The Cambridge History of the Bible*, i. 435 f. Hanson's survey of early Christian exegetical method is very useful, and recommended as an introduction. From the large bibliography which could be cited on Alexandrian exegesis, let us mention several of Daniélou's works on Origen: 'Origène comme exégète de la Bible', *SP* 1 (1957), 280–90; *Origen* (New York, 1955), 131–99; and the chapters on Alexandrian Christianity in *The Gospel Message and Hellenistic Culture* (London, 1964). See also Hanson, *Allegory and Event*; Grant, *The Letter and the Spirit*, ch. 5; and M. F. Wiles, 'Origen as Biblical Scholar', *The Cambridge History of the Bible*, i. 454–89.

[108] As evidence of the traditionalist resistance already in the third century, the *Refutation of the Allegorists* of the Egyptian bishop Nepos is often cited. Nepos' tract inspired Dionysius of Alexandria's celebrated literary analysis of the Johannine writings, preserved in Eus., *HE* 7. 24–5.

the later fourth and fifth centuries a more articulate opposition crys-
tallized among scholars identified with the celebrated school of
Antioch. The propriety of allegorical interpretation was the issue,
with the Antiochenes accusing the Alexandrians of neglecting or
even denying the literal meaning of scripture and the historical basis
of revelation.[109]

As this chapter has demonstrated, Eusebius was certainly sympathetic with the Alexandrian ambition to use the best of ancient
learning to unlock the meaning of the Bible. But a different intellectual orientation (more historical and factual) and a different interpretive situation (the Constantinian settlement) separated him from
his Alexandrian forebears. In important respects he resembles the
exegetical approach, especially to the Old Testament, that later became associated with the school of Antioch. The present section
places Eusebius in relation to these two schools of interpretation,
especially on the question of the nature and object of prophecy. This
poses some risk of anachronism, since the Alexandrian–Antiochene
debate did not emerge clearly until after Eusebius' death.[110] Nevertheless, as we noted in Ch. II, Eusebius was aware of attacks against
Origen's allegorically based philosophical theology, which may
have been the reason for his oblique and anonymous allusions to
Origenist interpretations. Perhaps the *Commentary on Isaiah's*
restrained and cautious allegory, in subservience to a broadly
historical interpretation, indicated trends to come. If the most pres-
tigious living representative of the Alexandrian tradition could write
such a commentary, it may have portended that the future of exegesis in the East lay with Antioch.

The ultimate root of Eusebius' confidence in Isaiah's prophetic
veracity lay in the traditional view that the text of the Bible, in its
entirety, was essentially oracular,[111] an assumption Christianity

---

[109] For general discussion of Antiochene exegesis, see R. M. Grant, *A Short History
of Biblical Interpretation* (New York, 1948), chs. 6 and 7; discussion of representative
authors in *The Cambridge History of the Bible*, i. 489–541 (Theodore of Mopsuestia
and Jerome); and *RAC* vi. 1220–4. A fascinating study which sets Antiochene exegesis
(Diodore of Tarsus and Theodore) in the context of the education received in
the schools of grammar and rhetoric is Christoph Schäublin, *Untersuchungen zu
Methode und Herkunft der Antiochenischen Exegese* (Bonn, 1974).

[110] Hanson, 'Biblical Exegesis in the Early Church', 435 f., notes that the
Antiochene is not much in evidence until the middle of the fourth century, unless we
want to find in Antioch and the martyred biblical scholar Lucian the roots of the early
Arians' precise and grammatical reading of scriptural tests.

[111] Ibid. 419 f.

inherited from Judaism[112] and incorporated in the church's catechetical and apologetic tradition. Since the resolution of the Gnostic crisis, Christians took the unity of the Bible for granted. Origen expounded scripture's unity with a highly developed theory of divine inspiration.[113] Proofs of Christian claims on the basis of prophetic interpretation were a constant feature of Christian literature from the New Testament onwards, as Daniélou has noted:

> In the Gospels Christ presents himself as the realization of the eschatological event proclaimed by the Prophets and adumbrated by the institutions of the old covenant; and during the first three centuries this continued to be the mainspring of Christian proofs of the faith. The fundamental argument, on which the Fathers base their affirmations about Christ, is that he fulfils the predictions of prophecy.[114]

Thus Eusebius' fundamental approach to the prophetic aspect of scripture derived from ancient and well-established assumptions. He stood in harmony with tradition when he observed that when the prophet speaks, Christ speaks through him.[115] His exegesis sought to demonstrate in what period, person, or event the prophetic oracles found their appropriate *ekbasis*.[116] Like flares in surrounding darkness, they illuminated the true contours of both Israelite and Christian history.

As we have demonstrated, the literal and historical meaning of a prophecy referred to the ordinary language meaning of the prophetic diction and to the actual events it foresaw. It was easy for Eusebius to concede that very often prophecy addressed a properly Jewish and Old Testament situation, because he was convinced that the history of Israel was the history of Christianity as well. The godly polity comprised both. Biblical prophecies did not always need to be allegorized in order to become relevant, since they could help his readers map out the antiquity of their religion. By the same token, Isaiah could be interpreted as referring directly and literally to events of the Christian era. The tools of biblical scholarship were

---

[112] C. K. Barrett, 'The Interpretation of the Old Testament in the New', *The Cambridge History of the Bible*, i. 410–12.

[113] Hanson, *Allegory and Event*, ch. 7, discusses Origen's understanding of biblical inspiration, see esp. 198–202. Ch. V of the present study examines in more detail Eusebius' view of prophetic inspiration.

[114] Daniélou, *Gospel Message and Hellenistic Culture*, 198. This is a main theme of Daniélou's treatment of second- and third-century exegesis in this volume.

[115] *CI* 278. 11–18 (on Isa. 43: 7).

[116] E.g. ibid. 46. 14–15 (Isa. 7: 5–9); 68. 21 (9: 7); 126. 31 (19: 4); 304. 3–5 (48: 3–4).

suitable for either interpretation, the 'Jewish' or the 'Christian'. These tools consisted of the ensemble of techniques for reaching the literal meaning studied above in Section 2, but also the restrained modes of figurative interpretation discussed in Section 3. For Eusebius they were complementary rather than incompatible ways to comprehend a prophetic text.

For purposes of comparison, let us look briefly at Origen's view of prophecy. Although Eusebius is rightly described as a protégé of Origen's, the character of their interest in the Bible was not the same. Their kinship depended more on common theological commitments and common exegetical techniques. Origen was certainly deeply interested in the apologetic significance of biblical prophecy, as shown by the attention he gives to it in *Against Celsus*, especially regarding the coming of Christ and the spread of Christianity.[117] Origen recognized that the prophets spoke to their contemporaries about Jewish history as well as about Christ.[118] But this aspect of prophecy was quite peripheral to him. In fact he made the disarming admission that the truth and divine inspiration of the prophecies were open to doubt until they were fulfilled in Christ,[119] a devaluation of the strictly Jewish-Old Testament function of prophecy that Eusebius did not share. What really interested Origen was the hidden meaning accessible only to allegorical interpretation.

The prophets, according to the will of God and without any obscurity whatever, could be at once understood as beneficial to their hearers and helpful towards attaining moral reformation. But all the more mysterious and esoteric truths, which contained ideas beyond the understanding of everyone, they expressed by riddles and allegories and dark sayings, and by what are called parables and proverbs. Their purpose was that those who are not afraid of hard work but will accept any toil to attain to virtue and truth might find out their meaning by study, and after finding it might use it as reason demands.[120]

In *On First Principles* he discussed at length the relation between the historical veracity of the biblical text and its allegorical interpretation. He concluded that the frequent obscurity of the text's literal

---

[117] *C. Cels.* 1. 2, 12, 31, 35–37, 42, 48–50; 3. 2–4; 7. 1–11. Cf. Henry Chadwick, 'Evidences of Christianity in the Apologetic of Origen', *SP* 2 (1957), 331–9.

[118] *C. Cels.* 1. 36, 3. 3.

[119] *De Princ.* 4. 1. 6.

[120] *C. Cels.* 7. 10 (trans. H. Chadwick, *Origen: Contra Celsum* (Cambridge, 1986)). Cf. also 4. 49.

meaning, or the literal impossibility of purportedly historical events, demonstrated that the hidden, spiritual meaning was paramount.[121] Many of his examples come from the prophetic literature, which he preferred to see as narratives about the heavenly world rather than the world of the ancient Near East.

It would appear to follow from this that the prophecies which are uttered concerning the various nations ought rather to be referred to souls and the different heavenly dwelling places occupied by them. Moreover in regard to the record of events that are said to have happened to the nation of Israel, or to Jerusalem or to Judaea, when they were besieged by this people or that, there is need of careful inquiry and examination, seeing that in very many cases the events did not happen in a physical sense, to discover in what way these events are more suitably ascribed to those nations of souls who once dwelt in that heaven which is said to 'pass away', or who may be supposed to dwell there even now.[122]

Grant summarizes Origen's discussion of allegory and history in *On First Principles*: 'This analysis in Origen's fourth book shows that while, like other allegorizers, he can admit the historical reality of much of his text, his ultimate concern is not with history at all. Like his theology, his exegesis is fundamentally spiritual and unhistorical.'[123]

In an excellent comparative study of Antiochene and Alexandrine exegesis, Jacques Guillet found illuminating differences in the way the two schools assessed biblical prophecy.[124] Both approaches occupied much common ground in a thoroughly traditional exegesis. They both recognized that the Old Testament was a foreshadowing of the New, and that its persons and events were in some measure types and figures of Christ. But they had different points of view on this fundamental principle. As Guillet presents them, the Antiochenes regarded typology from its prophetic aspect, and the Alexandrians from its symbolic aspect and its spiritual content.

Pour Antioche, le fait dominante de l'histoire biblique, le miracle qui atteste en permanence la continuité de l'action divine, et qui prépare directement l'avènement du Christ, c'est le prophétisme. Alexandrie, sans ignorer les textes prophétiques, n'y trouve pas un aliment suffisant pour nourrir la

---

[121] *De Princ.* 4. 1–3.

[122] Ibid. 4. 3. 10 (trans. G. W. Butterworth, *Origen: On First Principles* (New York, 1966)).

[123] Grant, *The Letter and the Spirit*, 96.

[124] J. M. Guillet, 'Les exégèses d'Alexandrie et d'Antioche: Conflit ou malentendu?', *RSR* 34 (1947), 257–302.

réflexion chrétienne et la vie spirituelle. Il lui faut retrouver la présence du Seigneur à chaque page. Elle voudrait ressaisir, de cette histoire passée, la substance imperissable, ce qu'elle contenait déjà de realité évangélique.[125]

Using Origen as his representative Alexandrian, he goes on to say that the Alexandrians saw at bottom only one object of the prophetic experience, the glory of the Word and the mystery of God. 'C'est une experience spirituelle plus qu'une vision de l'avenir, c'est la vision, par les parfaits, de l'éternité de Dieu, de son éternelle présence dans la création.'[126] He quotes Origen's *Commentary on John*: 'There is a coming of Christ before his physical coming, which is his spiritual advent in the perfect, for whom the fullness of time is already present, as for example the patriarchs, Moses and the prophets, who saw the glory of Christ.[127] For Origen, the historical events recorded by the prophets appeared superficial in comparison to the spiritual vistas and authentic realities they revealed to those able to understand. Every word and line of the text was filled with these mysteries, so that his exegesis was essentially a search for figures and correspondences.

The Antiochenes identified the prophetic experience not as a spiritual vision but as an ecstatic premonition of future events. Not every passage but only certain ones possessed true predictive significance, although the Antiochenes differed among themselves as to which types and figures were genuinely prophetic.[128] Theodore of Mopsuestia, for example, has long been recognized for the austerity of his Old Testament exegesis, which denied that even very traditional proof texts such as Zech. 9: 9–10 or Isa. 53 were direct Messianic prophecies, in the sense that the prophets themselves actually foresaw their Christian fulfilment.[129] In general, Antiochene scholars considered that prophecy should be understood literally, i.e. within the horizon of its own culture and times, unless the prophecy gave manifest indications otherwise.[130] The chief such

---

[125] Ibid. 274.

[126] Ibid. 287.

[127] Origen, *Comm. John* 1. 7, cited ibid.

[128] See his discussion of Antiochene views of prophecy, ibid. 275–87.

[129] Ibid. 278, with citations. On Theodore, see Wiles' survey in *The Cambridge History of the Bible*, i. 489–510. The standard monograph on his Old Testament exegesis is R. Devreesse, *Essai sur Théodore de Mopsueste* (Studi e Testi, no. 141; Vatican City, 1948), to which should be added the monograph of Schäublin cited above.

[130] In keeping with the grammatical principle that went back to Aristarchus, 'to interpret Homer by Homer', as Schäublin has shown (*Antiochenische Exegese*, 158–60).

indication was 'hyperbolic' expressions, disproportionate to the events which were predicted, so that their (Jewish) fulfilment was only partial, and a more complete fulfilment, or *ekbasis* as the Antiochenes called it, was still to come.[131] Guillet quotes a text from Diodore of Tarsus that illustrates this concept of prophetic fulfilment very clearly:

If people should say that this psalm [118], inasmuch as it was pronounced by God, applied to generations of humanity, and that it applied at once to present events and to events of a higher order, their interpretation would be right. This is almost what we are saying: the prophets, in predicting events in advance, have adapted their speech to the periods they are addressing, and to later periods; their words are found to be, for the contemporary period, 'hyperbolic' expressions, but they are also found to be in complete agreement with the events they are supposed to realize ... For it is the quality of the Spirit to give eternal and absolute gifts, that is, the divine oracles, capable of being adapted to all ages until the end of humanity ... But this is not a case of allegory, but of a reality susceptible of multiple adaptations.[132]

Prophecy for this Antiochene was 'a reality capable of multiple adaptations', a phrase which Guillet explains as envisioning a series of successive fulfilments oriented in the same direction, each one deepening the meaning of the prophecy but not arbitrarily adding to it, as Diodore presumed was true of allegory.

Even this brief summary throws interesting light on Eusebius. With Origen and the Alexandrians, Eusebius shares a strong sense of the unity of the scriptures—Isaiah as an apostle and an evangelist—and his idea of prophetic inspiration as a rational vision that enlightens the mind. He avoids any mention of prophetic ecstasy because of its Montanist associations, a reluctance not shared by the Antiochenes, who showed much more interest than Origen in the psychology of the prophetic experience.[133] According to Origen, the prophet was inspired to see and understand more clearly than his natural powers allowed; clear mental vision was the essence of inspiration.[134] Eusebius, while he recognized a contingent human element in a prophetic revelation, was certainly closer to Origen in his notion of prophetic inspiration than to the Antiochenes.

---

[131] Guillet, 280–3. See Bates, 'Some Technical Terms of Greek Exegesis', 63, for more on the use of *ekbasis* for a complete fulfilment of prophecy. Schäublin, *Antiochenische Exegese*, 169 f., explains the rhetorical background of the Antiochene concept of *hyperbolē*.

[132] Guillet, 280 f.

[133] Ibid. 276, 282–4.   [134] Cf. *C. Cels.* 7. 3–4.

Where Eusebius and Origen differ is in their attitude to history, because interest in the religious significance of historical process puts him closer to the Antiochenes. Like them, he was primarily interested in prophecy's fulfilment (*ekbasis*) in future events, and not in 'the spiritual vision of the glory of God' that Guillet found was characteristic of the Alexandrian view of prophecy. Eusebius shared the Antiochene orientation to the historical and the empirical, and so the literal sense of scripture, though his view of prophecy conceded the prophet a more detailed and exact knowledge of the future than theirs. In the prophecy of Zech. 9: 9, for example, Theodore of Mopsuestia believed that Zerubabel and not Christ was directly predicted; the prophet at best had only a certain apprehension (*tina phantasian*) of a messianic future.[135] In his *Proof of the Gospel* Eusebius saw this text as a direct and literal prophecy of Christ, in keeping with the traditional messianic interpretation.[136]

In the *Commentary on Isaiah* Eusebius showed a more differentiated awareness of the 'multiple adaptations' of the oracles, to use Diodore's phrase, but he does not try to explain how a text can have more than one historical fulfilment. The openness of a prophetic text is something he takes for granted, so that he does not feel the same need as the Antiochenes to justify prophetic prevision of events in the Christian era. For him supernatural foresight is the essence of prophecy. It is part of the solution, not part of the problem of the relation between the Testaments. Like the Antiochenes Eusebius seeks to recover the Jewish phase of salvation history, although he falls short of their rigour in historical interpretation. Finally, the commentary's prefatory remarks about confining allegory to texts where it is required by the literary form are in conformity with the practices of moderate Antiochenes.[137]

In a word, Eusebius showed his Alexandrian breeding by his notion of *how* the prophets understood revelation, and his affinity with Antioch by his grasp of *what* they understood as revelation. In reality, of course, he belonged fully to neither camp. As Wallace-Hadrill cleverly remarks, like Caesarea itself he was in between.[138] Alexandrian allegory was not as useful as Alexandrian philology for

[135] Theodore of Mopsuestia, *Commentary on Zechariah*, 9 (PG lxvi. 561A), cited by Guillet, 284.
[136] *DE* 8. 4.
[137] Bates, 'Some Technical Terms of Greek Exegesis', 60 f.
[138] *Eusebius of Caesarea*, 96.

seeking the historical lineaments of the people of God, the godly *politeuma*. Eusebius found the right medium in traditional expositions of the fulfilment of prophecy, as formulated and defended by the best contemporary scholarship, and construed so as to bring it into continuity with the stirring events of his own time. The resultant blend of literal and spiritual interpretation may have been too unstable a compound for Jerome's tastes, but it served Eusebius very well and stands as a fitting testimony to Christian biblical scholarship at a critical turning-point in the church's history. It enabled him to incorporate the church's traditional apologetic reading of the Old Testament in a form that could recommend it to learned Christians and pagans of his own time. It also provided a biblical justification for the contemporary optimism of the church in the age of Constantine.

IV

Eusebius' Political Discourse: Defining the Godly Polity

The central apologetic line of the *Commentary on Isaiah* is the ancient Christian theme of the rejection of Israel and the calling of the Gentiles. The commentary recasts the traditional theme around the notion of a godly polity (*to theosebes politeuma*) whose roots lay in biblical Israel. Although the idea of a prehistory of the Christian community was a core element in Eusebius' apologetic programme,[1] it was not original with him. The New Testament declared that the church had been created before the world itself and taught that Christ descended to hell to preach deliverance to the just of the Old Testament who had died before his birth.[2] Justin claimed as Christians before Christ all those, such as Socrates, who had lived according to reason.[3] According to the second-century homily known as 2 Clement, the church was created before the sun and the moon.[4] Similar notions of a pre-existing church emerged in contexts as diverse as Christian apocalyptic, Christian gnosticism, and Christian platonism.[5]

In Eusebius the treatment of the subject is characteristically historical. The double apology of *The Preparation for the Gospel* and

---

[1] See Sirinelli, *Les vues historiques*, chs. 4, 5, and 6. This topic is developed further in the next chapter of the present study.

[2] Eph. 1: 11; 1 Pet. 3: 19. On the descent into hell, see Daniélou, *Theology of Jewish Christianity*, 233–48.

[3] Just., *Apology*, 46. 4.

[4] 2 Clement, 14: 2.

[5] Cf. Hermas: *Shepherd*, Visions 2. 4. 1, where the world is created for the sake of the church. According to Irenaeus the pair Anthropos-Ecclesia is the fourth syzygy in the primordial ogdoad (*Adv. Haer.* 1. 1. 1.). See Johannes Beumer, 'Die altchristliche Idee einer präexistierenden Kirche und ihre theologische Auswertung', *Wissenschaft und Weisheit*, 9 (1942), 13–22, and Daniélou, *Theology of Jewish Christianity*, 293–301. On Origen see Jacques Chênevert, *L'Église dans le Commentaire d'Origène sur le Cantique des Cantiques* (Bussels and Montreal, 1969). The general subject of the pre-existence of the church in patristic, medieval, and counter-reformational theology is surveyed by Yves Congar, 'Ecclesia ab Abel', in *Abhandlungen über Theologie und Kirche: Festschrift für Karl Adam* (Düsseldorf, 1952), 79–108.

The Proof of the Gospel constituted an 'archaeology and legitimation' of the Christian church—already a topic in the *Church History*—that would disprove the allegation that Christians were a new people only lately arrived in world history.[6] *The Proof of the Gospel* secured Christianity's relation to the history of Israel, and *The Preparation for the Gospel* its relation to the cultural history of the whole human race. The *Commentary on Isaiah* is concerned almost exclusively with the former topic, Christianity's roots in Judaism. As we explained in our discussion of the purpose of the commentary, Eusebius took up the subject afresh because of the altered religious and political situation after 324, when Constantine's intervention in the affairs of the churches of the East brought a new urgency to Jewish–Christian relations and pressured the bishops to clarify the boundaries between the two religious communities.

   The dual historical focus is one reason for the commentary's practice of calling Christianity 'the godly polity'. Because Eusebius needed to establish Christianity's continuity with Israel during the first phase of the divine economy, he chose a terminology which was not as historically limited as the conventional Christian word *ekklêsia*. The more neutral 'polity' or 'community' expressed in the same term the consistent identity of the association of the just, whether before or after the Incarnation. Furthermore, abstract nouns derived from *polis* could still bear the old civil and corporate meanings that had not entirely been diluted in the Hellenistic and Roman periods. Eusebius was interested in the empirical history of a religious community. *The Preparation for the Gospel* had described a succession of pious men, beginning with Enos (Gen. 4: 26), who composed a history of virtue leading up to Moses.[7] Although Eusebius depended largely on Philo for his list, he considered them not merely as allegorical symbols of virtues but as definite individuals.[8] With Abraham these *dikaioi* became a *genos*, and among Jacob's descendants in Egypt they grew into an *ethnos*.[9] Moses legally established them on a political footing as a nation, the stage of their history at which the book of Isaiah took up the story. Eusebius' interpretation of this religio-political evolution is considered in more detail in the next chapter. He may also have used

   [6] Sirinelli, *Les vues historiques*, 135 f.
   [7] Eus., *PE* 7. 8. 1–39.
   [8] See the analysis of Sirinelli, *Les vues historiques*, 150 ff., and the comparison with Philo by Guy Schroeder in G. Schroeder and E. des Places (eds.), *Eusèbe de Césarée: Préparation Évangélique, Libre VII* (SC no. 215; Paris, 1975), 60–70.
   [9] Sirinelli, *Les vues historiques*, 156.

political language for the church as a way of signalling to pagans what kind of community the church properly was, on the analogy, as we shall see, of Josephus' presentation of Judaism to pagans.

The present chapter clarifies what Eusebius means in his works when he calls Christianity 'the godly polity'. Commentators have debated whether words like *politeia* and *politeuma* have a distinctive social and corporate weight, or whether they should be understood in the normal Christian sense of life-style and personal comportment.[10] To solve this problem we will examine how certain words derived from *polis* acquired a range of meanings in the Hellenistic and Roman periods much broader than their original meanings in the classical Greek polis in which they came into being. Because of their importance to Eusebius' ecclesiological vocabulary, of the many derivatives of polis only *politeia* and *politeuma* really concern us, although we shall mention the verbal form *politeuesthai* in passing. *Politês*, despite its relevance to biblical usage, has no special function in Eusebius and is therefore ignored. *Polis* itself is less common in Eusebius than the abstract nouns coined from it. We will briefly consider Graeco-Roman and Hellenistic Jewish sources before turning to Christian literature. Then we will examine Eusebius' own works.

1. Graeco-Roman and Jewish Usages

During the Hellenistic and Roman periods the set of words derived from polis underwent a fundamental expansion of meaning.[11] Their

---

[10] F. E. Cranz's article on Eusebius' political theology, 'Kingdom and Polity in the Theology of Eusebius of Caesarea', *HTR* 45 (1962), 47–66, first drew attention to this problem. Cranz was hampered by the unavailability of a critical edition of the commentary, since this was one of his chief sources, and by his failure to consider the historical structure of Eusebius' thought on the godly polity, hence his uncertainty on the relations between Judaism and Christianity as expressed on p. 62 n. 76. Sirinelli, *Les vues historiques*, 147–9, 157 f., also discussed the subject of terminology, but neglected the commentary because it was a post-Nicene book and outside the scope of his investigation. Sirinelli's analysis of the godly polity in Eusebius is criticized by M. Harl in a lengthy review of his book, 'L'Histoire de l'humanité racontée par un écrivain chrétien au debut du IVe siècle', *Revue des études grecques*, 75 (1962), 522–31. Her objections to the social interpretation of *politeia, politeuma,* and *politeuesthai* are on pp. 529–31. Walker, *Holy City, Holy Places?*, 368–76, recognizes the importance Eusebius attributes to 'the godly polity' in the commentary, but interprets it primarily in terms of an invidious contrast with the actual city of Jerusalem.

[11] For what follows, see the article *polis* in G. Kittel (ed.), *Theological Dictionary of the New Testament* (hereafter *TDNT*), 10 vols. (Grand Rapids, Mich., 1964–76), vi.

purely political associations went back to the classical period in Greece, when they were part of the vocabulary of civic and governmental life. *Politeuesthai* had meant to live and act as a citizen. *Politeia* had meant life in a civic order, forms of political activity, and the state order as such, the constitution. *Politeuma* first meant political acts and dealings, and then specific departments of government or government as such, state, commonwealth, and citizenship, eventually merging with *politeia* and *polis*.[12] A notable Hellenistic development was the use of *politeuma* for foreign colonies, publicly recognized national bodies with specific legal and political rights. Besides colonial settlements, the civic body of a community could be called a *politeuma*, as in the case of the *politeuma* of the citizens of Joppa mentioned in 2 Macc. 12: 7. By extension any legally recognized association could constitute a *politeuma*, whether formed for cultic, military, or fraternal purposes.[13] Jewish *politeumata* in the Diaspora, such as those in Cyrenaica, Antioch, and Alexandria, are especially well known.[14] These communities were colonial settlements in the midst of foreign peoples, possessing also a religious character as associations for the worship of God.

The strictly political connotations survived throughout the period of the empire, long after the demise of the city-states.[15] Alongside these older meanings, however, a much broader usage developed. *Politeuesthai* and *politeia* in particular came to indicate the whole range of human conduct, from business dealings to the execution of religious obligations. *Politeuesthai* is used of religious life already in a second-century BC papyrus: 'For I kept faith with you and the gods, towards whom I have kept myself blameless, having behaved (*politeusamenos*) holily and justly.'[16] Ethical behaviour in general,

---

511–35, supplemented by the discussion of Ceslas Spicq, *Notes de lexicographie néotestamentaire*, 2 vols. (Orbis biblicus et orientalis, no. 22; Fribourg, 1978), ii. 710–20.

[12] *TDNT* vi. 517–19.

[13] See the examples in Spicq, *Lexicographie néotestamentaire*, ii. 716.

[14] On the civic status of the Alexandrian Jews and the Hellenistic Diaspora generally, see Victor Tcherikover, *Hellenistic Civilization and the Jews* (New York, 1970), 296–332. On Jewish *politeumata*, see E. Schürer, rev. and ed. by G. Vermes and F. Millar, *The Jewish People in the Age of Jesus Christ* (Edinburgh, 1973–88), iii. 88–9.

[15] *Politeia*: Plutarch, *De unius in republica dominatione*, ii–iii, *Moralia*, 16 vols. (Loeb Classical Library, hereafter LCL; Cambridge, Mass., 1927–69), x. 307. *Politeian politeuesthai*: Epictetus, *Dissertationes* 3. 22. 85, *The Discourses*, 2 vols. (LCL; Cambridge, Mass., 1926–8) ii. 160. *Politeuesthai poleôs*: F. Preisigke (ed.), *Wörterbuch der griechischen Papyrusurkunden*, 3 vols. (Berlin, 1925–31), iii. 141 f.

[16] U. Wilcken (ed.), *Urkunden der Ptolemäerzeit*, 2 vols. (Berlin, 1927–57) i. 625 (no. 144, lines 12 ff.).

whether public or private, could be implied by the terms.[17] Under *politeutai* the lexicographer Hesychius listed only *prattei, anastrephetai*. For *politeia* he reported 'either *polis*, or *bios, anastrophê, praxis*'.[18] In the fifth century AD Proclus offers an interesting pagan example: 'I know that you live piously and act (*politeuêi*) honourably and embellish the renowned name of philosophy with the virtue of unexceptional and pure behaviour (*politeia*).'[19]

In general, however, it is first in Hellenistic Judaism and then in Christian authors that the non-civic meanings are best attested.

The Septuagint is for the most part lacking in polis derivatives, although *polis* itself is frequently used to translate Hebrew '*îr*. 2, 3, and 4 Maccabees use *politeia* and *politeuesthai* several times, always as religious and moral concepts. The lone occurrence of *politeuma* has the older political sense of civil commonwealth (2 Macc. 12: 7). Typical usages suggest that the words stood for the religious and ethical way of life enjoyed by the Mosaic ordinances. Judas Maccabeus defended the 'lawful ways of living' (*nomimous . . . politeias*, 2 Macc. 4: 11). 3 Macc. 3: 23 renders the *politeia* of 2 Maccabees as *embiôsis*. Similarly, *politeuesthai* means to live according to the law of God (2 Macc. 6: 11).

Philo and Josephus drew freely on polis derivatives to express philosophical, religious, and political ideas, but in rather different ways. Philo's typical meaning is 'a philosophical, spiritualizing transposition' of the ordinary political sense.[20] The philosopher is the world-citizen who lives according to the laws of the whole cosmos, and whose life is spent in contemplating the spiritual universe above. In his *On the Creation of the World* Philo described Adam as not just the first man but the first citizen of the world, adapting political language to philosophical and cosmological speculations.[21] He did the same in *On the Contemplative Life*, with his account of the way of life of the Therapeutae of Alexandria, whom he called citizens (*politai*) of heaven and the cosmos.[22] Eusebius

[17] Epictetus, *Diss.* 3. 22. 83–5 (LCL ii. 160).
[18] *Hesychii Alexandrini Lexicon*, ed. M. Schmidt, 5 vols. (Amsterdam, 1965), iii. 354.
[19] *Epistolographi Graeci*, ed. R. Hercher (Paris, 1873), 13.
[20] *TDNT* vi. 528.
[21] Philo, *De opificio mundi* 142–4, *Philo*, 10 vols. with 2 suppl. (LCL; Cambridge, Mass., 1924–62), i. 112–14.
[22] Philo, *De vita contemplativa*, 90 (LCL ix. 168).

believed that Philo had actually described the common life of Christian ascetics; his summary of Philo's account in the *Church History* called their life-style variously *politeia, diatribai,* or *agôgê tou biou*.[23] Such an equation of *politeia* with words of a broadly behavioural meaning became normal Christian usage.

Josephus, on the other hand, often retained the strictly political associations. Because of his interest in presenting Jewish institutions in terms comprehensible to Graeco-Roman readers, he used Greek political terminology for historic Jewish institutions and practices. In the *Jewish Antiquities* he announced his intention to describe for all readers 'the entire history and constitution [*diataxin*] of our polity [*politeumatos*]'.[24] There is an elaborate example of this in *Against Apion*, where he compared 'our lawgiver [*nomothetês*]', Moses, with Lycurgus, Solon, Minos, and Zaleucus, his laws with Greek laws, and the Jewish constitution (*politeuma*) with the governments established among the Greeks.[25]

There is endless variety in the details of the customs and laws which prevail in the world at large. To give but a summary enumeration: some peoples have entrusted the supreme political power [*tên exousian tôn politeumatôn*] to monarchies, others to oligarchies, yet others to the masses. Our lawgiver, however, was attracted by none of these forms of polity, but gave to his constitution [*politeuma*] the forms of what—if a forced expression may be used—may be termed a 'theocracy', placing all sovereignty and authority in the hands of God.[26]

This directly political usage suggests a parallel between Eusebius' terminology and Josephus'.[27] Like Josephus, he may have adopted the terminology to explain Christian concepts and institutions to readers of pagan background. Just as Josephus explained the religious community of Israel in political terms, so perhaps did Eusebius in describing the godly polity which was Israel's successor.

The terminological parallel may rest on something besides common apologetic needs. Since Eusebius held the Christian conviction that Christianity was the successor of Israel, I would like to

[23] Eus., *HE* 2. 16. 2.
[24] Josephus, *Antiquitates Judaeorum*, 1. 5, *Josephus*, trans. and ed. Ralph Marcus, 9 vols. (LCL; Cambridge, Mass., 1926–63), iv. 4.
[25] Josephus, *C. Ap.* 2. 145–286 (LCL i. 350–406).
[26] Ibid. 2. 164–5 (LCL i. 359).
[27] Josephus also knew the broader ethical and religious application; a letter of Antiochus III describes living according to Mosaic law as *politeuesthai kata tous patrious nomous* (*Ant.* 12. 142 (LCL vii. 72)).

consider here how Josephus' description of Israel as a polity founded by Moses may have influenced Eusebius' thinking on the church. Eusebius frequently relied on Josephus, whom he calls 'one of the most illustrious of the Jews',[28] as an authority for Jewish history and a useful source for Christian anti-Jewish apologetics. Josephus provided him with information on events like the end of political autonomy and the destruction of the Temple that were important for his interpretation of how Israel's prerogatives as the Chosen People had passed to Christianity. Another event that signalled Israel's fall from divine favour was the end of the authentic high-priestly succession under Herod the Great. He discussed this episode on three different occasions in relation to the prophecy of the seventy weeks in Daniel 9: 24–7.[29] The words of the prophecy that 'the anointing will be destroyed' (Dan. 9: 26) he referred to Herod's monopoly of the high-priestly succession, the authentic line of which ended with Hyrcanus. The words 'until an anointed one come' (*heôs christou hêgoumenou*, Dan. 9: 25) he applied to Christ. Daniel's prophecy was thus understood to embrace both developments, on the strength of the keyword 'anointing', and to order them according to Eusebius' reading of Jewish history.

The discussion of Dan. 9: 24–7 in the *Church History* co-ordinates the interruption of the high-priestly succession with the simultaneous loss of Jewish political autonomy. Both disasters are explained as the responsibility of the same person, Herod the Great, whose Idumean ancestry Eusebius emphasized. They serve as complementary manifestations of the fundamental reality of Judaism's fall from grace, which had consequences on both the political and religious levels. This complementarity of political and religious history may have seemed especially appropriate to Eusebius in view of Judaism's constitution as a temple state in the post-exilic period. 'After the return from Babylon', he observed, 'a constitution [*politeia*] of oligarchic aristocracy was maintained, for the priests were at the head of the state . . .'[30] This is almost a quotation of what Josephus says in Book 11 of the *Antiquities*.[31] Complementing the Danielic prophecy on the priesthood is Jacob's blessing of Judah in Gen. 49: 10, 'A ruler

---

[28] Eus., *HE* 3. 46 (GCS no. 2: 160. 2–3).

[29] Cf. Eus., *DE* 8. 2; *HE* 1. 6. Citations from Dan. 9: 24–7 in the version attributed to 'Theodotion'.

[30] *HE* 1. 6. 6, *Eusebius: The Ecclesiastical History*, ed. and trans. Kirsopp Lake and J. E. L. Oulton, 2 vols. (LCL; Cambridge, Mass., 1972), i. 51–2.

[31] Josephus, *Ant.* 11. 111 (LCL vi. 368).

shall not fail from Judah, nor a leader from his loins, until he comes for whom it is reserved', which Eusebius sees fulfilled through the ascendancy of the non-Jew Herod and through the coming of Christ.[32] Taken together, these prophecies anticipate the eclipse of Judaism as a distinct religio-political unity. The manifestation of Christ, founder of the true godly polity, thus coincides with the demise of the polity descended from Moses. In the *Commentary on Isaiah* Eusebius will say repeatedly that the godly polity has passed from Judaism to Christianity. I suggest that Josephus' 'political' description of the Mosaic polity, whether as theocracy or oligarchy, may have influenced Eusebius' conception of the church as the godly polity which succeeded Israel.

2. New Testament Usage

We turn first to the New Testament. Here we find *politeuesthai* in Acts 23: 1 (Paul's speech to the Sanhedrin) and Phil. 1: 27, both instances of the religious use found in the books of the Maccabees in the sense of fidelity to inherited or shared religious obligations; *politeia* in Acts 22: 28 (Paul's Roman citizenship, a secular usage) and Eph. 2: 12 ('you were . . . aliens from the commonwealth of Israel' (NRSV)); and *politeuma* in Phil. 3: 20.[33]

The translation of Phil. 3: 20 has inspired an instructive debate.[34] The Vulgate rendered *politeuma* as *conversatio*. Luther, after some hesitation, eventually settled on the similar *Wandel*.[35] The restoration of the eschatological perspective in modern New Testament studies made the individualizing and merely ethical implications of these translations unacceptable. Lohmeyer's Meyer commentary distinguished three possible meanings: the historical organization of

---

[32] *HE* 1. 6. 2.

[33] *TDNT* vi. 516–35; Spicq, *Notes de lexicographie néotestamentaire*, ii. 710–20; K. L. Schmidt, *Die Polis in Kirche und Welt* (Basel, 1939); W. Bieder, *Ekklesia und Polis im Neuen Testament und in der alten Kirche* (Zürich, 1941); Kurt Aland, 'Die Christen und der Staat nach Phil 3: 20', in *Paganisme, Judaisme, Christianisme* (Paris, 1978), 247–9.

[34] On the translation of *politeuma* here, see Schmidt, *Polis in Kirche und Welt*, 21–4; Bieder, *Ekklesia und Polis*, 19–21; *TDNT* vi. 535 n. 86; Spicq, *Notes lexicographie néotestamentaire*, ii. 717; E. Lohmeyer, *Philipperbrief* (Göttingen, 1964), 156–8; Aland, 'Die Christen und der Staat', 249 f.

[35] Bieder, *Ekklesia und Polis*, 21 n. 86. After 1545, *Wandel*, but before 1545, *Bürgerschaft*.

a community in time and space; its way of life; and the behaviour of the individual in relation to this way of life.[36] Strathmann's Kittel article considered all these to be just religious forms of the many diluted behavioural meanings assumed by polis derivatives in the post-classical period. He sharply distinguished them from the purely political meanings of classical usage. K. L. Schmidt on the other hand wanted to restore the full communal and social overtones to *politeuma* and like words by setting them in the larger context of New Testament and Jewish notions of the eschatological city of God, the heavenly/new Jerusalem.[37] He identified an essentially similar eschatological realism in Paul, Hebrews, and Revelation, all of which share convictions about a 'city whose maker is God', which exists as an eschatological reality in the plan of God and as an orientation point for Christians in the world.[38] Schmidt saw a strong polemical contrast between the old, civic connotations of polis derivatives and Christian notions of membership in a future city conceived as a theocracy, though a 'future theocracy of the kingdom of God', not to be confused with any present theocracy that would merely absolutize the existing Christian church.[39] He conceded that hope for the heavenly city is 'an inner disposition' in the sense that the present church is oriented to, but does not itself constitute the city of God; because the city of God is eschatological, there can be no direct continuity between human life now and then.[40] But he pressed for an acknowledgement of the social and political nature of the New Testament's terminology for this city, because it evokes the essentially corporate feature of Christian hope.[41]

The difference between these two approaches is perhaps illustrated by the Jerusalem Bible's translation of *politeia* in Eph. 2: 12 as 'membership in Israel' (no political metaphor expressed) and *politeuma* in Phil. 3: 20 as 'homeland', whereas the NRSV renders the first as 'commonwealth' and the second as 'citizenship'.[42] Strathmann appeared to leave the way open for a more inward sense

[36] Lohmeyer, *Philipperbrief*, 157.

[37] Besides the work cited, see his 'Jerusalem als Urbild and Abbild', *Eranos-Jahrbuch*, 18 (1950), 207–48.

[38] Gal. 4: 26; Phil. 3: 20; Eph. 2: 19; Heb. 11: 10, 16, 12: 22–3, 13: 14; Rev. 3: 12, 21: 1–22: 5. Cf. Schmidt, 'Jerusalem als Urbild und Abbild', 209–14.

[39] Ibid. 210 n. 2.

[40] Ibid.

[41] Aland adopts this same political interpretation in an even sharper form.

[42] 'Commonwealth' is listed as an alternative translation of Phil. 3: 20 in the *New Oxford Annotated Bible with the Apocrypha* (New York, 1991), 283 NT.

in which Christians belong to their homeland, as shown by his caustic references to 'totalitarian' and 'political' interpretations of religious community.[43] He denied that there was any parallel between Phil. 3: 20 and the Hellenistic legal institution of the *politeuma*,[44] whereas Schmidt thought Paul was making an allusion to Christians as a colony of heaven.[45]

The relevance of this discussion of Eusebius is twofold. First, Eusebius' terminology has something of the political resonance which Schmidt found in polis derivatives in the New Testament. This is not to suggest that Eusebius' terminology was directly inspired by the New Testament—in fact, the passages with *politeia*, *politeuma*, and *politeuesthai* do not play a major role in the commentary's proof texts, which deal more with the city of God—but only that the New Testament engages in a similar framing of political language for religious communities. Strathmann missed the real significance of this imitative language even in the Maccabean literature, because his categories and distinctions were too broad. Treating *politeia* and *politeuma* either as strictly political or as behavioural and religious is a false opposition. The non-political meanings need to be further distinguished from one another. When *politeia* and *politeuma* are used as designations of religious communities with their own history, structure, discipline, and legitimation, they function in ways much closer to the old civic meanings. Strathmann was right to say that in 2–4 Maccabees *politeia* stands for the Mosaic dispensation. But that religion's absolute and inclusive claim is misunderstood if its potential challenge to the civil order is ignored. The clash between competing allegiances is a fundamental subject of the Maccabean literature. Not just an individual's conduct and fidelity to God were at stake, but a whole people's. Whenever *politeia* and *politeuma* have a more than individual application, whenever the emphasis is on a shared way of life, obligation, institution, and the like, we need to be alert for parallelism and contrast.

Second, there is a notable contrast between Eusebius and the New Testament. As both Strathmann and Schmidt realized, the New Testament conception of the city of God is highly eschatological.

---

[43] E.g. *TDNT* vi. 526, 529, 531 f.
[44] Ibid. vi. 535.
[45] Schmidt, *Polis in Kirche und Welt*, 24; Spicq's survey of the Hellenistic and Roman background of *politeuma* as used in Phil. 3: 20 supports Schmidt (*Notes de lexicographie néotestamentaire*, ii. 711).

But eschatology plays only a secondary role in Eusebius' conception of the godly polity, and apocalyptic eschatology none at all. Instead, his thinking is more in line with the 'present theocracy of the church' derided by Schmidt in his study of the New Testament's eschatological vision of the heavenly Jerusalem.

3. Greek Christian Usage

The analysis here is limited to *politeia* and *politeuma*. Citations are drawn from the detailed entries in Lampe's *Patristic Greek Lexicon* and the lexical studies of Schmidt and Bieder.[46]

First, *politeia*. Departing somewhat from Lampe's classifications, we will distinguish four sets of meanings:

1. Civil and secular. Greek Christian writers continued to use *politeia* in its original civil and secular usage of citizenship, state, constitution, and the like.[47]

2. Ethical and behavioural. By far the largest number of Lampe's entries come under this heading. Since the dictionary did not distinguish between individual and social meanings, I examined the individual texts and found that the vast majority had a strongly individual sense and could be translated by life, conduct, deeds, or the like. The non-political and non-social applications show up very clearly in contexts where patently behavioural synonyms are also found. The *Shepherd* of Hermas, for example, says of the flesh of Christ, i.e. his humanity, that 'since it lived [*politeusamenên*] well and holily, and collaborated and co-operated with the spirit, acting [*anastrepheisan*] in every deed mightily and manfully, it was taken as a companion together with the Holy Spirit; for the life (*poreia*) of this flesh pleased God...'[48] In the same way the translation of the phrase in 1 Clement, 'those who live the godly life that admits of no regret' (*hoi politeuomenoi tên ametamelêton politeian tou theou*), is supported elsewhere by the letter's equation of *politeuesthai* with

---

[46] *PGL* 1113–14.

[47] Notably in the historians. Eusebius uses the plural to mean civic affairs: *HE* 8. 9. 7 (GCS no. 2: 782. 10), 9. 4. 2 (GCS no. 2: 808. 24); *MP* 11. 1 (GCS no. 2: 932. 17). The singular at *HE* 1. 2. 19 (GCS no. 2: 22. 5) means state or constitution. Socrates used *politeia* to mean a civil ordinance, but the usage was apparently unusual, because he felt compelled to add an explanation for his readers: *HE* 7. 13. 6 (*PG* 67. 761B).

[48] Hermas, *Shepherd, Similitudes* 5. 6. 6, in F. X. Funk (ed.), *Patres Apostolici* (Tübingen, 1901), 541. 18–542. 4.

poreuesthai and *badizein*.[49] Spiritual adornment by one's *politeia* became almost a topos.[50] Rhetorical contrasts of *politeia* with abstract nouns like faith, knowledge, and truth show how the word was thought to have a strongly practical and performative meaning. Origen expounded Paul's 'leaven of mercy and truth' (1 Cor. 5: 8) thus: '"Mercy" in respect to our deeds (*politeia*), "truth" in respect to our knowledge, since by both is the real leaven characterized.'[51] John Chrysostom claimed that Paul always combines action (*politeia*) with faith.[52] A further practical application of *politeia* developed in the vocabulary of asceticism and monasticism. In a prefatory letter to his *Lausiac History*, Palladius explained his intention to describe the manner of life (*biou diagôgê*) of the monks who wished to achieve an imitation of the life of heaven (*mimêsin tês tôn ouranôn politeias*).[53]

3. Communal and 'political'. Under this heading fall instances where *politeia* means either the way of life of a community or the community itself as a distinctive entity. The old civil resonances are usually discernible, especially when the emphasis is shaded towards the community as a body. The rather colourless 'system' is often a good translation test, because it can convey both senses. Most of the entries in *PGL* for *politeia* as a way of life which seem social rather than individual can be rendered this way. Not surprisingly, they frequently occur in comparisons of Christianity and Judaism as distinctive systems or regimens. An excellent example, discussed below, is Eusebius' own comparison of Judaism, Hellenism, and Christianity as three distinct communally ordained ways of life.[54]

---

[49] 1 Clement, 54. 4, ed. Funk (168. 10–11), cf. 3. 4 (102. 15). The translation is discussed by Schmidt, *Polis in Kirche und Welt*, 44 f. Cf. also 1 Clement, 2. 8 (102. 4); *Mart. Poly.* 13. 2, ed. Funk (330. 3), 17. 1 (334. 9).

[50] One third of the references to *politeia* in Clement's works qualify the noun with *orthê*. Cf. *Clemens Alexandrinus*, ed. O. Stählin, 4 vols. (GCS nos. 12, 17, 19, 39; Leipzig, 1905–9, 1936) iv. 312 f.

[51] Origen, *Comm. on 1 Corinthians*, ed. C. Jenkins, *JTS* 9 (1908), 365.

[52] Cf. John Chrys., *Homilies on Colossians* 1. 1 (11: 334A); also *Homilies on Hebrews* 7. 1 (12: 70D) and *Homilies on Genesis* 8. 5 (4: 62C). Other sources: *Pseudo-Clementine Homilies* 2. 6. 4, ed. B. Rehm (GCS no. 41; Berlin, 1953), 38. 7–9. Greg. Naz. *Ep.* 238 (PG xxxvii. 381B).

[53] Palladius, *Historia Lausiaca* pref. (PG xxxiv. 995). Cf. also Eus., *MP* 11. 2 (GCS no. 2: 934. 5–6), with reference to Pamphilus' way of life, and John Chrys., *Homilies on John* 57. 3 (8. 336B), with reference to virginity as a way of life.

[54] Eus., *DE* 1. 2. 2, 5, 16 (GCS no. 6: 7. 28, 8. 9, 10. 12). Similar usage in Clem., *Stromateis* 5. 98. 4, ed. O. Stählin, rev. L. Früchtel, ii of *Clemens Alexandrinus* (GCS no. 55; Berlin, 1960), 391. 3.

The presence of other juristic or political vocabulary, such as *nomos* or *prostagma*, may signal that the text presumes a close relationship between the *politeia* as behaviour and the community which defines correct behaviour. Such will often be the case in works of an explicitly apologetic nature, written to present the group's self-understanding *ad extra*, and thus devoted to matters of a social and political nature, or in works like 1 Clement that treat administrative and jurisdictional issues.[55]

4. A minor and for our purposes irrelevant use of *politeia* is its Christological application to the incarnate life of Christ.[56]

Although *politeuma* has a range of meanings in Christian literature similar to that of *politeia*, in absolute terms the word is much less common, and its original communal, political, and social associations are more unequivocal.

1. Civil and secular. As with *politeia*, the old secular usages survived, usually to indicate the government and the political order, or the Roman Empire as a whole.[57]

2. Mode of life, conduct. *Politeuma* can also have the behavioural sense of ethical conduct, although this meaning is not as frequent as with *politeia*.[58] This meaning seems increasingly common from the fourth century, for example in the literature of the ascetic movement.[59]

3. Communal. *Politeuma* was more successful than *politeia* in retaining the 'political' associations of the original civil usage in contexts that are explicitly religious. Many of the citations in *PGL* are patristic allusions to Phil. 3: 20. All the ones listed understand *politeuma* as heavenly citizenship, as proven by the common juxtaposition of life on earth with citizenship in heaven. A passage from the pseudo-Macarian homilies is particularly interesting in this

---

[55] Schmidt's study of the apostolic fathers and the apologists points out repeatedly how these writers graft the older political connotations onto polis-derivatives even in cases where the translation is properly 'way of life' or 'conduct'. Cf., e.g. Tatian, *Oratio ad Graecos* 40, ed. E. Schwartz (TU, no. 4, pt. 1; Berlin, 1888), 41. 11–12.

[56] *Life of Barlaam and Joasaph*, 8 (PG xcvi. 924A); Eus., *HE* 1. 4. 1 (GCS no. 2: 38. 7).

[57] For government, cf. Evagrius Scholasticus, *Ecclesiastical History*, ed. J. Bidez and L. Parmentier (London, 1898), 5. 11 (207. 24, 31); for the empire, ibid. 5. 9 (204. 14), 5. 22 (217. 15).

[58] Clem., *Paedagogus*, 2. 10 (GCS no. 1: 220. 10); Tatian, *Or. ad Graec.* 19 (21. 12).

[59] *Historia Monachorum in Aegypto*, 10. 2, ed. A. J. Festugière (Subsidia Hagiographica, no. 53; Brussels, 1971), 76. 13, 15.

respect, because it also contains *politeia*: 'For while we are on earth, we hold our citizenship [*politeuma*] in heaven, by keeping our conduct and action [*diagôgên kai politeian*] fixed on that world, both in our mind and in our inner man.'[60] Here *politeia* stands for the conduct which marks our citizenship, *politeuma* for the citizenship itself.

It is a revealing measure of Eusebius' vocabulary that all the lexicon's instances for *politeuma* as a designation for historic Christianity (and Judaism) are from his works. The reference to the 'communities of the monks' (*politeumata*) in the *Historia Monachorum* is a little misleading, since it occurs in a celestial vision of the whole heavenly host, in which monks are mentioned along with angels, martyrs, etc.[61] A citation from Clement of Alexandria actually refers to pagan civil communities, although the same passage does also mention the church on earth as the city of God.[62]

4. The Christological use is unusual but not unknown.[63]

4. *Politeia* and *Politeuma* in the Works of Eusebius

The vast majority of Eusebius' uses of *politeia* and *politeuma* occur in his exegetical works and in *The Proof of the Gospel*, which is composed mainly of exegetical material. *The Preparation for the Gospel* is also relevant, though the words occur much less frequently, and so too is the *Church History*. Among the later works we find only scattered instances, which correspond wholly to the civil and behavioural meanings. The *Life of Constantine* restricts *politeia* to secular political usage, consistent with its subject; Eusebius must have avoided vocabulary which might suggest that the church was a community rivalling the state in its constitution and the obligations it laid on its members.[64] The late dogmatic tracts *Against Marcellus* and *On the Ecclesiastical Theology* reveal only one instance of *politeia*, the conventional ethical meaning.[65]

[60] Pseudo-Macarius, *Hom.* 17. 4, *Die fünfzig geistlichen Homilien des Macarius*, ed. H. Dörries, E. Klostermann, and M. Kroeger (Patristische Texte und Studien, no. 4; Berlin, 1964), 168. 52–4.
[61] *Historia Monachorum*, 11. 7 (91. 34).
[62] Clem., *Stromateis* 4. 36 (GCS no. 2: 325. 4). This is the earliest instance known to me of this identification.
[63] Basil of Caesarea, *On the Holy Spirit*, 35 (*PG* xxxii. 128D).
[64] Eus., *VC* 1. 11. 1 (GCS no. 1: 20. 21), 4. 14. 1 (GCS no. 1: 125. 13).
[65] *Gegen Markell*, ed. E. Klostermann, iv of *Eusebius' Werke* (GCS no. 14; Leipzig, 1906), 1. 2 (1. 24–2. 1).

Of the relevant books we shall begin with the *Church History*, the earliest in the order of composition. Though comparable in length to both *The Proof of the Gospel* and the *Commentary on Isaiah*, the *Church History* has a much lower frequency of *politeia* (ten times) and *politeuma* (once). Three other occurrences of *politeia* come from documentary citations. In the sole use of *politeuma*, it is difficult to tell whether the ethical or collective sense is paramount.[66] A contrast of the Lyons martyrs with soldiers who die for their country uses the formula *to kata theon politeuma*, which may be an earlier form of *to theosebes politeuma*, the phrase favoured by the *Commentary on Isaiah*. Of the uses of *politeia*, five clearly refer to mode of life and conduct. Four others are secular. There is also a theological reference to Christ's fleshly *politeia*.[67] Eusebius evidently avoided calling the institutional church a godly polity, even though church order, or at least the office of the bishop in the great sees, was a central theme.[68] Most of the *Church History* was written in the shadow of the persecutions, and he may have decided it was prudent not to use language which might exaggerate the tension between the church and the empire.

The references in *The Preparation for the Gospel* are suggestive, though not abundant. *Politeia* frequently bears the conventional ethical connotation, but also is used in ways recalling the 'political' usage of Josephus. *Politeuma* always refers to religious life in its corporate and collective aspect, usually Jewish but also Christian. This pattern will be repeated in *The Proof of the Gospel*.

While life-style is an acceptable rendering of *politeia* in several instances, a collective meaning is also intended in passages where Eusebius is talking about Judaism under the Mosaic convenant, especially in Books 7 and 8 on the doctrines of the Hebrews and the Mosaic constitution.[69] Here he says that Moses was the first, as

---

[66] *HE* 5. Prol. 4 (GCS no. 2: 400. 18).

[67] Life or conduct: *HE* 2. Prol. 1 (GCS no. 2: 102. 4), 2. 17. 5 (GCS no. 2: 148. 9), 4. 7. 13 (GCS no. 2: 318. 25), 4. 23. 2 (GCS no. 2: 374. 8), 7. 32. 30 (GCS no. 2: 730. 7), and *MP* 11. 2. 3 (GCS no. 2: 934. 5). Secular applications: *HE* 1. 2. 19 (GCS, no. 2: 22. 5), 8. 14. 9 (GCS no. 2: 782. 10), 8. 9. 7 (GCS no. 2: 758. 17), 9. 4. 2 (GCS no. 2: 808. 24), and in *MP* 11. 1 (GCS no. 2: 932. 17). Christological: *HE* 1. 4. 1 (GCS no. 2: 38. 7).

[68] On the succession motif, see Eger, 'Kaiser und Kirche', 99, and Grant, *Eusebius as Church Historian*, 45–59.

[69] Ethical meaning: 6. 6. 39 (GCS no. 8, pt. 1: 305. 29), 10. 4. 25 (GCS no. 8, pt. 1: 572. 10–11), 12. 15. 1 (GCS no. 8, pt. 2: 103. 16), 15. 61. 11 (GCS no. 8, pt. 2: 422. 7).

theologian and legislator, to found a polity consonant with piety.[70] 'Because of the depravity of their conduct, they were unable to match the virtue of their forebears, so he (Moses) handed down the polity appropriate to their souls, prone to passion and diseased.'[71] The Mosaic regime provided a collective discipline to restrain the vices of a people no longer equal to the high ascetic and philosophical attainments of their ancestors, the 'Hebrews', Eusebius' designation for the pre-Mosaic worthies of Genesis.

Book 8 of *The Preparation for the Gospel* is devoted to the Mosaic polity. The preface declares that, having dealt with the lives and teachings of 'the Hebrews', Eusebius will proceed to the next in rank, the Mosaic polity, 'which claims a second degree [*bathmos*] of piety after the first one, having been enacted for the Jewish people alone'.[72] Book 8 cites passages from Philo and Josephus relevant to the Mosaic polity, in which *politeia* and *politeuma* seem indistinguishable.[73] The quotation of Josephus, the comparison of Moses with famous Greek legislators found in *Against Apion* and cited above,[74] is another indication that Josephus influenced his conception of a religious society as a *politeuma*.

Unlike *politeia*, Eusebius never uses *politeuma* except to mean a society, religious or civil. Most often it indicates 'the polity of the Jews, which began from Moses and lasted until the coming of our saviour Jesus Christ, according to the words of their own prophets: for this was the prediction of Moses and the subsequent prophets, that the laws and commandments would not pass away [*eklipein*, cf. Gen. 49: 10, *ekleipsei*] before the Christ appeared'.[75] The reminiscence of Gen. 49: 10, a traditional Christian proof text, reminds us that Eusebius is thinking not just of the supersession of the Old Testament ritual law, but of Israel's political structure as well. The 'Jews' (as opposed to the 'Hebrews') took their origin from Judah, 'from whose tribe the kingdom of the Jews was established long afterwards'.[76] Thus the origin and passing of the Jewish *politeuma*

---

[70] *PE* 7. 9. 1 (GCS no. 8, pt. 1: 378. 15–18).
[71] Ibid. 7. 8. 39 (GCS no. 8, pt. 1: 377. 20–2).
[72] Ibid. 8. Prol. 2 (GCS no. 8, pt. 1: 419. 9–11).
[73] Ibid. 8. 5. 11 (GCS no. 8, pt. 1: 427. 4), 8. 6. 10 (GCS no. 8, pt. 1: 429. 14–16), 8. 7. 21 (GCS no. 8, pt. 1: 433. 15), 8. 8. 56 (GCS no. 8, pt. 1: 443. 10).
[74] Ibid. 8. 8. 1–55 (= Josephus, *Con. Ap.* 2. 163–228). Ibid. 7. 8. 40 (GCS no. 8, pt. 1: 378. 2–7).
[75] Ibid. 7. 8. 40 (GCS no. 8, pt. 1: 378. 2–7).
[76] Ibid. 7. 6. 2 (GCS no. 8, pt. 1: 368. 23–4).

are co-ordinated with the traditional Christian Messianic reading of Old Testament prophecy.

The Preparation for the Gospel refers once to Christianity as a *politeuma*. In Book 12 Eusebius says that, 'Our whole school [*didaskaleion*] ought not to be blamed if some appear to live wickedly, apart from a leader or ruler, or with wicked rulers; rather one ought to marvel at those who adhere to the godly polity.'[77] Possibly he means the Donatists of North Africa, since Constantine was forced to abandon coercion and to concede their right to exist during the years when Eusebius was composing the *Preparation*. If this is correct, we have an echo of the bitter African disputes on the nature and boundaries of the godly polity that would ultimately inspire Augustine's reflections on the city of God.

5. *Politeia* and *Politeuma* in *The Proof of the Gospel*

Politeia is used almost thirty times in *The Proof of the Gospel*. In only one instance does it have a directly institutional meaning, in a passage commenting on Isa. 19: 1–4.[78] The majority of cases, about two-thirds, involve the sense of *politeia* as a way of life shared by members of a religiously defined community. The remaining third refer to the broader sense of life-style and conduct. Because of the importance of what Eusebius says in the *Proof* about Christianity as a middle way between Hellenism and Judaism, we shall consider briefly his analysis of these three *politeiai*. The material is to be found chiefly in Book 1.

The fundamental purpose of *The Proof of the Gospel* is to justify Christian appropriation of the Jewish scriptures, while rejecting the Mosaic law, the Jewish way of life (*ton . . . tou biou tropon*).[79] His secondary aim is to accomplish this 'by a more logical demonstration', a reference to his plan of an integrated Christian apology directed against both Jews and Greeks, with the hope of silencing critics who ridiculed Christianity as credulity.[80] He wishes to demonstrate that Christianity is not in fact derivative from Judaism but prior to it, and therefore to 'Hellenism', since the religion founded

---

[77] Ibid. 12. 33. 3 (GCS no. 8, pt. 2: 128. 5–7).
[78] DE 6. 20. 16 (GCS no. 6: 288. 8–9).
[79] Ibid. 1. 1. 15 (GCS no. 6: 6. 35–7. 3).
[80] Ibid. 1. 1. 12 (GCS no. 6: 6. 8–12).

by Christ is actually the same as that professed by the pre-Mosaic saints or 'friends of God' (*theophileis*) spoken of in Genesis.[81] The identity of patriarchal and Christian religion is the basic thesis, but a key step in the demonstration is the assertion that Moses had introduced an entirely new stage in the economy of salvation, indeed virtually a new religion. That Judaism is a creation of Moses and a declension from the pure religion of the patriarchs is a position we have just encountered in Book 7 of the *Preparation*. In the *Proof* he says that 'Judaism would be correctly defined as the polity [*politeia*] constituted according to the law of Moses, dependent on the one, omnipotent God. Hellenism you might summarily describe as the worship of many gods according to the ancestral religions of all nations.'[82] Monotheism and the Mosaic law characterize Judaism, ancestral polytheism characterizes Hellenism. Between the two and older than both is Christianity, which Eusebius wants to show has preserved Judaism's virtues but not its defects.

> Christianity would therefore be not a form of Hellenism nor of Judaism, but something between the two, the most ancient regimen for holiness [*to metaxu toutôn palaiotaton eusebeias politeuma*], and the most venerable philosophy, only lately codified as the law [*nenomothetêmenê*] for all mankind in the whole world.[83]

We meet again the distinction between Hebrews and Jews. The former are the pre-Mosaic friends of God who adhered to a pure, ethical monotheism. The latter are all those who kept the Mosaic Law and hence belonged to the polity of Moses. The distinction, though not invented by Eusebius, is deepened and clarified to serve a central apologetic role.[84] Moses, though himself a 'Hebrew of the Hebrews', is pre-eminently the leader and legislator who established the constitution of the Jews.[85] *The Proof of the Gospel* repeatedly uses legal and political language in discussing Moses. Judaism is 'the polity ordained according to the law of Moses' (*tên kata ton Môseôs nomon diatetagmenên politeian*), recalling Josephus' similar lan-

---

[81] His central thesis is announced in *DE* 1. 2. 1 (GCS no. 6: 7. 18–23) and worked out in the rest of Book 1.

[82] Ibid. 1. 2. 2 (GCS no. 6: 7. 27–30), trans. W. J. Ferrar, *The Proof of the Gospel*, 2 vols. repr. in one (Grand Rapids, Mich., 1981), i. 8.

[83] Ibid. 1. 2. 10 (GCS no. 6: 8. 33–6), trans. Ferrar (slightly altered), i. 9.

[84] The distinction, already put forth in *HE* 1. 4. 5, is taken up again in *PE* 1. 6. 2, 6 (GCS no. 8, pt. 1: 23. 3–10, 24. 4–8) and worked out in more detail in *PE* 7. 6–8.

[85] *PE* 7. 7. 1 (GCS no. 8, pt. 1: 369. 14), 7. 8. 38 (GCS no. 8, pt. 1: 377. 16).

guage in the *Antiquities*.[86] Moses founded (*katabeblêmenos*) a polity for the Jewish people by his legislation (*nomothesia*).[87] His polity is 'more rational and well-ordered', leading to a civilizing way of life that lifts men beyond savage and beastly manners through its legislation, which he was the first to commit to writing.[88] We are reminded again of the comparison in Josephus with the law-givers of the Greeks. In *The Proof of the Gospel* Moses' work as legislator is paralleled by the regime of Christ, the new law-giver.[89] The interpretation is found already in Justin,[90] but Eusebius gives it a strongly institutional expression. He sees the double name of Jesus Christ foretold in Moses' appointment of Joshua and Aaron. Joshua, being the Hebrew form of the proper name Jesus, is rendered in the Septuagint as *Iêsous*. His renaming by Moses anticipates the supersession of the Mosaic polity by one who would be 'leader of another and superior polity'.[91] Similarly, Aaron's selection as anointed high priest points to the real high priest, 'the person named with the name of the real Christ'.[92]

And so Moses, the most wonderful of the prophets, understanding by the Holy Spirit both the names of our Saviour, Jesus Christ, honoured the choicest of all his rulers by bestowing them as kingly crowns, naming worthily the two leaders and rulers of the people the high priest and his own successor, Christ and Jesus, calling Aaron Christ and Nauses Jesus, as his successor after his death.[93]

Though Eusebius does not extend the parallel to cover the successors of Jesus, the *Commentary on Isaiah* will declare that the rulers of the Christian polity exercise an authority like their Jewish and apostolic predecessors.

To round out the legal-political parallel, recall that Eusebius' definition of Christianity as the middle way between Hellenism and Judaism declares that Christianity's establishment as a law (*nenomothetêmenê*) marks the phase of its history since the Incarnation.[94] In certain respects, then, Eusebius sees the Christian polity in

---

[86] Josephus, *Ant.* 1. 5.
[87] *DE* 1. 2. 16 (GCS no. 6: 10. 12).
[88] Ibid. 1. 6. 34 (GCS no. 6: 28. 2–5).
[89] Ibid. 3. 2. 6 (GCS no. 6: 97. 15).
[90] Justin, *Dial.* 12. 2.
[91] *DE* 4. 17. 4 (GCS no. 6: 196. 17).
[92] Ibid. 4. 16. 53 (GCS no. 6: 194. 10).
[93] Ibid. 4. 17. 5 (GCS no. 6: 196. 19–26), trans. Ferrar, i. 217.
[94] Ibid. 1. 2. 10 (GCS no. 6: 8. 36).

terms resembling the Jewish. But while Christianity shares with Mosaic Judaism its character as a legally defined community or polity founded by a legislator, it is distinguished by the material content of its law. Christianity does not adopt the ceremonial law and sacrificial cult descending from Moses. The Christian 'polity for holiness' (*DE* 1. 6. 1) is not based on circumcision, dietary laws, purification rites, Sabbath observance, or temple cult, but on a pure worship in spirit and truth which no longer depends on 'symbols and types'.[95] The typological interpretation of the law, in itself an apologetic commonplace, is given a distinctive expression by being framed in Eusebius' historical correlation of the pure and natural religion of the patriarchs with that of Christ. The virtues of the pre-Mosaic friends of God, celebrated already in *PE* 7. 8, are rehearsed in *DE* 1. 5–6 to demonstrate that they and the Christians uphold the same ideals of justice, continence, faith, monotheism, blameless life, spiritual priesthood, and the like. The Mosaic law, while appropriate for a people still suffering from the effects of slavery in Egypt, was not suitable for a world-wide movement because of its localization in Jerusalem.[96] But Christianity, 'the renewal of the ancient, pre-Mosaic religion in which Abraham, the friend of God, and his forefathers are shown to have lived', is applicable to men of all nations and suffers from none of Judaism's geographical restrictiveness.[97]

The dialectic of religious history moves from the *dikaioi*, the Hebrews, to the Jewish *ethnos*, from a succession of historically attested individuals to the life of a religio-political community. Christianity shares with the former the purity of its doctrine and morals, with the latter its organization as a community. Like the former it is universal in its appeal, not confined to a single locale, but like the latter it can embrace multitudes. Eusebius had already implied that Moses was moved to establish his polity because the prolific growth of the people in Egypt demanded a written law.[98]

Before concluding this section, we need to examine an important discussion in *The Proof of the Gospel* of the composition of the Christian church (1. 8), in which Eusebius defends the existence of two ways of life (*tropoi*) which Christ legislated for the church. The one is supernatural, beyond ordinary human life (*politeia*), and does

---

[95] *DE*. 1. 6. 42 (GCS no. 6: 29. 17–20).
[96] This thesis is defended in *DE* 1. 3.
[97] Ibid. 1. 5. 1–3.
[98] *PE* 7. 8. 37 (GCS no. 8, pt. 1: 377. 10).

not accept marriage, procreation, property, or the possession of wealth, but 'by an excess of heavenly love' is dedicated to God's service alone.

Like some celestial beings they gaze on human life, performing the duty of a priesthood [*hierômenoi*] to Almighty God for the whole race, not with sacrifices of bulls and blood, nor with libations and unguents, nor with smoke and consuming fire and destruction of bodily things, but with right principles of true holiness, and of a soul purified in disposition, and above all with virtuous deeds and words; with such they propitiate the Deity and celebrate their priestly rites [*hierourgian*] for themselves and their race. Such is the perfect form of the Christian life. And the other more humble, more human, permits men to join in pure nuptials and to produce children, to undertake government, to give orders to soldiers fighting justly; it allows them to have minds for farming, for trade, and the other more secular interests [*politikôteras agôgês*], as well as for religion, and it is for them that times of retreat and instruction, and days for hearing sacred things are set apart. And a kind of secondary grade of piety [*bathmos*] is attributed to them, giving just such help as such lives require . . . [99]

The renunciations of the perfect Christians—marriage, offspring, property, wealth—appear to come from the list of renunciations mentioned in Matt. 19: 10–26. Eusebius introduces the higher way as given by the disciples of the master 'to those who can accept it' (*tauta tois hoioiste chôrein paredidosan*), which recalls Jesus' closing exhortation to continence, 'Let anyone receive this who can' (Matt. 19: 12, *ho dynamenos chôrein, chôreitô*).[100] The four renunciations repeat Matthew's order of topics: *gamous* (cf. Matt. 19: 10, *ou sympherei gamêsai*); *paidopoiïas* (Matt. 19: 13, *paidia*); *ktêsin* (Matt. 19: 22, *ktêmata*); and *periousias hyparxin* (Matt. 19: 23, *plousios*). Perhaps Eusebius is reflecting an exegetical tradition which used Matt. 19 to undergird an organized ascetic life in the church.

Eusebius seems to consider the distinction between two orders in the church as a parallel to or recapitulation of the historical distinction between the Hebrews and the Jews. In conventional Christian fashion he contrasts the written law of Moses with the perfect commandments of the new covenant, written not on lifeless tablets but on living minds (cf. 2 Cor. 3: 3). To see Jeremiah's new covenant (Jer. 31: 31–4) as a prophecy of Christianity was a primitive Christian conviction (cf. Heb. 8: 8–12). But Eusebius goes on to say that

---

[99] *DE* 1. 8. 2–3 (GCS no. 6: 39. 19–31), trans. Ferrar, i. 48–50.
[100] Ibid. 1. 8. 1 (GCS no. 6: 39. 7–8).

the disciples of the master also handed over (*paredidosan*, authoritative tradition) for others to keep 'some things in writing, others in unwritten ordinances', as a discipline accommodated to the weakness of the majority.

The distinction between a spiritual law for a moral élite and an authoritative legislation for the many exactly resembles the one separating Hebrews from Jews. Mass Christianity has therefore something in common with Judaism's inclusion of larger numbers of people who were no longer equal to the high ethical demands of their Hebrew forebears. Like such 'Jews', ordinary Christians are legally organized as a cultic collectivity: they are provided with written books and unwritten laws which 'fit souls still empassioned and in need of therapy', just as *The Preparation for the Gospel* had described the Mosaic polity as 'appropriate to their souls, prone to passion and diseased'. The Greek shows the verbal parallel: *tois eti tas psychas empathesi kai therapeias deomenois*, said of the weaker Christians in the *Proof*, and *tas psychas empathesi kai nenosêleumenois*, said of the Jews in the *Preparation*.[101] For the benefit of these humbler Christians a regimen of scriptural instruction served as a 'secondary grade of piety' (*deuteros eusebeias... bathmos*). So too Eusebius had described the Mosaic polity as a secondary grade of piety (*deuteron... eusebeias... bathmon*).[102] The parallel is not complete, however, since, as noted above, the new law is more spiritual than the old. A heightened spirituality applies to the new law as a whole, even the portion of it adapted to weaker and humbler Christians. Eusebius says that the regimen appropriate to these ordinary Christians consists of regular scripture readings and days for instruction, but he gives no analogue to the corporeal worship of sacrifice and ritual observance.[103]

In *The Proof of the Gospel* Eusebius uses *politeuma* only nine times, less than a third as often as *politeia*. *Politeuma* always expresses the notion of a religious collectivity, twice with an emphasis on its way of life, the rest of the time indicating a religious association as such, whether Jewish, Christian, or pagan.[104] As we have

---

[101] *DE PE* 7. 8. 39 (GCS no. 8, pt. 1: 377. 21).

[102] *DE* 1. 8. 4 (GCS no. 6: 39. 33–4); *PE* 8. 1. 1 (GCS no. 8, pt. 1: 419. 9–10).

[103] *DE* 1. 8. 4 (GCS no. 6: 39. 32–3). The *askêseôs kairoi* mentioned here must be scriptural study, not special ascetic disciplines, which are cultivated by perfect Christians. For *askêsis* as scriptural study in Eusebius, cf. *HE* 6. 2. 15 (GCS no. 2: 524. 3) and *DE* 8. 3 (GCS no. 6: 393. 13).

[104] *DE* 1. 1. 10 (GCS no. 6: 8. 35), 7. 18. 12 (GCS no. 6: 276. 20).

shown, *politeuma* as generally used by Christians was more likely than *politeia* to have this collective meaning. The greater frequency of *politeuma* in the *Commentary on Isaiah* (about thirty-five times) is a rough statistical measure of the prominence of the church in the *Commentary* as compared to the *Proof*.

A passage in *The Proof of the Gospel* commenting on Isa. 52: 5–10 offers three interpretations of Sion and Jerusalem. According to the first they stand for heavenly realities, which is how Eusebius understands the New Testament texts on 'the Jerusalem above'. In the *Commentary on Isaiah* he is inclined to historicize Gal. 4: 26 and Heb. 12: 22. Sion and Jerusalem can also refer to the Christian church and the godly polity (*to theosebes politeuma*). The 'godly polity' is therefore the bond of continuity between Israel and Christianity. First it existed as the special prerogative of Israel and then in a superior and pre-eminent way in the Christian church. Finally, Sion and Jerusalem can refer to the soul of the individual believer, an interpretation whose immediate source must be Origen.[105] Although an individualized and mystical meaning is found in the *Commentary on Isaiah*, it is rare and marginal to its main ideas.

6. *Politeia* and *Politeuma* in the *Commentary on Isaiah*

In the *Commentary on Isaiah* Eusebius prefers *politeuma* to *politeia* by almost two to one, the only instance in his books of a reversal of the normal dominance of *politeia*. Furthermore, in almost every instance we can translate *politeuma* as polity, organization, community, association, or the like. It never has the moralizing sense of principle, behaviour, or way of life. As we have seen, both Christians and pagans were more likely to give the looser sense of behaviour to *politeia* rather than *politeuma*. The unusual frequency of *politeuma* reflects Eusebius' concern with the church as a historical and social reality. But his terminology is not rigid, and the two words are sometimes used interchangeably.

The basic meaning of *politeia* recalls its use in *The Proof of the*

---

[105] Passages in Origen where Jerusalem is equated with the soul: *Comm. John*, 10. 28. 174, C. Blanc (ed.), *Origène, Commentaire sur S. Jean* (SC no. 157; Paris, 1970), 488. 15; *Hom. Luc*, 38. 3–4, H. Crouzel, F. Fournier, P. Périchon (eds.), *Origène, Homélies sur S. Luc* (SC no. 87; Paris, 1962), 444; *Hom. Jos.* 21. 2, A. Jaubert (ed.), *Origène, Homélies sur Josué* (SC no. 71; Paris, 1960), 436; *Hom. Jer.* 13. 2 and 19. 14 (SC no. 238: 56. 1–58. 37 and 234. 54–63).

Gospel to indicate a religiously defined community, its constitution, organization, and shared way of life. In the *Commentary on Isaiah* pagan communities are 'the godless *politeiai* of the impious' (162. 10). They can be called *politeiai* both for their civil organization and for their ancestral cultivation of polytheism, which Eusebius calls 'political religion'.[106] The godly polity (usually *hê kata theon politeia*) existed formerly among the Jews (341. 27–8). It was governed by the law of Moses, which was unsuitable (*akatallêlos*) for the government of Gentiles, a doctrine identical to that expounded in Book 1 of the *Proof* (323. 2). This is the godly polity, the 'Jerusalem above, the mother of us all', which Paul spoke of in Gal. 4: 26 (371. 17).[107] The 'city of God' spoken of in the psalms (Pss. 45: 5, 86: 3) is scripture's way of naming the godly polity (121. 17–18). Since its transferral from Judaism the godly polity is now established in the churches (340. 27–8). In an institutional application of the word, we learn that the church is divided into five ecclesiastical orders or *politeiai* (133. 12, 273. 1). The passage happens to be the only instance in *PGL* of *politeia* used of the church with an explicitly institutional meaning.[108] Capitalizing on the special administrative terminology used in Egypt since the Ptolemaic period, Eusebius interprets Isa. 19: 3 (*nomos epi nomon*) to mean that the *nomos* of the gospel has subverted the ancestral customs (*nomima*) of the Egyptians, whose godless life (*bios*) was in opposition to the godly polity (126. 4–11). Here *politeia* refers to religious customs, beliefs, and way of life. Practical, ethical, and pious connotations appear in Eusebius' description of the marvellous works to be performed by the members of the Jerusalem to come after the end of the ages, but even here the emphasis is on the community which shall do the deeds, 'the godly *politeia* of "those who serve me"' (cf. Isa. 65: 15) (397. 23).

Politeuma in the *Commentary on Isaiah* means a concrete human association[109] based on devotion to God, whether in Israel, in the church, or in heaven. Scripture calls it indifferently Sion, Jerusalem, or the city of God.[110] Very often Eusebius speaks of this *politeuma* as something distinct from the land or city in which it exists. 'For those worthy of salvation must offer the salvific and supreme service to the

---

[106] See Sirinelli, *Les vues historiques*, 199–204, and *PE* 4. 1.
[107] Also at *CI* 373. 36–374. 1.
[108] *PGL* 1113, s.v. *politeia*, no. D.
[109] 'An association of souls', as Eusebius says, *CI* 312. 34.
[110] E.g., ibid. 321. 32–3; 326. 36–7; 331. 14, 19, 27, 35; 368. 2; 369. 16; 383. 11.

city of God, that is, the church, and the godly *politeuma* in her [*en autêi*]' (375. 28–31). The godly *politeuma* exists 'among men' (*en anthropois*) (332. 16–17). The prophecy that 'his people will dwell in a city of peace' (Isa. 32: 18) is fulfilled in the city which God will build, 'the catholic church and the godly *politeuma* in her' (212. 17–18). Isaiah spoke to 'the godly *politeuma* which existed of old among the Jews' (313. 2). The priests, prophets, and patriarchs of Israel 'preserved safely the *politeuma* of godliness, so that they were no small part of the city of God' (370. 20–3). Such language recalls Paul's assertion in Philippians 3: 20 that our *politeuma* is in heaven [*en ouranois*]. It derives, as noted in Section 1, from the Hellenistic juridical concept of the *politeuma*, according to which members were enrolled in legally recognized corporations, whether civil, ethnic, cultic, or military in nature. Eusebius speaks of the godly *politeuma* existing 'in' a city or region, or 'among' a people in two different senses. When he says that it exists in the church, he seems to have in mind the analogy of a citizen body and the city in which it lives: Christians are the citizens of the city of God, the church. When he says that the godly *politeuma* exists among men [*en anthropois*], he uses the word in the stricter legal sense of the union of citizens of a common origin and sharing a common law, but living in the midst of strangers.[111] Now the Pauline text does not fit either of these senses exactly, and it is striking that, for all Eusebius' interest in proof texts on the city of God, he quotes this passage only once in the commentary (342. 18–19). The reason perhaps is that Paul does not equate the church with the city of God, which for him is an eschatological reality. Eusebius does not ignore the eschatological or heavenly dimension of the godly polity, but he is more interested in its historical or earthly dimensions, its life 'in the church' and 'among men'.

The godly polity, he says, also existed among the Jews. Here the ambiguity of the metaphor of the *politeuma* serves him well. In one sense, the godly *politeuma* was the 'citizen body' of Judaism, just as it is in the church. Judaism was the proper home and setting of the godly *politeuma*, until its definitive apostasy in the rejection of the Saviour. But if we take the analogy with the stricter legal sense of *politeuma*, then the godly polity becomes something distinct from and even alien to Judaism, which is reduced to being only the host body of this association of holy men, who sojourned in its midst as

---

[111] Cf. Spicq, *Notes de lexicographie néotestamentaire*, ii. 716.

strangers, united by a common devotion that set them apart from fellow Jews. In the same legal sense Christians constituted the godly *politeuma* in relation to the rest of men (*en anthropois*).

Let us turn now to Eusebius' commentary on Isa. 54: 11–13, since this text provoked one of his longest ecclesiological expositions, and illustrates his use of both *politeia* and *politeuma*.

But 'your parapets' I will rebuild from stone 'of jasper', or, according to Symmachus: 'and I will make your dwellings of *karchêdonion*, and your gates of carved stone'; according to the Seventy: 'and your gates of stones of crystal and your wall of choice stones'. We should understand all these things of worthy and precious souls, from which God promises to build the godly *politeuma*. He compares them to sapphire because of its resemblance to the colour of heaven. And their *politeia* is heavenly and angelic, as Paul teaches, saying: 'Our *politeuma* is in heaven' [Phil. 3: 20]. In the prophet Ezekiel the place under the throne of God is said to be like sapphire. So these are all the prophets and apostles who are foundations [cf. Eph. 2: 20], firm and secure, of the godly *politeuma*, and are likened to 'sapphires' because of 'the heavenly *politeuma*' and because of their 'bearing the image of the heavenly man' [cf. 1 Cor. 15: 49]. Therefore it is said: 'I will place sapphire as your foundations.'

And 'the parapets' of this new Jerusalem would be 'jasper' stone, or *karchêdonion* according to Symmachus, which is choice and splendid. Such would be those in the church who strengthen the faith with intellectual means, being like battlements of the godly *politeuma* to destroy 'every obstacle raised against the knowledge of God' [2 Cor. 10: 5] and to disprove every false argument hostile to the truth. For as the parapets are battlements equipped with the means of resistance against the enemy, so too those in the church who are gifted in thought and wisdom might properly be called 'parapets'.

With these he lists others, likening them to stones of crystal, of which he prophesies the gates of the city will be built, and indicates the clarity and purity of sound faith of those who have believed the first, elementary and introductory teaching. In addition to these he declares that he will place the wall of the new city of God from 'choice' stone. These would be those who encircle and make secure, in the place of every fence, by means of their prayers to God, the whole edifice of the city, and its great, precious, and worthy buildings.

'And all your sons are taught of God, and your children in deep peace' [Isa. 54: 13]. Such are the rest of the masses who shall be enrolled to dwell in that city, with God himself as their teacher.[112]

---

[112] *CI* 342. 11–343. 10. Isa. 54: 11–13 is only mentioned by a few writers before Eusebius; Irenaeus, *Adv. Haer.* 5. 34. 4, A. Rousseau, L. Doutreleau, C. Mercier

Eusebius almost certainly adopted this allegory from Origen, although it is not found in this precise form in any of Origen's extant writings. The closest parallel is *C. Cels.* 8. 19–20, where Origen breaks off abruptly, saying that he has treated the subject more fully elsewhere. He had already interpreted the 'sapphire' of Lam. 4: 7 as representing the heavenly *politeia* of the elect.[113]

Isa. 54: 11–13 is one of the texts which served as a starting point for Jewish reflection on the eschatological Jerusalem.[114] In Eusebius' interpretation of the allegory, it is a blueprint or charter not for the heavenly Jerusalem but for the historical Christian church and its predecessor in Israel. The godly *politeuma* built of worthy souls is a corporate and historical reality, whose various social segments are represented by the fortifications of the new city of the biblical prophecy. Its history reaches back to Israel ('apostles and prophets') and forward into the history of the church. Although Eusebius here quotes Phil. 3: 20—for the only time in the commentary—he is not describing a *politeuma* in heaven but on earth. He appears to understand Paul to mean that the community of Christians displays a manner of life in this world that could appropriately be called heavenly or angelic (342. 17–18). He shows less interest in the Pauline doctrine that we have or expect an eschatological homeland in heaven. The emphasis is on the life of Christians now, on their membership in the present community of worthy souls. *Politeia* occurs here, for the only time in this lengthy passage, because Eusebius was aware that the word possessed a greater range of meaning. In the passage as a whole he prefers *politeuma* (three times), in keeping with his sociological allegorization of the biblical text.

The phrase 'angelic *politeia*' is found one other time in the *Commentary on Isaiah* (312. 30–313. 5). Commenting on Isa. 49: 11, Eusebius explains that Sion and Jerusalem can be understood in three ways (*tropoi*): as the historical Jewish capital; as the godly *politeuma*, that is, as an association or gathering (*synkrima*) of souls;

(eds.), *Irénée de Lyons, Contre les hérésies, Livre V* (SC no. 153; Paris, 1969), 434. 93; an anonymous writer, perhaps Clement of Alexandria, whose work survives in a papyrus fragment published in *JTS* 9 (1908), 244; and other references listed under Isa. 54: 11–13 in *Biblia Patristica*. None of these yields a parallel to Eusebius' exegesis, except for Origen, *C. Cels.* 8. 19–20.

[113] Origen, *Comm. Lam.* 4: 7 (*PG* xiii. 653B).

[114] Schmidt, *Polis in Kirche und Welt*, 28 ff.

and as the angelic *politeia* in heaven. The third of these, grasped by spiritual exegesis (*epanabebêkota tropon*), is clearly a celestial community composed of angels (and men?), inspired by the words of Heb. 12: 22 ('you have drawn near . . . to myriads of angels') and further buttressed by appeal to the Jerusalem above of Gal. 4: 26. The second interpretation, the godly *politeuma*, is the historic community of the faithful in Israel, and then in the church gathered from the nations, the same corporate and historical understanding we have just observed in the commentary on Isa. 54: 11–13.

V

The Prehistory of the Godly Polity: Eusebius' Assessment of Judaism in the Commentary on Isaiah

1. Eusebius' Attitude to Judaism[1]

Having committed itself definitively to the Old Testament as a consequence of the struggles with gnosticism and the dualism of Marcion, Christianity thereby also bound itself to a vindication of its claim to the Jewish Bible against the Jews themselves.[2] The need of this vindication continued so long as the existence of a vigorous and substantial Jewish community provided a living counter-argument to the Christian reading of the scriptures. The Christian attitude to the Jewish tradition had to remain fundamentally positive or expose Christianity again to the dualist critique. From the starting point of basic acceptance of the Old Testament, a variety of options were available to Christian apologists who wanted to demonstrate how and why Christianity claimed precedence over Judaism as the true portion of the Lord. Adapting a formulation of Harnack, Marcel Simon identified three different strategies used to justify this claim.[3]

[1] On Eusebius' attitude to Judaism: R. M. Grant, *Eusebius as Church Historian*, 97–113; J.-R. Laurin, *Orientations maîtresses des apologistes chrétiens de 270 à 361* (Rome, 1954), esp. 124–30, 344–80 (rather disappointing); J. Parkes, *The Conflict of the Church and the Synagogue: The Origins of Antisemitism* (London, 1934), 160–2 (cursory and selective); G. Schroeder, E. des Places (eds.), *Eusèbe de Césarée, Préparation Évangélique, Livre VII* (SC, no. 215; Paris, 1975), 7–93, 127–36 (very helpful). Eusebius is an important source in Marcel Simon's fundamental study of Jewish–Christian relations in the Roman Empire, *Verus Israel* (2nd edn.; Paris, 1964), esp. chs. 3, 5, and 6. See now the numerous articles in the valuable collection edited by H. Attridge and G. Hata, *Eusebius, Christianity and Judaism* (Detroit 1992).
[2] Simon, *Verus Israel*, 92 f.
[3] 'The gospel was preached simultaneously as the consummation of Judaism, as a new religion, and as the restatement and final expression of man's original religion' (A. Harnack, *The Mission and Expansion of Christianity in the First Three Centuries* (New York, 1961), 240).

They are by no means mutually exclusive and on different occasions may be used by the same writer.

1. The first option considers the relation between Judaism and Christianity in terms of rupture, contrast, and cancellation, based on dichotomies like old/new, letter/spirit, law/Christ, and the like.[4] The Old Testament law and cultus were abrogated by Christ, who freed men from servitude to an external law or cult. This approach is evident in the radical anti-legalism of Marcion, Pauline mitigated anti-legalism, and the purely symbolic interpretation of the Old Testament ceremonial prescriptions in the *Letter of Barnabas*. Paul's anti-legalism had been tempered in practice by his experiences with his churches. Simon observed that Paul's spiritual man would not act significantly different from a virtuous Jew, being distinguished more by the source of his motivation than the nature of his conduct.[5] After Paul the church formalized a distinction between the ceremonial and the moral law, enabling a new moralism to grow which paralleled that of the Jews and led to the second apologetic strategy.

2. The rise of a new nomism among Christians[6] suggested a pattern not of rupture but of smooth development between old and new covenants, based on precedents like Matt. 5: 17, in which a gradual and developmental process leads from earlier to later stages of revelation. The law of Christ subsumed and replaced the law of Moses, but still retained its character as law. Examples of this Christian nomism range from 1 Clement's emphasis on works and Old Testament precedents for the Christian priesthood to popularity of the *traditio legis* motif in early Christian art. Conceiving Christianity as a new law involved the related idea of thinking of Christians as a new people subject to this law who transcend the local and ethnic limitations of the former people. The continued existence of the former people, however, posed the question whether the Jews' priority in time was not a convincing rebuttal of Christian claims. This polemical need, plus the political difficulties which Roman law created for new religious movements, led Christians to extend their claim to supplant Israel in the present back into the past as well, by asserting that Christianity was even then the true Israel. Thus Chris-

---

[4] Simon, *Verus Israel*, 93–9.   [5] Ibid. 98 f.
[6] Ibid. 100–5.

tianity, in Simon's words, having revelled in its youth, was brought gradually to age itself.[7]

3. The third option circumvented the revelation to Israel entirely by going even further back and identifying Christianity with the true, primitive religion of humanity, restated and republicized by Christ.[8] Eusebius' distinction between the Hebrews and the Jews, mentioned in the previous chapter, is an outstanding example of this approach.

In the *Commentary on Isaiah*, however, the second strategy dominates. Christianity is repeatedly described as the evangelical law, the divine law, the new law.[9] The new people constitute the godly polity in place of the former people. Commenting on Isa. 51: 4, Eusebius says,

Who would be so foolish to think that 'people' here means the one to whom is said, 'Behold, for your iniquities you were sold, and for your sins I sent away your mother?' [cf. 50: 1]. But the present people would be 'saved by the grace of God' from the nations . . . For a new 'law' had to be given to a new 'people' to arise 'from the nations'. For that given by Moses was inappropriate for the *politeia* of the nations, since it prescribed the whole physical cult for a single site in Jerusalem.[10]

The last remark echoes the objection already raised in *The Proof of the Gospel* about the geographical restrictiveness of the old law.[11] Consistent with the second apologetic strategy, Eusebius goes further to identify Christianity as the true Israel even in the Old Testament. The sanctions enjoyed by biblical Israel were assimilable on the literal level once they could be understood as sanctions of the godly polity—its city, laws and citizens. When the prophet exulted in the Lord's protection of Jerusalem, spiritual interpretation was unnecessary. In this way Eusebius avoided having to yield to Jewish opponents the rich historical terrain charted in the book of Isaiah. He could map it with his customary equanimity because the land was part of his history as well as theirs.

[7] Ibid. 104.   [8] Ibid. 105–11.
[9] *Nomos evangelikos: CI* 16. 27, 17. 9, 60. 33, 61. 29, 126. 7; *nomos theios*: ibid. 61. 36, 233. 30–1; *nomos kainos*: ibid. 8. 12, 9. 5, 7, 14. 29, 15. 12, 34–5.
[10] Ibid. 322. 28–31, 322. 37–323. 3.
[11] From very early in his association with Christianity, Constantine was in the habit of referring to Christianity simply as 'this law'. *HE* 10. 5. 17, 10. 7. 1; *VC* 2. 67, 70. Cf. Kraft, *Konstantins religiöse Entwicklung*, 165, and Dörries, *Selbstzeugnis Kaiser Konstantins*, 296 ff.

2. The History of Israel and the History of Salvation

The most fundamental elements of Eusebius' view of Judaism go back to the New Testament itself and represent common Christian tradition, such as the election of Israel (e.g. Rom. 9: 1–4) and the doctrine of the faithful remnant (Rom. 11: 5).[12] From the apologists and the Alexandrians he adopted the doctrine of the Old Testament epiphanies and tutelage of the Logos.[13] The historical shape he gives to them is neatly expressed in a gloss on Isa. 63: 19 ('We became as in the beginning, when you neither ruled us nor bestowed on us your name.'), which he casts as a national lament:

And these things happened [i.e. the trampling of the sanctuary mentioned in the preceding verse] because we turned away from you. Thus abandoned and bereft of your oversight we are now as we were before you ruled us. For as there was once a time when we had 'neither prophet nor priest nor king', nor any of your gifts [*charismata*], so now we are brought to that bereavement again. We are as when we drifted so long in Egypt, even before Moses led us. For at that time your name did not adorn us nor were we called your people nor a portion of your inheritance, and now once again we have come round to the same end.

Eusebius adds as an apostrophe: 'All these things seem to be referred to the time after the coming of our Saviour, when they were utterly abandoned because of the crimes against him.'[14]

The *Commentary on Isaiah* is not much concerned with the beginnings and early course of Israel's role in the history of salvation, which appear only as solemn echoes.[15] Instead it is taken up with the 'new things' declared by God (Isa. 42: 9): the tumultuous history of the prophet's own lifetime, which spanned the reigns of four kings of Judah; the catastrophe of 587 BC, the liberation granted by Cyrus, the rebuilding of the temple, and ensuing phase of Jewish history; and the rejection of Christ and the denouement of AD 70. The flow of events (*ekbasis*) verified Isaiah's prophecies.[16] The final word of the prophet's oscillation between weal and woe was a decisive con-

[12] *CI* 12. 18 f.; 86. 28, 33; 87. 33; 90. 7, 9; 407. 3.
[13] Moses talked not with the invisible God but with his Christ (*CI* 391. 30–392. 2). The theophany of Isa. 6 was not a vision of the unbegotten divinity but of his only begotten son (ibid. 36. 2–11).
[14] Ibid. 390. 29–391. 6.
[15] For example, ibid. 86. 18–21.
[16] e.g. on Isa. 7: 5–9 (ibid. 46. 14–15), the fall of Samaria, or ibid. 276. 10–26, where Israel's history up to AD 70 is clearly intended.

demnation, expressed in the baleful words with which the book of
Isaiah ends ('Their worm shall not die, nor their fire go out'). 'Who
these are', he writes of the damned in Isa. 66: 24, 'he made plain in
the beginning of the prophecy, "I have begotten and raised up sons,
but they have disobeyed me"' (Isa. 1: 2). The lamentable fate of the
former people is anticipated in the very structure of Isaiah's book,
framed at beginning and end by God's judgement against his disobe-
dient sons.[17] This bleak mood occasionally descends to the railing
and violence typical of anti-Jewish polemics.

But balancing the theme of judgement is the theme of blessing.
Eusebius concedes that the prophet's words of consolation are addressed not only to the Christians of the distant future, but to the
people of Isaiah's own time. This is possible because the history of
Israel is constituted by two factions composed of those who are
faithful to God and those who are not. The former belong to the
godly polity, the latter to the rebellious portion which brought on
the disaster of AD 70 by their crucifixion of the saviour. The former
group, usually called simply 'friends of God', actually have more in
common with the Christians who came after them than with their
Jewish co-religionists.[18] There are two orders (*tagmata*) of those
who are saved: those who lived among the Jews before the proclamation of the Gospel, and those among the Jews and Gentiles who lived
after it and heeded its call. In Judaism the order of the saved included
'prophets, patriarchs, priests, pious men, high priests, thousands of
men and women who of old constituted the godly polity, no small
part of the city of God'.[19] Eusebius is not talking about a mere
sprinkling of pious souls lost in a sea of iniquity. A very significant
part of the history of Israel stands under God's approving sanction.
An insistence on vast numbers of faithful Jews is also found in his
comments on Isa. 11: 11, where the 'remnant' of the text is applied,
according to his custom, to Jewish Christians who were the first to
receive the Gospel and then preached it to the Gentiles. These numbered in the 'thousands', according to Eusebius' estimate, under the
influence of Luke (Acts 2: 41, 4: 4, 21: 20).[20] The godly polity existed
within the community of Israel but was not coterminous with it—a

---

[17] Cf. his comment on Isa. 1: 4, ibid. 5. 18–20.
[18] Ibid. 6. 15.
[19] Ibid. 370. 18–23; cf. also *to kreitton tagma . . . apo tou laou*, 276. 33.
[20] Ibid. 87. 5–31. On the Lucan theme, see Ernst Haenchen, *Die Apostelgeschichte*
(Göttingen, 1956), 151 f.

kind of *ecclesiola in ecclesia*, provided that we discount the sectarian imputation that the pious must be a minority.

Nor should the metaphor of an *ecclesiola* suggest that the godly polity is an invisible communion essentially removed from the empirical history of the rest of Israel. Eusebius' basic conviction is that biblical history is a real history of men and events which stands in its totality under the dispensation of the Logos. The literal and historical meaning of the text carries a sacred significance in addition to whatever predictive or symbolic function it may also serve. The history of Israel is itself salvation history, or a manifestation of the divine *oikonomia*.[21]

Let us turn to several examples of how Eusebius assessed Israel's history, its peak events and its most impressive achievements.

Our first illustration is the Emmanuel prophecy Isa. 7: 14. Eusebius had already treated it in the *Prophetic Selections*, where he showed his familiarity with the Jewish–Christian debate over the meaning and accuracy of the LXX reading *parthenos*.[22] Christian exegetes had long been aware of Jewish appeals to the general meaning of *'almah* and the alternative translation *neanis*.[23] In the *Commentary on Isaiah* Eusebius dismisses the translation difficulty by treating *parthenos* and *neanis* as equivalent, since the Mother of Christ was 'not an unmarried youth but a young matron (*neanis*) in her age and married state'.[24] The harmonizing interpretation seems to be original with him; it is typical of his practice of adopting as many of the Greek versions as he can.[25]

---

[21] See Sirinelli's discussion of Eusebius' use of this word, *Les vues historiques*, 259–61, 365 f. Sirinelli established that *oikonomia* means not merely the incarnate life of the Word but his whole providential dispensation. On *oikonomia* generally, see Prestige, *God in Patristic Thought*, 57–68, and *PGL* 940–2, where only one reference is given to *oikonomia* as the Old Testament as a whole (Origen, *C. Cels.* 4. 9). I have been unable to find a place in the commentary where Eusebius speaks directly of Israel's history as part of the divine *oikonomia*, a word he uses either for the Incarnation (207. 6; 345. 3–4; 85. 28) or in the general sense of ministration, service (of the Old Testament priesthood, 148. 11; the service of the righteous man, 351. 31).

[22] *EP* 4. 4 (177. 9–28).

[23] Justin, *Dial.* 43, 66–7. Origen also draws attention to it, *C. Cels.* 1. 34. See further Irenaeus, *Adv. Haer.* 3. 21. 1 (SC no. 211: 399) and Tertullian, *Adv. Marc.* 3. 13 (CSEL xlvii. 397. 2–5).

[24] *CI* 49. 28–50.

[25] Origen (*C. Cels.*) 1. 34) appealed, mistakenly, to the precedent of the MT of Deut. 22: 23–7 to justify rendering *'almah* as *parthenos*, because the Hebrew words in the passage he cites are *bethulah* and *na'ar*. Presumably Eusebius was under Origen's influence when he appealed to Hebrew usages in the *Prophetic Selections* (*EP* 4. 4), though he cites Leviticus rather than Deuteronomy, a sure sign that he was quoting

From the earliest times Christians were accustomed to interpret 7: 14 as a messianic prophecy (Matt. 1: 23). Eusebius is no exception. Nevertheless, he prefers to see the prophecy primarily in terms of its relevance to Israel.[26] The prophet's injunction, 'You will call his name Emmanuel', is properly addressed to Israel, even though its complete fulfilment lies in the distant future. The prophecy of the birth of the Saviour is supposed to be a source of consolation to Israel even now (*enteuthen êdê*)[27] if the people will only have faith that their God is truly with them and if they will not appeal to the gods of Damascus. Isaiah is calling for confidence based on faith in God's great deeds (*ta megala*), though their full, visible manifestation will not be evident for ages to come. The proof that Isaiah is appealing to his contemporaries is the second person of the verb, *kaleseis to onoma autou Emmanouêl*. Not all men, but only the people of Israel, can use this divine name, which is a token or symbol of God's protection. Otherwise the prophecy would be mistaken, since in fact the Saviour was not named Emmanuel but Jesus (Matt. 1: 21). The misquotation of Isa. 7: 14 (LXX) in Matt. 1: 23 rendered *kaleseis* by the third person plural *kalesousi*, a mistake which Eusebius attributed to careless copyists.[28] He notes carefully that the Matthean rendering, if original, would have diverted the attention of Isaiah's listeners to the future, as if that were the whole substance of the prophecy, when in fact its relevance was to the prophet's own time as well.

Our second example of Eusebius' understanding of biblical history is taken from his treatment of the Babylonian exile, about which he believed the historical Isaiah (to whom of course he attributed the whole book) had prophesied frequently. We will focus on his exegesis of the passages in Deutero-Isaiah which speak explicitly of the Persian king Cyrus (Isa. 44: 21–45: 23).

Eusebius is the first Christian writer to comment at length on these verses in a predominantly historical way, aside from scattered references in Origen. Christians had hitherto practised a narrowly apologetic interpretation of 45: 1 that required the substitution of *tôi christôi mou kyriôi* ('to Christ my lord') for the Septuagint's *tôi*

---

from memory. When he came to write the *Commentary on Isaiah* he may have learned from his Jewish contacts of Origen's error, because he omitted it.

[26] *CI* 48. 22–49. 28.
[27] The phrase is repeated three times (49. 2, 21; 48. 22).
[28] Ibid. 49. 24–8.

christôi mou Kyrôi ('to Cyrus my anointed').[29] This virtual Midrash on the text transformed it into a Christian prophecy. Eusebius, followed by the learned exegetical tradition, limits himself to saying that the Hebrews were accustomed to call their kings anointed ones, hence the prophet's address to Cyrus as the anointed one.[30] For him, the whole passage is in the first instance a prophecy of events almost two centuries in the future, the purpose of which is the provision of 'light and peace' to the repentant Jewish people after the chastisement (*paideia*) of the exile.[31] The disasters inflicted by the Babylonians were the ultimate fulfilment of the threats uttered by the prophet, and so the liberation was the decisive redemption wrought by the God who makes weal and woe (45: 7). Similarly, the rain of righteousness promised in 45: 8 answers to the restraint of the rain in the parable of the vineyard in 5: 6.[32] Everything that happened to Israel is the work of the one who alone is God; even the affairs of those who do not acknowledge him stand under his direction, hence Eusebius' repeated references to the divine *pronoia* in this section.[33]

The universal disposition of Providence is most boldly portrayed in God's sponsorship of Cyrus, God's servant. Eusebius has already anticipated the introduction of Cyrus in discussing an earlier oracle against Babylon (13: 17), which he thought alluded to

[29] See the critical apparatus of *Isaias, Septuaginta*, xiv. 290, and Ziegler's comments in his Introduction (p. 100). Before Eusebius only Origen understood the text as applying to Cyrus, cf. *Comm. Gen.* 3. 5, in *Philocalie 21–7 (Sur le libre arbitre)*, ed. E. Junod (SC, no. 226; Paris, 1976), 144. 5–6. All the following testify to the Christological reading: *Barn.* 21. 11, ed. F. X. Funk (Tübingen, 1901), (78. 5–6); Irenaeus, *Dem.* 49, *Démonstration de la prédication apostolique*, trans. with introduction and notes by L. M. Froidevaux (SC 62; Paris, 1959), 109; Tertullian, *Adv. Iud.* 7. 2, ed. Tränkle (13. 22); id., *Adv. Prax.* 11. 8, 28. 11, ed. Kroymann and Evans (*CCL* ii. 1172. 55–6, 1202. 49–50); Novatian, *De Trin.* 26. 7, ed. Diercks (*CCL* iv. 62. 24–5); Cyprian, *Test.* 1. 21, ed. Weber (*CCL* iii. 23. 49–50); Lactantius, *Inst. div.* 4. 12. 18, *Institutions divines*, ed. P. Monat (SC no. 377; Paris, 1992), 108. 79–80. The erroneous reading may have been inspired by the very similar language of Ps. 109: 1. Its wide attestation was one of the reasons for the thesis, popularized by J. Rendel Harris, of a Christian book of Old Testament testimonies in circulation from earliest times. See the discussion of R. A. Kraft, 'Barnabas' Isaiah Test and the Testimony Book Hypothesis', *JBL* 79 (1960), 341 f.

[30] *CI* 288. 30. 32. Jerome says the same, adding a tart comment about the *stultitia* of the many Greek and Latin writers who expounded the Christian interpretation, *Comm. Is.* 12. 45. 1 (*CCL* lxxiii A. 504. 17–505. 54). Likewise, Theodoret, *Commentary on Isaiah* 45. 1 (*PG* lxxxi. 421C–423A).

[31] *CI* 289. 23–30.

[32] Ibid. 290. 3–10.

[33] Ibid. 291. 12, 37; 292. 19, 22.

Cyrus.[34] The present prophecy, besides consoling the exiles, is intended to encourage Cyrus, whose resolve should be strengthened by learning that a Hebrew prophet foresaw his day and called him by name.[35] Isaiah even predicts the stratagem by which Cyrus would capture Babylon, when he describes the drying up of the abyss and the rivers.[36] According to Josephus, Cyrus actually read this prophecy after Babylonian Jews provided it for him, a non-scriptural detail which Eusebius is pleased to repeat.[37] Curiously, he also repeats Josephus' determination of a 210-year interval between prophecy and fulfilment, even though he himself remarks a few pages before that it was actually less than 200 years.[38]

It is true that Eusebius does not limit himself to a purely historical interpretation of Isaiah's prophecy about Cyrus. The Christological understanding, passed over at 45: 1, emerges when Eusebius comes to 45: 13, the verse which rounds off the whole section: 'I have raised a king with righteousness, and all his ways are straight; he will rebuild my city and will overturn the captivity of my people, not with payments or gifts, says the Lord of hosts.'[39]

Eusebius names Cyrus, Zerubbabel, and Christ as possible identifications of this righteous king. Cyrus' claim rests on his magnanimous ('not with payments or gifts') release of the Jews to return home, which amounts to a virtual (*dynamei*) reconstruction of the city of Jerusalem (293. 2–4). Zerubbabel, of royal descent from the tribe of Judah and the Davidic succession, actually led the people back and rebuilt the temple, with the prophetic sanction of Haggai and Zechariah.[40] Both these figures have undeniable historical evidence in their favour. A typological interpretation, however, enables Eusebius to see the actual fulfilment of Isa. 45: 13 in Christ, whom the Father raised from the dead, who built the true city of God, the church built upon the rock (Matt. 16: 18), by the spread of the godly polity throughout the world, and who liberated men from the captivity of demonic error.[41] Cyrus' and Zerubbabel's achievements,

[34] Ibid. 99. 27–36.
[35] Ibid. 290. 17–24.
[36] Ibid. 288. 18–22.
[37] Josephus, *Ant.* 11. 1–7 (LCL vi. 314–16) = *CI* 290. 21–31.
[38] Ibid. 287. 11–12. See the comments of the Loeb editor on Josephus' chronological confusion here (LCL vi. 316–17 n).
[39] The reading *basilea* instead of *auton* (MT) is found in numerous authorities (*Isaias*, ed. Ziegler, *Septuaginta*, xiv. 293).
[40] *CI* 293. 6–12, cf. Zech. 4: 9.
[41] Ibid. 293. 12–13.

besides being genuine historical events, are 'images and symbols' of what God will accomplish spiritually through Christ, to whom we can now see that 45: 1 applies more truly. Cyrus was not in reality the Christ of God, says Eusebius in reverting to the traditional reading *christôi* as a name rather than a title, nor did he see the completed reconstruction of Jerusalem, but only its foundations, since the site remained waste until the reign of Darius (Ezra 3–6). No evidence is offered why the prophecy should not apply to Zerubbabel.[42] Eusebius may have been acquainted with a Jewish messianic interpretation of Zerubbabel, judging from what he says about Isa. 32: 1 ('a righteous king shall rule').[43] When he closes his remarks by saying that the present passage 'would fit the Christ of God more than the king of the Persians, and our Saviour more than Zerubbabel', the parallelism suggests that he knew of someone who had portrayed Zerubbabel as a saving king.

Our last example of Eusebius' positive valuation of Jewish history is his assessment of the Second Temple period as a whole, or to be more accurate, the portion of it lasting until Maccabean times. His views on post-exilic Judaism can be inferred from his discussion of Isa. 3: 1–3, a prophecy which was fulfilled neither during Isaiah's time nor during the Babylonian captivity, but only after the death of Christ, when the Jews lost their *charismata* by 'binding the just man' (3: 10).[44] Isaiah's list of public offices in fact endured, at least in part, until the final crisis.

For there were then among them many prophets, both in Jerusalem, both before and throughout the captivity, and in Babylonia too, and after the return from there, there were also 'judges' among them who ruled the people. In Babylonia Daniel judged 'the elders', and after the return Jesus the son of Josedek and Zerubbabel the son of Salathiel both led the people, and in still later times Ezra and Nehemiah, both elders honoured for understanding and wisdom, adorned their people. Then you will find, too, splendid 'warriors' who lived among them in the times of the Maccabees, with whom were 'leaders of fifty' in the military ranks. And there were probably 'marvellous counsellors' among them, 'wise in speech' and 'master builders'. There were also 'shrewd hearers', who weighed the words of the prophets,

---

[42] *CI* 294. 1–2. Jerome seems to have felt this omission, and offered his own rebuttal: Zerubbabel didn't rebuild the city, nor did he end the captivity, nor was he even called a king, but lived under the power of the Medes and Persians. *Comm. Is.* 13. 45. 9–13 (*CCL* lxxiiiA. 510. 82–6).

[43] See *infra*, Section 3. 1, and Eusebius' remarks on Zerubbabel at *CI* 206. 2–21.

[44] Ibid. 21. 19–27, 23. 12–14.

testing those of the pseudoprophets, and doing this with a discerning spirit. Of old all these flourished among the Jewish people.[45]

Taken together, these legal, religious, and military offices are a kind of *ordo* of dignities in the godly polity.[46] In the previous chapter we noted how Eusebius used the extinction of some of these institutions, the high priesthood and native kingship, to mark the incipient divine judgement against Israel, although his prophetic touchstone was taken from the book of Daniel. Here Isaiah gives him an opportunity for a similar analysis on a much broader social base, although he tactfully passes over the dubious office of diviner (*stochastês*).[47] As a consequence of their rejection of Christ, the Jews have lost the illustrious leadership of old and suffer from the debased guidance foretold by Isaiah in 3: 4. His remark about youthful leaders may reflect an actual deterioration in the quality of the Jewish patriarchs of Eusebius' own time.[48]

In general Eusebius saw the post-exilic period as a time of great peace and prosperity for the Jewish people, when the twin monuments of city and temple were rebuilt and remained secure against attack until the Maccabean period. This extended peaceful interlude between the catastrophes of 587 BC and AD 70 was granted as a recompense to the righteous in Israel, just as the captivity in Babylonia had been inflicted as a punishment upon the wicked. Such an interpretation was inspired by passages like 30: 18–26, an exilic or post-exilic addition to the book of Isaiah. Here Eusebius finds a succinct statement of the this-worldly eschatology and retribution which he believes is characteristic of Judaism. He speaks frequently in his discussion of the 'deep peace' enjoyed by Second Temple Judaism.[49] Peace for Eusebius is not just an incidental circumstance

[45] Ibid. 22. 18–31.

[46] In the introduction to Book 8 of the *The Proof of the Gospel*, Eusebius refers to the disappearance of three outstanding dignities (*axiômata*) of kingship, prophecy, and high priesthood, as marks of the coming of Christ. The whole of Book 8 expands this theme, but with an exclusively Christological focus rather than the *Commentary on Isaiah*'s theme of the transfer of the godly polity to Christianity.

[47] An indication that this omission is intentional is Eusebius' failure to mention that Aquila, Symmachus, and Theodotion rendered the Hebrew original as *mantis*, also a word offensive to Christian ears—even though otherwise in this section he notes their diversions from the LXX. Jerome, and Theodoret both mention the non-LXX diversions on this point, cf. Jerome, *Comm. Is.* 2. 3. 2 (*CCL* lxxiii. 43. 20–6) and Theodoret, *Commentary on Isaiah* 2. 3. 2 (SC no. 276. 212. 246–7).

[48] *CI* 23. 15–16, *pace* the suggestion of M. Avi-Yonah, *The Jews of Palestine*, 167.

[49] Ibid. 197. 15; 199. 2–3, 5.

of history to which Christians can afford to be indifferent. As the work of divine providence, it represents an authentic sign of God's sanction. The prolonged immunity of Jerusalem and its temple is therefore evidence of God's special favour to Israel at this time. If the prophecy warned that the Jews were still to be given 'the bread of adversity and the water of affliction' (30: 20), this could only be a reference to the temporary resistance of neighbouring peoples to the rebuilding of the temple, following which the prophet assures them of abundance and prosperity.[50] Possibly Eusebius reflects the prophecies of imminent prosperity found in Haggai and Zechariah, the contemporaries of Zerubbabel and the high priest Joshua (e.g. Hag. 2: 9, Zech. 8: 12), who foretold that great abundance would accompany the reconstruction of the temple. But he also demonstrates how Christians like himself conceded a provisional legitimacy to the religious institutions of Judaism under the old dispensation. Finally, Eusebius' stress of the *euthênia* of the Jewish temple-state may be another indication of his affinity for the priestly post-exilic theocracy.

The disappearance of idolatry and polytheism was one of the strongest indications of the religious superiority of the post-exilic Jewish community, as compared to the nation in the days of Isaiah. For Eusebius, idolatry, the denial of the unity and transcendence of God, was error (*hê planê*) par excellence.[51] The emergence of polytheism in human history had been the surest sign of the depravity of primitive humanity, just as its disappearance was the decisive consequence of the spread of the Gospel. Although the book of Isaiah makes frequent and vehement denunciations of idolatry, historical honesty compels Eusebius to recognize that these charges became irrelevant after the exile. Commenting on Isa. 31: 7 ('For on that day, everyone shall cast away his idols of gold and silver'), he admits that the prophecy had its fulfilment within Jewish history.[52] The propagation of Christianity would be marked above all by the definitive rolling back of idolatrous polytheism, but the Jews had already anticipated this triumph by eliminating it from their own community.

[50] *CI* 198. 18–21.
[51] Ibid., index, s.v. *planê* (e.g., 45. 27). See Sirinelli's discussion of Eusebius' view of polytheism, *Les vues historiques*, ch. 5.
[52] *CI* 204. 20–5.

3. The Privileges of the Godly Polity

During the Jewish phase of its history, the godly polity was marked by the possession of visible tokens of its election. These gifts (*charismata*)[53] were lost definitively when the Jews killed Christ, the 'just man', as Eusebius remarks in commenting on Isa. 3: 9–10. Although he nowhere gives a complete list, the following classification comprises the aspects of Judaism which most preoccupy him in his commentary.

1. The first and most important of these is the *written revelation* itself, the Old Testament. To make the Christian interpretation of the text persuasive to pagans who regarded the Christian claims as a theft of the sacred book of the Jews, Eusebius took over the literary techniques developed by Origen and discussed in Ch. III. We omitted at that time a discussion of Origen's acquaintance with Jewish exegesis. Eusebius copied Origen in this respect as well. 2. The second charisma is the phenomenon of *prophecy*, its nature and purpose, and the role of the prophet as an evangelist before the Gospel. 3. Besides the written revelation and prophecy, Israel possessed *holy people*, the righteous of Israel who constituted the godly polity and who are distinguished from the corrupt leadership which eventually condemned Jesus. 4. The *sacred institutions* of temple cult, ritual law, kingship, and priesthood play a role, though little is said here that is distinctive. 5. The *holy city* of Jerusalem receives a great deal of attention. In this chapter we will be speaking of the historic status and fate of Jerusalem rather than of its symbolic and transcendent references.

The Written Revelation: Eusebius' Use of Rabbinic Exegesis

Though Christians insisted that the Bible spoke everywhere of Christ, the truth remained that the Jews had possessed it for centuries before the Incarnation (Rom. 9: 4). To explain why they had failed to recognize the one who was promised, Christians resorted to forms of prophetic or allegorical exegesis and belittled Jewish 'literalism'.[54] Consequently, there could be little appreciation for Jewish exegesis, even though the Jews were able to claim a special access to

[53] Cf. ibid. 23. 13–14, 21. 21, 115. 16–28, 174. 19–39, 390. 32.
[54] Simon, *Verus Israel*, 177 ff.

the Old Testament by virtue of the continuity of language and religious practice. In Christian eyes the futility of reading scripture according to the letter was demonstrated by the Jews' rejection of Christ and by their commitment to the Mosaic law.[55] Eusebius spoke for a long tradition of Christian polemic when he echoed the harsh denunciations of Titus 1: 14 and I Timothy 4: 7 about adhering to Jewish myths, especially those having to do with a human messiah.[56] The Jews, he said, rejected Christ because they failed 'to grasp the *nous* hidden in the depth of the words, but busied themselves with the word alone [*peri de monên tên lexin*]'.[57]

Besides the incomprehension of the Messianic texts and the obstinate clinging to the ritual law, a third Christian objection to Jewish exegesis was its reliance on rabbinic tradition as a supplement to written revelation. Eusebius expressed an ancient Christian view when he criticized Jewish dependence on the 'traditions of the elders'.[58] Nevertheless, there is contrasting evidence that in practice Eusebius recognized the value of Jewish expertise for grasping the literal sense of scripture. There is an analogy in his attitude to the land of Israel. When Israel fell away from the godly polity, its land and cities continued to be invested with a sacred aura as the sites of God's deeds on behalf of the former people. Eusebius' *Onomasticon* was designed as a scholarly aid to help Christians recover the ancient past of their polity.[59] Similarly with the literal meaning of the scriptures, which shared the same degree of national determination as the godly polity as a whole—written in the language of a particular people, set in their land, and devoted to the events of their history. These particularizing qualities were not arbitrary ciphers to provoke allegorical ingenuity. There were the essential cultural conditions for embodying and transmitting scripture's spiritual meaning.

The literary remains required guides as much as did the physical. Providing an intelligible past for Christians was one of the purposes

---

[55] See for example Justin, *Dial.* 11–13.

[56] *CI* 362. 24–9.

[57] Ibid. 364. 32–3.

[58] Cf. Matt. 15: 2, 3, 6.

[59] See Barnes' discussion of the importance of the *Onomasticon* as evidence of the originality of Eusebius' historical orientation (*Constantine and Eusebius*, 106–10), and Dennis Groh, 'The *Onomasticon* of Eusebius and the Rise of Christian Palestine', *SP* 18 (1983), 23–32. On the general subject of Eusebius and the holy land, see Robert Wilken, 'Eusebius and the Christian Holy Land', in Attridge and Hata (eds.), *Eusebius, Christianity, and Judaism*, 736–60, and, with a rather different emphasis, Walker, *Holy City, Holy Places?*

of the *Commentary on Isaiah*, and Eusebius felt free to exploit traditional Jewish learning if it illuminated obscurities in the literal meaning. Such learning was readily available in the Jewish community of Caesarea.[60] Origen's example gave him a precedent for consulting Jewish experts on textual, linguistic, and exegetical matters.[61]

Eusebius says that these experts are called *deuterôtai* and their interpretations are known as *deuterôseis*, Greek coinages which Jews themselves had invented to express Hebrew *Mishnah* and Aramaic *tannâ* and *tnh*.[62] The *deuterôtai* revealed for the more advanced the deeper *nous* of scripture, by interpreting the things which were concealed in riddles (*di' ainigmatôn*).[63] Their *deuterôseis* are contrasted with the mere stories (*historiai*) told to the simple and uneducated.[64] He gives an example in *The Proof of the Gospel*, which says that Josephus consulted *tas exôthen ioudaikas deuterôseis* in order to expound the meaning of the leprosy of King Uzziah.[65] Origen, from whom Eusebius may have learnt this terminology, says in his *Commentary on the Song of Songs* that the *deuterôtai* expounded selected passages in scripture which young students were prohibited from studying: the creation account, the passages in Ezekiel on the cherubim, the end of Ezekiel on the building of the temple, and the Song of Songs.[66] These are texts which inspired esoteric interpretation, although Eusebius' reference to Josephus suggests that the interpretations could also be public (*exôthen*).

Eusebius seems to have been ambivalent about this Jewish expertise. The *Commentary on Isaiah* occasionally denounces it. An allegorization of Isa. 22: 11 ('You made a reservoir between the two walls for the water of the old pool. But you did not look to him who did it, or have regard for him who planned it long ago') contrasts the

---

[60] On Caesarea's Jews at this time, see the study of L. I. Levine, *Caesarea Under Roman Rule* (Studies in Judaism in Late Antiquity, no. 7; Leiden, 1975), esp. 86–106.

[61] See Nicholas de Lange, *Origen and the Jews* (Cambridge, 1976) and Hans Bietenhard, *Origenes und die Juden* (Berlin, 1974), esp. 19–38.

[62] On the terminology: de Lange, *Origen and the Jews*, 34–5; Simon, *Verus Israel*, 115–17; and E. Schürer, *History of the Jewish People*, rev. and ed. G. Vermes and F. Millar, i. 70.

[63] Cf. *PE* 12. 1. 4 (GCS no. 8, pt. 2: 88) and 11. 5. 3 (GCS no. 8, pt. 2: 11).

[64] Ibid. 12. 4. 2.

[65] *DE* 6. 18. 36 (GCS no. 6: 281).

[66] *Comm. Songs*, Prol. 1. 7. Rufinus transliterated *deuterôseis* (plural) into Latin, which suggests that it was a technical term. Cf. Origen, *Commentaire sur le Cantique des Cantiques*, ed. with trans., text, introduction and notes, P. Monat (SC no. 377; Paris, 1992), 108. 79–80.

biblical interpretation of the Jewish *deuterôtai* with that of the new covenant of the city of God. Eusebius takes the diverted water of the old pool that was in the city (cf. 22: 9) to be the rabbinic distortion of the revelation entrusted to the city of God, appealing also to Jer. 2: 13, 'They abandoned me, the spring of living water, and dug for themselves ruined cisterns.'

Thus 'they diverted the water of the old pool' that was in the city and fashioned for themselves alien 'water between the two walls', that is, of the old and new convenant. For these two walls of the city of God are plainly the godly polity [*tês kata theon politeias*], in the midst of which those who are denounced conceived strange and 'alien water' for themselves, the 'traditions of the elders' [cf. Matt. 15: 2] upon which those among them who are called *deuterôtai* pride themselves.[67]

The perversion of the scriptures by the *deuterôtai* is the decisive mark of their defection from the city of God.

But Eusebius' exegetical practice often belies this negative attitude. Perhaps he introduces his allegorical defence of Christian exegesis at this point in the commentary because he is thinking ahead to 22: 15–25, the episode about Somnas (Shebnah in Hebrew) the steward, where he will exploit Jewish exegetical lore, and he may have felt it necessary to protect himself against the charge of undue Jewish sympathies. The table lists passages in the commentary where Eusebius refers to Jewish interpretations of scripture. The numbered passages will be examined in the analysis which follows.

Several of the references in the table are merely stock criticisms of Jewish exegesis, such as the conventional Christian trope on water and wine.[68] Besides these, there are appeals to Jewish exegesis on matters having to do with dating the fulfilment of prophecy, the city of Jerusalem, the temple cult, and religious and political leaders. It appears that Eusebius resorted willingly to Jewish assistance when he was interested in the literal interpretation of texts bearing on the godly polity's *charismata*.

Eusebius' Jewish traditions were either mediated to him by Josephus or came directly from a rabbinic source. Although Origen is also a likely source, none of the interpretations listed in the table

---

[67] *CI* 146. 2–8.

[68] See patristic comments on, e.g. Gen. 49: 11, Song of Songs, John 2: 1–11, Acts 2: 13, in *PGL* s.v. *oinos* 3. Origen was very fond of the metaphor, as in *Comm. Joh.* 13. 62, ed. E. Preuschen, iv of *Origenes' Werke* (GCS; Leipzig, 1903), 295. 1: 'For before Jesus scripture was water, but since him it has become for us wine.'

TABLE 1. Citations of Jewish exegesis in the *Commentary on Isaiah*

Isaiah	Source (acc. to Eusebius)	Summary
1: 22–3	(none listed)	Jewish exegesis of the tent/ city of David based on Jewish myths; Jews dilute wine of scripture
1: 30	(none listed)	Jewish exegesis is sterile
5: 18–20	(none listed)	Polemic against Jewish myths (1 Tim. 4: 7)
(1) 7: 8	Sons of the Hebrews	Proof of the prophecy is the fall of Samaria 65 years after the 25th year of King Uzziah
22: 7–11	(none listed)	Allegorization of the 'two walls' (=OT and NT) between which Jewish *deuterôtai* introduce 'the traditions of men'
(2) 22: 15–25	The Hebrew	Midrashic lore about Somnas the steward
(3) 29: 1	Sons of the Jews	Ariel is Jerusalem, but also the altar set up in front of the temple, because it consumes everything set upon it
30: 1–5	Children of the Hebrews	The prophecy is fulfilled about 150 years later, in the time of the prophet Jeremiah (Origen's commentary ended here)
(4) 30: 30–1	Children of the Hebrews	*hoi Assyrioi* is traditionally taken by Jews to mean all those in authority who are proud and arrogant in their rule
(5) 32: 1–4	Children of the Hebrews	'A righteous king shall rule' is said by Jews to apply to Zerubbabel
36: 3	Children of the Hebrews	Reference is made to earlier passage on Somnas

Table 1. *Continued*

Isaiah	Source (acc. to Eusebius)	Summary
(6) 38: 13	(none listed)	Non-scriptural detail: Hezekiah's lament is due to his facing death childless and without a successor
(7) 39: 1–2	Teacher of the Hebrews	Jewish traditions about Hezekiah's illness, caused by (also 'the Hebrew') his omission of a prayer of thanksgiving after Sennacherib's defeat
(8) 40: 1–2	The Hebrew	Hezekiah's prayer was reprehensible in God's eyes because he prayed for himself rather than for his people. Therefore Isaiah is bidden to console the people
59: 4–5	(none listed)	Polemic against Jewish myths and human traditions
59: 9–10	(none listed)	Critique of Jewish literal exegesis

are found in Origen's extant works.[69] Furthermore, several of the references are from the last half of Isaiah, for which Origen never completed his commentary.[70] Eusebius' reference to 'the Hebrew' and 'the teacher of the Hebrews',[71] with whom he discussed Isa. 39: 1–2, recalls the unidentified informant mentioned frequently in Origen's works.[72] It happens that Jerome was not above passing off

[69] See the list of Origen's references to Jewish exegesis in G. Bardy, 'Les traditions Juives dans l'œuvre d'Origène', *RB* 34 (1925), 217–52.

[70] On Isa. 30: 30–1, 32: 1–4, 36: 3, 38: 13, 38: 19–20, 39: 1–2, 40: 1–2.

[71] *CI* 245. 29–30; cf. 147. 25.

[72] On 'the Hebrew' in Origen, see Bardy, 'Les traditions Juives', 221–3; Nautin, *Origène*, 417; Hanson, *Allegory and Event*, 174; de Lange, *Origen and the Jews*, 23–8.

as Jewish tradition revealed to him by a Jewish consultant what he had actually learned from the commentaries of his Christian predecessors.[73] For example, he attributes to 'the Hebrew' the tradition about Somnas that Eusebius says 'the Hebrew' had revealed to *him*.[74] It is doubtful, however, that Eusebius was concealing anything, since, as noted, some of the Jewish traditions he cites come from parts of Isaiah not discussed by Origen.

Let us examine the numbered passages.

(1) Isa. 7: 8. In order to explain the obscure figure of 65 years until the fall of Samaria, which was manifestly impossible if uttered in the reign of Ahaz, Eusebius appealed to a calculation of the 65 years from the reign of Uzziah, on the grounds that it derives from the prophecy of Amos, 'Israel will be led away captive from its own land' (Amos 7: 11, 17). Since Amos' ministry began 'two years before the earthquake' (Amos 1: 1), Eusebius' Jewish source felt justified in dating Amos' prophecy to the twenty-fifth year of Uzziah's reign, and the earthquake to the twenty-seventh year, when Uzziah entered the sanctuary to offer sacrifice and was struck with leprosy for his arrogant presumption. Since Uzziah reigned for 52 years, 27 (Uzziah) + 16 (Jotham) + 16 (Ahaz) + 6 (Hezekiah, cf. 2 Kgs. 18: 10) = 65 years from Amos' prophecy to the capture of Samaria. Who or what was Eusebius' source? As just noted, Eusebius says in *The Proof of the Gospel* that Josephus, on the basis of Jewish *deuterôseis*, had correlated Uzziah's sacrilege with an earthquake.[75] Furthermore, Eusebius credited himself, not Josephus or Josephus' *deuterôseis*, with the identification of that earthquake with the one mentioned at the beginning of Amos (Amos 1: 1). But here in the commentary he acknowledges his indebtedness to a Jewish source which cannot be Josephus, who has nothing to say about how to calculate the 65 years. The most plausible explanation is that Eusebius consulted another Jewish source when he found his earlier comments in the *Proof* inadequate for explaining Isa. 7: 8 intelligibly.

[73] For references in Jerome's own works and some modern critical studies, see Nautin, *Origène*, 326–8. S. Gozzo, 'De commentario s. Hieronymi in Isaiae librum', 59–61, is too lenient in assessing Jerome's evasiveness in this regard.

[74] Jerome, *Comm. Is.* 5. 22. 2 (*CCI* lxxiii. 201. 2–6).

[75] *DE* 6. 18. 36. Cf. Jos., *Ant.* 9. 10. 4. Other Midrashic attestations are listed and discussed by Louis Ginzberg, 'Die Haggada bei den Kirchenvätern VI: Der Kommentar des Hieronymus zu Jesaja', in S. W. Baron and A. Marx (eds.), *Jewish Studies in Memory of George A. Kohut* (New York, 1935), 287. See also id., *The Legends of the Jews*, 7 vols. (Philadelphia, 1946), vi. 357 nn. 29–31.

A plausible candidate is the *Seder Olam*, which has the same explanation for the 65-year period. And yet Eusebius' gloss is not in all respects derivable from it. For one thing, the *Seder Olam* identifies the earthquake with the theophany in the temple (Isa. 6), even though this is clearly incompatible with the statement that Isaiah's vision occurred in 'the year that King Uzziah died' (Isa. 6: 1), a contradiction which gave rise to later Midrashic speculation that Uzziah could be said to have 'died' when he became leprous.[76] Furthermore, Eusebius also says that he learned from his source that during the earthquake the fat of the altar of sacrifice was poured out, a motif for which I could not find a rabbinic parallel.

Whatever the full explanation, Eusebius' borrowed exegesis saved the plain meaning of the text by providing an inner-Jewish *ekbasis tôn pragmatôn* for the prophecy.

(2) Isa. 22: 15–25. Eusebius was aware of Haggadic traditions that the steward Somnas had attempted to betray Jerusalem during the siege of Sennacherib.[77] Eusebius says that 'the Hebrew' told him that Somnas was actually a high priest and a man of dissolute character given over to pleasure (*truphêtês*). Both these details are attributed by Jewish sources to a rabbi Eleazar. The Babylonian Talmud says that rabbi Eleazar explained the title *skn* (steward), said of Somnas in 22: 15, by reference to the nurse (*sknt*) given to King David in his old age (1 Kgs. 1: 2, 4).[78] *Midrash Rabbah* on Leviticus also credits a rabbi Eleazar with the information that Somnas was a high priest.[79] Unfortunately, no patronymic or native city is given, and he cannot be further identified.

(3) Isa. 29: 1–2. The identification of both Jerusalem and the place of sacrifice in front of the temple as 'Ariel' was almost certainly taken from Origen. Jerome says that Origen ended the thirtieth book of his *Commentary on Isaiah* with the teaching of the Jewish patriarch Huillus on Isa. 29: 1 ff., but he does not tell us what that interpretation was.[80] He also notes in his own *Commentary on*

---

[76] S. *'Olam Rab.* 20, cited in Ginzberg, 'Die Haggada bei den Kirchenvätern VI', 288. Ginzberg cites the Targum for Isa. 6: 1 and *Ex. Rab.* 1. 34 for the concordizing interpretation.

[77] Ginzberg, 'Die Haggada bei den Kirchenvätern VI', 301; id., *Legends of the Jews*, vi. 364–5 n. 64.

[78] *Sanhedrin* 26a, in *The Babylonian Talmud*, ed. I. Epstein, 18 vols. (London: The Soncino Press, 1948), xii. 153–4.

[79] *Leviticus Rabbah* 5. 3, trans. J. Israelitam and Judah Slotki, iv of *Midrash Rabbah*, ed. H. Freedman and M. Simon, 10 vols. (London, 1939).

[80] Jerome, *Contra Rufinum* (PL 23. 408), cited in de Lange, *Origen and the Jews*, 23.

Isaiah that 'some think' that Ariel is the temple and the altar, besides Jerusalem as a whole, but it is impossible to tell whether this was the doctrine taught by Huillus.[81] As elsewhere in his commentary, Jerome is probably quoting Eusebius in his anonymous reference. The etymology of Ariel as 'lion of God' was known to both Eusebius and Jerome from *The Interpretation of Hebrew Names*.[82] Only Eusebius, however, explains how the etymology applies to the altar of sacrifice: 'They (the Jews) say that Ariel is translated lion of God, since the altar was God's, and he consumed all the animal sacrifices offered on it, for which reason it has received this name.'[83]

(4) Isa. 30: 30–1. The probable source for the allegorical explanation of 'Assyrians' as all those who are proud and arrogant in their rule is the etymological handbook, which says that *Assyrioi* means *dirigentes*.[84]

(5) Isa. 32: 1–4. The identification of Zerubbabel as the just king of the prophecy has no parallel that I know of. It seems very likely that Eusebius knew Jewish applications of royal-messianic texts to Zerubbabel, though the rabbis never declared him as the promised Messiah, despite allotting him various roles in the messianic age.[85] Origen says that the Jews denied that an identical prophecy in Isa. 45: 13 could apply to Christ ('I have raised him up, a king with justice' (LXX)), since he had not fulfilled the prophecy by rebuilding the city.[86] This Jewish critique of Christian exegesis may have gone on to speak of Zerubbabel as the righteous king, as we noted in our earlier discussion of Isa. 45: 13.

(6) Isa. 38: 13. Josephus says that Hezekiah's lament was due to his childlessness and his fear of dying without a successor.[87] The Babylonian Talmud expands this to mean that Hezekiah was a celibate, and asserts that he asked Isaiah for his daughter in marriage, a request the prophet denied.[88] Eusebius Christianizes this Haggadah by explaining that the tragedy of his childlessness would be his deprivation of the Saviour from among his descendants, since Christ was born of the seed of David (Rom. 1: 3).[89]

---

[81] *Comm. Is.* 9. 29. 1–8 (*CCL* lxxiii. 370. 55–7).
[82] For Ariel as lion of God, cf. *Int. Heb. nom.* 37. 19, 44. 17, and 56. 27.
[83] *CI* 187. 33–5.
[84] *Int. Heb. nom.* 60. 16–17. The same interpretation is found in *DE* 7. 1. 57 ff.
[85] So Ginzberg, *Legends of the Jews*, vi. 438.
[86] Origen, *Commentary on Romans* 8. 8, cited in Hanson, *Allegory and Event*, 155.
[87] Josephus, *Ant.* 10. 25–7.
[88] *Ber.* 10a (*The Babylonian Talmud*, xiv. 54–5).
[89] *CI* 243. 31–3.

(7) Isa. 39: 1–2. The tradition that Hezekiah suffered his illness because he failed to sing a thanksgiving song for the destruction of the Assyrian army is unknown in Christian sources before Eusebius.[90] Among Jewish sources, Josephus is excluded, because he says that Hezekiah *did* sing such a song.[91] The preservation of the Haggadah in the late Midrashic compilation *Song of Songs Rabbah* may point to the same Jewish tradition Eusebius drew from, since it is of Palestinian provenance.[92] Eusebius' source also told him that the Babylonians discovered about Hezekiah's cure because their astronomers had noticed the miracle of the sun's retrogression. Having made inquiry, they learned that the God of the Hebrews was great and that his cure of the sick king was the cause of the marvel of the sun, and therefore sought an alliance with him.[93] Eusebius quotes this tradition at length, then makes an instructive correction. He rejects the explanation for the Babylonian embassy as fanciful, because the diplomatic mission took place in the same year as the flight of Sennacherib and the revolt of his sons. The political situation provided sufficient reason for a rival king to look for foreign allies, especially such potent ones as the Jews apparently were.

(8) Isa. 40: 1–2. This Haggadic explanation for the prophecy of consolation which follows the Hezekiah cycle is also taken from 'the Hebrew', and like the previous discussion is only found in late Midrashic works.[94] The *Commentary on Isaiah* is its earliest instance in Jewish or Christian literature. Jewish exegesis seems to have encouraged Eusebius to see the great prophecy of consolation with which Deutero-Isaiah begins as applying not just to Christians but to Jews as well, both in the time of the prophet and in subsequent ages. The source told him that 'God, out of concern for his own people, commanded those who were capable of it to "console" the

---

[90] As noted above, Jerome simply borrowed from Eusebius without acknowledging him; Ephrem the Syrian also has this exegesis, presumably independent of Eusebius, as cited in Ginzberg, 'Die Haggada bei den Kirchenvätern VI', 308.

[91] Josephus, *Ant.* 10. 24.

[92] *Song of Songs Rabbah* 4. 8. 3, trans. Maurice Simon, ix of *Midrash Rabbah*. This Midrash is dated to the mid-sixth century: *Encyclopedia Judaica*, 16 vols. (Jerusalem, 1972), xv. 154. Other citations in Ginzberg, *Legends of the Jews*, vi. 366 nn. 70–1.

[93] *CI* 245. 34–246. 7.

[94] Cf. *Yalqut* on Isa. 40: 1, cited in Ginzberg, 'Die Haggada bei den Kirchenvätern Vi', 309. Once again the same tradition turns up in the works of Ephrem (ibid.). Jerome has it likewise, along with other information not found in Eusebius; see *Comm. Is.* 11. 39. 3–8 (*CCL* lxxiii. 453. 51–63).

people',[95] since Hezekiah had selfishly neglected his responsibility. In a long exposition of Isa. 40: 1–2, Eusebius develops the kind of bifocal interpretation typical of the commentary as a whole.[96] The Christian interpretation, an important example of his ecclesiastical reading of Isaiah, must wait until the next chapter. In the Jewish construction of the text, he sees the 'heart of Jerusalem' to whom the consolation is addressed as those among the larger body of corporeal-minded folk who are eminent for their understanding and wisdom. These spiritual Jews suffered the same historic tribulations as the wicked ones, specifically the 'double chastisement' (Isa. 40: 2) of the two captures of Jerusalem. To them the prophet addresses his announcement of the coming of Christ (40: 3) as a proleptic consolation. Jewish exegesis has thus been admitted as worthy of serious consideration and applied to the historical experience of Israel, but within a fundamentally Christian framework. Jewish experience has its own integrity placed within the greater framework of the history of the godly polity in its pre- and post-Incarnational phases.

The Charism of Prophecy

Eusebius shared the general patristic view of prophetic inspiration, which saw the prophet as one who spoke what he had learned from God's Spirit through illumination, hearing, or sight. Ever since the church's experience with Montanism, it had been customary to understand the Spirit's use of a human agent as not restricting or cancelling the prophet's conscious mind but somehow enhancing or ennobling it.[97] Justin's statement that the prophets spoke in ecstasy became suspect. Writers like Origen emphasized that the prophets did not lose control of their rational faculties under the agency of inspiration. Compare Justin's assertion of Zechariah that 'he did not see the Devil or the Angel of the Lord with his own eyes, since in his revelation he was not in a normal state [*katastasei*], but in an ecstasy [*ekstasei*]',[98] with Origen's defence of biblical inspiration against Celsus.

[95] *CI* 247. 11–12.

[96] Ibid. 247. 13–249. 17.

[97] On the reaction to Montanist New Prophecy, see Pierre de Labriolle, 'La polémique antimontaniste contre la prophétie extatique', *Revue d'histoire et de littérature religieuses*, 11 (1906), 97–145.

[98] Justin, *Dial.* 115. 3. Origen's view of inspiration is discussed in Hanson, *Allegory and Event*, 187–209. Origen's most extended discussion of prophecy, Jewish and

Furthermore, it is not the work of a divine spirit to lead the alleged proph-
etess [i.e. the Delphic oracle] into a state of ecstasy and frenzy so that she
loses possession of her consciousness. The person inspired by the divine
spirit ought to have derived from it far more benefit than anyone who may
be instructed by the oracles to do that which helps towards living a life
which is moderate and according to nature, or towards that which is of
advantage or which is expedient. And for that reason he ought to possess the
clearest vision at the very time when the deity is in communion with him.
From this ground, by collecting evidence from the divine scriptures, we
prove that the prophets among the Jews, being illuminated [*ellampomenoi*]
by the divine Spirit in so far as was beneficial to them as they prophesied,
were the first to enjoy the visitation of the superior Spirit to them. Because
of the touch, so to speak, of what is called the Holy Spirit upon their soul,
they possessed clear mental vision and became more radiant in their soul,
and even in body, which no longer offered any opposition to the life lived
according to virtue, in that it was mortified according to the 'mind of the
flesh' as we call it.[99]

Origen's doctrine that inspiration was supra-rational did not keep
Eusebius from seeing a genuinely human and contingent element in
prophecy. At one point he paraphrases the prophet's admonitions
this way: 'For what God had revealed to me [*apokalypse*], that he
has also shown [*exephênen*] to you, namely, by my interpretation
[*hermêneôs*].'[100] Unlike the ecstatic prophets described by Plato in
the *Timaeus*, the biblical prophet is his own interpreter.[101] He may
even require time and the rich texture of historical experience to
reach the proper perspective on his prophecy. Eusebius says that the
heading of the book of Isaiah, which sets Isaiah's prophecies in
the reigns of the four kings Uzziah, Jotham, Ahaz, and Hezekiah,
indicates how lengthy an interval Isaiah needed to achieve a full and
accurate knowledge of the future in his partial revelations.

[The heading] indicated the ages of the kings, since there was a different state
of affairs among the Jews, and events were to transpire in the distant future
which never entered the mind or suspicion of the people of that time.

---

pagan, is in the *C. Cels.* 1. 35–7, 48; 2. 28–9, 37; 3. 2–4; 6. 19–21; and 7. 1–10, with the
whole of Book 7 being a defence of the Christian interpretation of Old Testament
prophecy.

[99] *C. Cels.* 7. 3–4, trans. Chadwick.

[100] *CI* 142. 1–3.

[101] *Timaeus*, 72a–b. Contrary to Chadwick's note, *Origen: Contra Celsum*, 397 n.
2, the idea that the prophet can interpret his own prophecies because his inspiration
is supra-rational contradicts Plato's statement that the prophet's madness requires an
independent expositor.

Furthermore, it needs to be noted that the whole book, which only seems to be a single composition, was actually spoken over long periods of time, since there was need of extensive and precise understanding to discern the future, to determine the meaning [*dianoian*] of the events of the time, and to suit [*epharmozein*] the prophecy for the events that occurred in each reign. For the age of these kings covered fifty years in all, during which the things contained in this whole book were spoken.[102]

Eusebius recognizes considerable freedom in the prophet's judgements, which he describes as a meditation on both the present and the long-range implications of contemporary events. The prophet is a man who, by virtue of divine inspiration and his own effort and capacity, can seen through the maze of history to grasp its fundamental meaning (*dianoia*).

We turn now to the scope of prophecy and its role in Jewish history. For Origen, the real value of biblical prophecy, when it was not interpreted in utterly allegorical terms, was its prediction of Christ.[103] Until it had been fulfilled in Christ, doubters might have been justified in their indecision and hesitation, because of scripture's obscurities. Writes Origen in a highly characteristic passage:

It would be a long business if we were to record at this point the ancient prophecies relating to every future event, in order that the doubter might be struck by their divine origin and, putting away all hesitation and indecision, might devote himself with his whole soul to the words of God. But if in every passage of the scriptures the superhuman element of the thought does not appear obvious to the uninstructed, that is no wonder. For in regard to the works of that Providence which controls the whole world, while some show themselves most plainly to be works of Providence, others are so obscure as to appear to afford grounds of disbelief in the God who with unspeakable skill and power superintends the universe. The skilful plan of the providential rulers is not so clear in things on earth as it is in regard to the sun and moon and stars, and not so plain in the events that happen to men as it is in regard to the souls and bodies of animals, where the purpose and reason of the impulses, the mental images and the natures they possess and the structures of their bodies are accurately discovered by those who investigate these matters.[104]

This is eloquent testimony to Origen's preference for finding the *vestigia Dei* in the regularities of the cosmic order than in the

[102] *CI* 4. 15–23.
[103] *De Princ.* 4. 1. 6.
[104] Ibid. 4. 1. 7, trans. Butterworth.

contingencies of history. In the economy of Jewish history, the only purpose of prophecy was to keep the Jews from resorting to the 'soothsayers and diviners' of the Gentiles (cf. Deut. 18: 14). The prophets addressed trivial business like the whereabouts of lost asses (1 Sam. 9: 20) as a concession to human myopia.[105] Eusebius repeats this condescending view, and even cites the same episode of Samuel's prophecy on the lost asses of Saul, which must have been something of a topos in Jewish–Christian debates on prophecy.[106] Nevertheless, he recognizes a far broader scope to biblical prophecy, including matters which to him, if not to Origen, were far from trivial. At the beginning of *The Proof of the Gospel* he summarized the kind of events which fell within the purview of prophecy, the thoroughly secular nature of which shows his fundamentally different approach.

What sort of [prophetic] fulfilment, do you ask? They are fulfilled in countless and all kinds of ways, and amid all circumstances, both generally and in minute detail, in the lives of individual men, and in their corporate life, now nationally in the course of Hebrew history, and now in that of foreign nations. Such things as civic revolutions, changes of times, national vicissitudes, the coming of foretold prosperity, the assaults of adversity, the enslaving of races, the besieging of cities, the downfall and restoration of whole states, and countless other things that were to take place a long time after, were foretold by these writers.[107]

The prologue of the *Commentary on Isaiah* has a similar catalogue in shorter form.

A 'vision' [Isa. 1: 1] he says, not ordinary or perceptible with physical eyes, but a prophetic vision of things to come in far distant times; for just as one sees in a great tablet the invasion of enemies, ravagings of countryside, sieges of cities and enslavements of men, represented with the brilliance of colour, the same way he seems to see a dream, but not a vision in sleep, when the divine spirit enlightens the soul.[108]

The engraving tablet or book (*pinax*) which Eusebius appeals to in this comparison is actually a description of the contents of the very book he is preparing to discuss in his commentary. Origen may have disparaged scripture's demonstration of divine providence in 'the events that happen to men', but Eusebius was fascinated by it.

---

[105] *C. Cels.* 1. 36.
[106] *CI* 237. 9–24; *EP* 4. Prol. (167. 9–10).
[107] *DE* 1. Prol., trans. Ferrar, i. 2.
[108] *CI* 3. 18–23.

The proper subject of prophecy is thus identical with the subject of history as such. It is not concerned with purely religious matters but with the historical process as a whole, both the secular and the religious. Prophecy does not in fact recognize a distinction between secular and religious history in the sense of dual or parallel realities, but sees history as a unity. As explained in our discussion of exegetical method, for Eusebius the terms *kata lexin/kata historian* and *kata dianoian* indicate history as observed and history as interpreted. It is the privileged role of the prophet to declare before the event what the meaning of the event will be. This view of prophecy seems closer to the Old Testament than to Origen. The prophet serves not only to leave a record of accurate prediction to corroborate Christian apologetics, but even in the present and the purely Jewish/Old Testament future to provide counsel and guidance for the godly polity. Isaiah's prophecies of the disasters to be visited upon Babylon (Isa. 47: 1 ff.) are delivered out of God's *philanthropia* for his people; he wants the Jews even of Isaiah's time (*enteuthen*, as in the Emmanuel prophecy of 7: 14) to know that the Lord alone is God and only his prophets declare the future. All else is deception (*apatê*). Babylon will suffer 'so that the unbelieving among you may know from the course of events [*ek tês tôn pragmatôn ekbaseôs*] that the words of my prophets are not human . . .'.[109]

The fulfilment of prophecy already in the Old Testament creates a continuous skein of providentially directed history leading out of the Old Testament into the Christian era, and beyond to the *eschaton*. The prophets are privy to this development as a whole, but the accuracy of their predictions is important in the near (Jewish) as well as the very distant (Christian) future. Remarking on the oracles on the nations contained in Isa. 13–23, Eusebius admits that it would be superfluous to study them if they contained nothing relevant to Christian piety, which is the reductionist view associated above with Origen. Nevertheless, he continues (and this is the really characteristic comment) even the prophecies on the nations contain edifying meaning *as well as* their local and specific reference. 'It is remarkable how things are prophesied of each nation that are pertinent to it, and in the same [prophecies] are contained things touching particularly on the worshipful Word.'[110]

---

[109] *CI* 304. 2–4. Compare the similar use of *enteuthen* in Eusebius' discussion of Isa. 7: 14, *CI* 48. 22, 49. 2, 21.

[110] Ibid. 149. 9–11.

The prophetic charisma deserted the godly polity after the return from the Babylonian exile. All prophecy worthy of the name came to an end with Ezra, as foreseen in Isaiah's prediction of poverty and destitution in 7: 21-5.[111] Historical fact and apologetic agenda coincided on this point, for post-exilic prophecy did not flourish for long. Eusebius saw its demise as the first step in the divine abrogation of Israel. The use of *ekleipô* recalls the theology of Israel's rejection based on Gen. 49: 10, a prophecy of the failure of native Jewish kingship, an association supported here by Eusebius' reference to the passing away of the Davidic line at the same time as the eclipse of prophetic inspiration. This roughly correct dating of prophecy's decline did not agree with the traditional Christian apologetic theme, based on Jesus' own words, that prophecy lasted until John the Baptist (Luke 16: 6). Origen himself had expounded this view.[112] Elsewhere in the *Commentary on Isaiah* Eusebius seems to contradict himself by defending the traditional motif, but the way he distances himself from the view—introduced with the disclaimer 'some think'—shows his doubt about it. The subject is the vineyard parable in Isa. 5. Almost certainly following Origen, he says that the withholding of rain in the parable is the suspension of prophecy, for the clouds stand for the prophets' purity and brilliance of life, and the rain (*hyetos*) is the Word of God preached by them.[113] 'Some think' (30: 28) that prophecy did not expire until John. Although Eusebius knows that this dating is wrong, he tries to save it by observing that the prophecy as a whole was not fulfilled until the Romans destroyed Jerusalem, and thus one might say that no single detail had been truly fulfilled until all had.

The Friends of God

The prophets were the greatest religious figures in Israel, but they were not its only saints. The godly polity also embraced Jews who showed in their contrite hearts (Ps. 50: 19) that they were true followers of the preaching of the prophets. Eusebius' comment on Isa. 57: 15 ('I will dwell with him who is of a humble and contrite heart') shows that he thought of the pure of heart in Israel as having a real membership in the city of God.[114] By their humility and lowliness they demonstrated the self-denying way of life praised by

[111] *CI* 53. 20-3.   [112] C. *Cels.* 2. 8; *Comm. Songs*, 3. 13.
[113] *CI* 30. 21-32.4.   [114] Ibid. 354. 26-355. 26.

Heb. 11: 37. In this passage Eusebius says that they were only a few in number, but elsewhere he numbers them in the 'thousands'.[115] These are the ones whom Isa. 44: 23 says that the Lord has redeemed and in whom he will be glorified: the 'foundations of the earth' (LXX) are 'all the prophets and just and pious men', the members of the former people who assisted the prophets and repudiated idolatry.[116] From these Old Testament saints come 'the seed of the sons of Israel' (Isa. 45: 25) who would be the Jewish nucleus of the Saviour's followers.[117] A continuous line thus connects the prophets, their persecuted righteous followers, and the saving remnant, the first Jewish Christians.

Set over against these are the leaders of the Jews, whose condemnation of Jesus was the ultimate betrayal of their responsibilities in the godly polity. They are the crown of pride (Isa. 28: 1) from Ephraim—the alliance of Pharisees, high priests and other leaders who plotted against Jesus.[118] The 'flower fallen from glory' is Judas, grouped with the crown of pride because he too, a member of the tribe of Ephraim, says Eusebius, was a 'hireling of Ephraim' (28: 1, LXX). Ranged against the company of the persecuted saints in Judaism is a criminal element in the religious leadership that would eventually conspire with one of Jesus' own followers to bring him to death. The numerous prophetic denunciations of corrupt religious leaders gave Eusebius ample opportunity to develop this theme, to the point of monotony.[119] These two factions, *tagmata* he calls them, warred for the soul of the godly polity, issuing in the death of Jesus and the fall of Judaism from the godly polity. The friends of God did not disappear wholly from Judaism until the Roman capture of Jerusalem, when its moral disease became incurable, when all were punished, from least to greatest.[120] Up to that time, wise men survived who could interpret the prophecies, though prophecy itself ceased not long after the return from the Exile.[121] Eusebius' grudging recognition of their abilities is probably an acknowledgement of their exegetical competence, such as we discussed in Section 3.1 of the present chapter.[122]

---

[115] Ibid. 370. 18–24.   [116] Ibid. 286. 26–9, 36; 287. 2.
[117] Ibid. 298. 14–21.
[118] Ibid. 178. 19–179. 12.
[119] See, e.g. his comments on Isa. 1: 24, 3: 13–15, 22: 2–3, 28: 7–8, 28: 15, 37: 18–19, 53: 8–10, 56: 10–11, etc.
[120] Cf. ibid. 6. 7–29, on Isa. 1: 5–6.
[121] Ibid. 52. 26–54. 14.   [122] Ibid. 53. 28–54. 4.

Holy Institutions

We have already discussed in this and the previous chapter Eusebius' attitudes to the special institutions of the godly polity, especially prophecy, kingship, and priesthood.[123] Here we will only say a few words about Eusebius' assessment of the temple and its cultus, since the *Commentary on Isaiah* has nothing original to say on these subjects.[124] The cultus was a physical worship, made necessary, according to the *The Preparation for the Gospel*, by the spiritual weakness of the people.[125] In itself it possessed dignity and worth, being 'beautiful to see and attractive, but transitory', but nevertheless lacked true divine meaning.[126] Now it has been left behind, as a first introduction to the Word, by those ready for a perfect teacher.[127] The temple will be destroyed, the prophet foresaw, along with the rest of the city, when it will be consumed by fire, as symbolized by the smoke of Isaiah's vision in the temple.[128]

Jerusalem

The exegesis of Isaiah's many references to the holy city of the godly polity is one of the most apologetically and theologically sensitive parts of the *Commentary on Isaiah*, as indeed of Eusebius' apologetics in general.[129] As theological symbol and apologetic focus, Jerusalem had a rich history long before Eusebius. His treat-

---

[123] The best short statement of the centrality of these three institutions and the significance of their collapse as the precursor of the incarnation, is in the preface to Book 8 of the *The Proof of the Gospel*. Most of the book is given over to the eclipse of kingship (*DE* 8. 1) and priesthood (*DE* 8. 2).

[124] On Eusebius' view of the temple, see now Walker, *Holy City, Holy Places?*, 376–96.

[125] *PE* 7. 8. 38.

[126] *CI* 7. 18–19; 255. 5–6.

[127] Ibid. 181. 14–22.

[128] Ibid. 40. 9–20.

[129] For the importance of the fall of Jerusalem in the *Church History*, see Grant, *Eusebius as Church Historian*, 97–113; also E. Fascher, 'Jerusalems Untergang in der urchristlichen und altkirchlichen Überlieferung', *Theologische Literaturzeitung*, 89 (1960), 81–98. K. L. Schmidt, 'Jerusalem als Urbild und Abbild', *Eranos-Jahrbuch*, 18 (1950), 207–48, discusses the general significance of Jerusalem as a religious symbol. The detailed analysis of Eusebius' attitude to Jerusalem in Walker, *Holy City, Holy Places?*, 347–401, is a valuable summary of the data, but seems over-determined by the author's concern to show how Eusebius opposed the contemporary movement to treat Jerusalem as a Christian holy city. The contemporary focus leads him to underestimate the importance Eusebius attached, not just to the city of Jerusalem, but to the

ment of it tells much about his most fundamental concerns. Here we will examine the basic range of his understanding of the city as a theological symbol, then explain the place of the historical Jerusalem in his construction of the history of the godly polity.

In a development whose roots lay in Judaism itself, both Old Testament and inter-testamental, Jerusalem came to be regarded pre-eminently as the 'heavenly Jerusalem', the apocalyptic new city of God laid up in heaven, waiting to be revealed at the end of time.[130] In general patristic writers saw five possible meanings to Jerusalem: (1) the historical city; (2) the new Jerusalem to descend as part of an earthly millenium, as in Revelation; (3) the heavenly Jerusalem whose transcendence was grasped in more platonic than apocalyptic terms; (4) the historical church; (5) the individual soul.[131] The Alexandrian theological tradition in which Eusebius was nurtured rejected the biblical literalism of the millenarian interpretation.[132] Origen himself favoured the transcendental and psychological inter-pretations, according to which biblical references to Jerusalem were allegorized as either the spiritual Jerusalem laid up in heaven or the soul of the individual Christian.[133] For him the biblical Jerusalem, like all topographical references, actually stood for a heavenly geo-graphy. His interest in the actual city was limited to its role in Christian apologetic, since he stood in the tradition which saw the Roman capture of Jerusalem as a divine punishment of the Jews for the crucifixion of Jesus.[134] In the *The Proof of the Gospel* Eusebius developed a four-fold interpretation of Jerusalem that seems to owe much to Origen.

whole of biblical Israel's history, in revealing and 'demonstrating' God's plan to save humanity. This is shown most clearly in his depreciation of the fundamental impor-tance of typology in Eusebius' approach to the Old Testament; he prefers to empha-size the spiritualizing side of Eusebius' Origenist heritage and to downplay his character as a historically minded apologist. But the rhetorical power of typology is precisely its integration of past and present (and future), and requires the legitimacy (however provisional) of the type—as Walker recognizes on pp. 375–6.

[130] For the development, see A. Causse, 'Le mythe de la nouvelle Jérusalem du Deutero-Esaie à la IIIe Sibylle', *Revue d'histoire et de philosophie religieuse*, 18 (1938), 376–414; id. 'De la Jérusalem terrestre à la Jérusalem céleste', *Revue d'histoire et de philosophie religieuse*, 27 (1942), 12–36; Eduard Lohse, 'Sion, Ierousalem', *TDNT* vii, s.v.; Paul Volz, *Die Eschatologie der Jüdischen Gemeinde im neutestamentlichen Zeitalter* (Hildesheim, 1966), 372–5.

[131] For citations, see *PGL* 671.

[132] Origen, *De Princ.* 2. 11. 2.

[133] Ibid. 4. 3. 8.

[134] *C. Cels.* 1. 47.

Sion and Jerusalem that here [Isa. 52: 5–10] have the good news told them the apostle knew to be heavenly, when he said, 'But Jerusalem that is above is free, that is the mother of us' [Gal. 4: 26], and, 'You have drawn near to Mount Sion and the city of the living God, heavenly Jerusalem, and to an innumerable company of angels' [Heb. 12: 22]. Sion might also mean the church established by Christ in every part of the world, and Jerusalem the godly *politeuma* which, once established of old time among the ancient Jews alone, was driven out into the wilderness by their impiety, and then again was restored far better than before through the coming of our Saviour. Therefore the prophecy says, 'Let the waste places of Jerusalem break forth into joy together, for the Lord has pitied her and saved Jerusalem.'

Nor would you be wrong in calling Sion the soul of every holy and godly man, so far as it is lifted above this life, having its city in heaven, seeing the things beyond the world. For it means 'a watch tower'. And in so far as such a man remains calm and free from passion, you could call him Jerusalem— for Jerusalem means 'vision of peace'.[135]

Eusebius has omitted the millenarian interpretation, as we might have expected, but the other four distinctions have been maintained. In the *Commentary on Isaiah* he twice reduces the list to three, now omitting the Origenist psychological interpretation: the city of the Jews; the godly polity on earth; and the heavenly Jerusalem, also called an angelic *politeia*.[136] Commenting on Isa. 52: 1, he employs a very Origenist-sounding interpretation of the Jerusalem which is bidden to arise: it is the rational soul that possesses the power and strength to stand up from its subjection to the hostile powers of sin.[137] Nevertheless, he promptly historicizes this exegesis by applying it to the unfaithful people of the historical Jerusalem: 'And these things are said not to the buildings nor the physical city but to its unfaithful people . . .' Eusebius' exemption of the physical remains of the city from the prophecy may reflect nervousness about possible Jewish claims that Jerusalem will be rebuilt in the Messianic age. More likely it is a disclaimer against Christian millenarians who looked for the reconstruction of the actual city of Jerusalem as part of the apocalyptic scenario of Revelation.[138]

---

[135] *DE* 6. 24, trans. Ferrar, ii. 45–6; see also the individualist interpretation at 6. 7.

[136] *CI* 312. 32–313. 5; 326. 33–327. 1.

[137] Ibid. 328. 30–329. 11.

[138] e.g. Irenaeus, *Adv. Haer.* 5. 34. 4, 35. 2; Justin, *Dial.* 81. See Daniélou, *The Theology of Jewish Christianity*, ch. 14. Jerome seems to have been much more concerned than Eusebius with millenarian beliefs, both Christian and Jewish, in his exegesis of Isaiah's prophecies of the new Jerusalem; see the useful summary of Gozzo, 'De S. Hieronymi commentario in Isaiae librum', 201–7.

The next chapter will discuss Eusebius' conception of the relation between the historical Christian church and the heavenly Jerusalem. We turn now to the place of Jerusalem itself in the historical economy of salvation developed in the *Commentary on Isaiah*. In keeping with the character of the godly polity as a community of souls in some sense embodied in the empirical form of the nation of Israel, it is not surprising that Eusebius conceded a special divine solicitude to Israel's capital. Ever since David had captured Jerusalem from foreigners, it had been a city of virtuous men, Eusebius admitted, and the home of 'justice' and 'judgement', in the words of Isa. 1: 21.[139] Jerusalem enjoyed the protective custody of God, 'like a mother bird hovering over her nestlings', as he notes in interpreting 31: 4–6.[140] The prophet rightly reproved those who had fled to Egypt for protection (31: 1), since they ignored the promises of God to fight like a raging lion on behalf of his people (31: 4). Nevertheless, biblical history showed that this divine sanction was not an absolute buffer against the vicissitudes of history whenever the faithlessness of the city's inhabitants exposed them to divine judgement. In an absolute sense the prophet's description of Jerusalem as 'a quiet habitation, an immovable tent' (33: 20) must apply to a city yet to come, since historical Jerusalem had actually succumbed to siege and capture. The prophet therefore summoned its citizens to anticipate a 'city of feasts' with truly redoubtable fortifications, namely the Jerusalem to come which is the church of God, the house built firmly upon a rock (Matt. 16: 18).[141]

The Roman occupation of Jerusalem in the most decisive and final way marks God's repudiation of Israel and the transfer of the godly polity to its new embodiment in the Christian church. This irreversible judgement for the murder of the Saviour is the pivotal event in Jewish history. As noted at the beginning of this section, this interpretation was commonplace in Christian apologetics, and certainly in the works of Eusebius.[142] The *Commentary on Isaiah* places the fall of Jerusalem in the broad framework of the Jewish and Christian history of the godly polity. Again and again Eusebius applies prophetic threats and denunciations against Jerusalem to the ultimate disasters of AD 70 and 135 Vespasian and Hadrian assume the same

---

[139] *CI* 10. 26–11. 2.
[140] Ibid. 204. 13–14.
[141] Ibid. 218. 15–34.
[142] E.g. in *DE* 6. 7. 5–7; 6. 25.

role of divinely commissioned chastisers once played by Assyrian and Babylonian kings. The Roman conquerors are described in realistic biblical language as the pagans they were, guilty of idolatry and licentiousness, but nevertheless absolved of their brutal conquest because they were enacting the just judgement of God.[143] In a now familiar distinction Eusebius saw prophecies of destruction like 5: 11–17 fulfilled literally (*pros lexin, rêtôs*) in the Roman conquest and settlement of Jerusalem, and spiritually (*kata dianoian*) in the Jews' deprivation of the spiritual nourishment of scripture. Historical event expressed and ratified spiritual reality.[144] Hadrian's prohibition against Jewish entry into their former holy city was also foreseen by the prophet.[145] In an ironic coda to the Jewish phase of the history of the godly polity, the Jews were now shut out of the same city from which they had once excluded the Amorites, Hivites, and Jebusites.[146]

---

[143] *CI* 220. 6; 189. 19–20.
[144] Ibid. 31. 27–32. 17.
[145] Ibid. 43. 15–19.
[146] Ibid. 18. 6–24; 117. 9–16.

VI

The Christian Church As the Godly Polity: The Doctrine of the Church in the Commentary on Isaiah

1. General Considerations

The present chapter deals principally with the place of the church in Eusebius' exegesis of Isaiah. A statement early in the *Commentary on Isaiah*, describes how the new form of the godly polity has superseded the old:

The one [sc. *politeuma*] established of old among the Jews has fallen away, whereas now it has been awakened, 'founded upon a rock' [cf. Matt. 7: 25, 16: 18] throughout the whole world by the Church of Christ. The *proestôtes* of 'this fair city', the 'judges and counsellors' [*kritai kai symbouloi*] have received rule [*archê*] from the apostles and disciples of our Saviour, and even now from this succession [*diadochê*], as though from the seed of good things, the presidents [*proedroi*] of the church of God bring forth fruit and shine brilliantly.[1]

This passage expresses concisely much that the commentary has to say about the church: the supersession of the godly polity of old, its foundation by and on the Logos, and its organization under legally constituted rulers who are the successors of the apostles. The new community laid claim to its own *charismata* endowed by the Holy Spirit.[2] It arose and spread with a speed astonishing in comparison to the slow development of its predecessor. The godly polity, the new Sion, the wonder which 'eye has not seen' (1 Cor. 2: 9), was truly a divine creation (*theion gennêma*). The prophet had predicted its rapid proliferation and divine heritage in order to instil confidence in its members by the realization of his predictions in the events of church history (*hê ekbasis tôn pragmatôn*).[3]

---

[1] *CI* 12. 22–8.
[2] Ibid. 315. 1–12; 321. 29–322. 17.
[3] Ibid. 402. 30–403. 26.

The incarnate Logos is the one to whom Isa. 45: 13 applies most fully: 'I raised up a king with righteousness, and all his ways are straight. He will build my city and will overturn the captivity of my people, not with ransom money or gifts, says the Lord of Hosts.' (LXX) This prophecy was fulfilled historically in Cyrus and Zerubbabel, who were images and symbols of its spiritual fulfilment in the Christ of God, whom the Father 'raised up' from the dead and established as king.[4] Eusebius habitually identifies the Logos as the rock of Matt. 16: 18, on whom the church is built.[5] This is natural for him in view of the traditional identification of Christ with rock (*petra*) and stone (*lithos*) proof texts, especially Isa. 28: 16: 'Therefore, thus says the Lord: "Behold, I will cast for a foundation of Sion a precious and choice stone, a worthy cornerstone for her foundation."' This text appeared already in the New Testament (Rom. 9: 33) and is considered one of the most primitive Christian testimonia.[6] Eusebius quoted Matt. 16: 18 in his commentary on this verse.[7] The related Matthean image of the house built on the rock (7: 25), able to withstand the force of the elements, reinforced the interpretation of Christ as the *petra* which supports the Church.[8]

Another biblical image for the intimate bond between the church and the Word which is the source of its life is the river which the psalmist says gives joy to the city of God in Ps. 45: 5 and the related texts in Ps. 86: 3 ('Glorious things are said of you, O city of God') and Ps. 64: 10 ('The river of God is filled with water'). The symbolism of water for inspiration and grace is thoroughly biblical; early Christians connected it with baptism and the spiritual regeneration of which Jesus had spoken in John (John 4: 13–14, 7: 37–8).[9] Origen was very fond of water and river as allegorical allusions to the Logos.[10] Eusebius shared this fondness, but always set the image in a clearly ecclesial context.

---

[4] *CI* 292. 32–294. 2 discusses Isa. 45: 13.

[5] As when discussing Isa. 45: 13, *CI* 293. 17–19.

[6] Dodd, *According to the Scriptures*, 31–57, quoted in Hanson, *Allegory and Event*, 75.

[7] *CI* 183. 16 f., 19 f. A related proof text, Dan. 2: 34 ('the stone cut without hands'), is also cited here. See *PGL* s.v. *lithos*, for references of other Christian writers to Dan. 2: 34.

[8] E.g. at *CI* 218. 25–34, where Matt. 16: 18 and 7: 25 are quoted in tandem.

[9] Modern bibliography on patristic interpretation of John 7: 37–8 in J. B. Bauer, 'Zions Flüsse, Ps. 45(46), 5', *Memoria Jerusalem* (Freundesgabe Franz Sauer zum 70. Geburtstag; Graz, 1977), 71 n. 55.

[10] For Origen's exegesis of Ps. 45: 5, cf. Bauer, 'Zions Flüsse', 67–70.

As we have often interpreted 'Mt Sion which is heavenly' [cf. Heb. 12: 22], so the 'many mansions with the Father' [John 14: 2] are heavenly mountains, where will dwell those worthy of the kingdom of God. Through each of these mountains or mansions, he says, 'water will flow' [Isa. 30: 25], bubbling up from the 'spring', of which it is said, 'From you is the spring of life' [Ps. 35: 10], from which flows 'the river of God', about which is said that 'the rushings of the river give joy to the city of God' [Ps. 45: 5], and 'the river of God is filled with water' [Ps. 64: 10], the only-begotten, lifegiving, and saving Word of God being thus meant.[11]

Similar associations of the Logos with the river and city of God psalm texts are found in Eusebius' discussion of Isa. 18: 4, 'Thus said the Lord to me: "There will be safety in my city, like the light of the noonday heat, and like the cloud of dew on the day of harvest."' Scripture is accustomed, he notes, to call the godly polity a city, as shown by the familiar texts in Pss. 45: 5 and 86: 3. The light is the illumination of the church by the Logos. The cloud of dew is the Holy Spirit which obscures the profound truth of Christ's divine generation (*theologia*) from those unable to understand it.[12]

The first generation of Christians were the Jews who accepted Christ as the Saviour and from whom he had chosen his apostles to be the college (*choros*) of leaders for his church. They are the gleanings left in Israel which the prophet foresaw. Isa. 17: 4–6 reads:

And on that day there will be a failing [*ekleipsis*] of the glory of Jacob and the richness of his glory will be shaken. And it shall be as when someone gathers the standing harvest and harvests the seed of the grapes with his arm. And it shall be as when one gathers an ear of grain in a difficult valley, and a gleaning shall be left in it, either two berries on an olive tree, or three at the very top, or four or five on the branches shall be left. Thus says the Lord God of Israel.

The text inspired Eusebius to an ecclesiastical allegory. Biblical numbers being a conventional invitation to allegory, he thought this prophetic parable (*paradeigma*) hinted at (*ainittomenos*) the apostolic *choros*. 'Two' referred to the Saviour's habit of picking his followers by pairs (*kata syzygian*). 'Three' referred to Peter, James, and John, the inner college of the apostles, who were present at the Transfiguration. Four and five introduce the remainder of the twelve. The initial 'two' might also be taken to mean Paul and James,

---

[11] *CI* 200. 9–17. Other ecclesial settings of Ps. 45: 5 in Eusebius are listed by Bauer, ibid. 71–4 (e.g. *CI* on Isa. 41: 17–18, 44: 1–4).

[12] *CI* 121. 13–28.

the brother of the Lord and bishop of Jerusalem, who have as much right as the other twelve to be called apostles. All of them stand in the succession (*diadochê*) of the Jewish religious leadership of old.[13]

The apostles and other disciples were the remnant or seed of which Isaiah speaks so often. He intended them to be a *paradeigma* for the whole people, as in 1: 9, the vineyard parable of Chapter 5, and 65: 8–9. According to the last passage, the chosen ones will inherit and dwell upon God's holy mountain, 'Mt Sion and the city of the living God, the heavenly Jerusalem' (Heb. 12: 22).[14] By his Resurrection Christ has rendered a judgement over the whole cosmos and has established the administration of the church, both of which he handed over to his apostles.[15] The apostles have replaced the wicked counsellors condemned by the prophet in 32: 7–8; they are the pious counsellors who advise with understanding. Symmachus' version of 32: 8 says that a ruler will counsel on matters of government and a leader shall arise. Eusebius likes to interpret such a text ecclesiastically. Symmachus' use of *hêgemôn* led him to quote Ps. 54: 14 (LXX). He argues that Christ addressed Ps. 54: 14 ('But you, O like-minded [*isopsyche*] man, my leader [*hêgemôn*] and familiar friend [*gnôste*] . . .') to his apostles, because they have the rule over the church. Since the bishops also enjoy the prerogative of rule (*archê*) in the church, by extension they share in the intimate bond uniting Christ and the first leaders and rulers of the church, the apostles. This bond is further implied by the liturgical overtones of the next line, Ps. 54: 15, though Eusebius does not cite it: 'You who sweetened my food together with me by your presence, when we walked in concord in the house of God . . .' Thus Eusebius not only reinforces his theme of the apostolic supersession of the old leadership of the godly polity, but also affirms the administrative, liturgical, and fraternal bonds which link Christ, the apostles, and the leaders of the church.[16]

The *diadochê* of apostles and bishops recurs in other parts of the commentary. Isa. 54: 2–5 was an apt text because it associated the inheritance of the nations with the seed of Israel. The *sperma* of

---

[13] *CI* 116. 3–25.

[14] Ibid. 393. 36–394. 19.

[15] Ibid. 269. 20–3. Note the legal and administrative language in this passage: *dioikêsis, diataxasthai, krisis, paredôke*.

[16] Ibid. 208. 1–209. 9.

Israel which will inherit the nations is the succession of apostles and bishops, 'through whom the godly *politeia* has been established in the churches which of old were devastated and bereft of God'.[17] The messianic prophecy of Isa. 9: 1–6 is applied both to the public ministry of Christ in Galilee and to the successors of the apostles. The surface meaning (*procheiros lexis*) of the prophecy is realized in the events of the public ministry, especially the Cana miracle and the multiplication of the loaves. These are not obvious associations even for an interpreter convinced of Isaiah's supernatural prevision, and Eusebius must depend on the LXX version of 9: 1 for his slender support: '*Drink* this first, do it quickly . . .' The addition of the loaves miracle is justified in Eusebius' eyes by the reference in 9: 2 to 'a large number of people' (*pleiston tou laou*), which relates to the crowds of four and five thousand at the two multiplications (Matt. 14: 21, 15: 38). We discover his real interest in these exegetical contrivances in his spiritual (*kata dianoian*) interpretation that the apostles and their successors, and those who were currently presidents of the church, are meant by 'those who rejoice in the harvest', since they were accustomed to feast together in the manner of harvesters, and were engaged in the joyful harvest of the souls of the Gentiles.[18] Verses 5–6 are also applied to the rulers of the church, since they possess from Christ the peace and dominion which the prophet says will be without end.[19] Once again, Eusebius has brought together juridical, liturgical, and fraternal themes in projecting the contemporary role of the episcopacy back into the text of Isaiah.

A major preoccupation of the *Commentary on Isaiah* is the exegetical establishment of a hierarchical differentiation of orders (*tagmata*) in the church, primarily in order to assert the dominance of the clergy. Eusebius commonly applies texts with keywords like *archontes*, *presbyteroi*, *leitourgoi*, *hēgemones*, and the like to the leaders of the church—unless of course the text condemned corrupt or derelict leadership. Thus the *archontes* of Isa. 41: 25 are either the angels who guard God's kingdom, or the presidents of his church.[20] The same alternative is found in his comments on Isa. 66: 12–13, one of the Jerusalem prophecies. The 'river of peace' is predictably the

---

[17] Ibid. 340. 3–341. 6.
[18] Ibid. 64. 12–14.
[19] Ibid. 67. 9–14.
[20] Ibid. 267. 3–6.

peace which the nations will enjoy in the new Sion and the new Jerusalem, the church, with the obligatory allusions to Pss. 45 and 64. Those on whom the children are carried are either their angels in heaven (cf. Matt. 18: 10) or the teachers and presidents of the church. They in turn are encouraged, 'as a mother encourages someone' (66: 13), by God himself, though Eusebius alters the image to say God's *paternal* rights (!) over the church's leaders, better to fit his preferred view of *their* own rights over the inferior ones in the church.[21]

An important passage on clerical supremacy is Eusebius' discussion of Isa. 40: 1–2. The Septuagint reads: ' "Console, console my people", says the Lord. "Priests [*hiereis*], speak to the heart of Jerusalem, console her, because her lowliness is fulfilled, her sin has been pardoned." ' Eusebius' interpretation capitalizes on the LXX reading to defend a clerical monopoly of teaching and pastoral guidance. The keyword 'console' (*parakaleite*) suggests the Gospel of John's doctrine of the paraclete (cf. John 14: 16–17; 16: 7–15), so Eusebius asserts that the divine injunction to console Jerusalem is addressed to all those who have received the spirit of Christ, namely, the evangelists, apostles, disciples, and 'those like them'. To prove unambiguously that the clergy are included here, Eusebius adopts the LXX reading of *hiereis* in verse 2, even though the word was obelized in the Hexapla and therefore was absent from the Hebrew and the other Greek versions. He allegorizes 'heart of Jerusalem' as 'those who are distinguished for intelligence, understanding and thinking', since the heart was scripture's way of indicating the living and rational principle in a man. In normal Alexandrian parlance the ones who would speak to the people were those who were intellectually and spiritually competent to interpret scripture. They were not necessarily priests. Thus Eusebius is stating in no uncertain terms that those who constitute the heart of the church, the *logikôteroi*, are indeed the better part (*tagma*) of the body of the church. None the less they are only part of the *laos* (which here certainly means laity); they themselves must be addressed by the *hiereis*.[22]

Interpreting the five cities which Isaiah says the Lord will one day establish in the land of Egypt (Isa. 19: 18), Eusebius asserts that 'the five cities of God in the church would be the various states (*politeiai*) divided into five ranks [*tagmata*]'. The five are, first, the order of presidents (*proedroi*), the bishops; second, the priests (*presbyteroi*);

---

[21] *CI* 404. 13–31.
[22] Ibid. 247. 13–248. 17.

third, the deacons; fourth, the enlightened, the baptized laity; and fifth, those still under catechetical instruction (*en eisagogêi*). Since the same verse predicts that there will also be one city alone that will be called 'city of the land'—so Eusebius interprets the reading 'Areopolis'[23]—he can also say that these five orders that constitute the church are the only city established by God throughout the whole earth, being the city of God spoken of by Ps. 86: 3.[24]

Eusebius frequently mentions the 'simpler ones' in the church who need instruction. The sons and daughters whom the nations bring on their arms are the catechumens, who were 'young in their thoughts'.[25] Adopting Paul's vocabulary (1 Cor. 3: 2), he describes the 'milk of the nations' (Isa. 60: 16) as the elementary teaching of the new covenant.[26] The providers of sound instruction in the church are the teachers, closely identified as we have seen with the bishops. When Isa. 60: 10a says, 'Foreigners will build your walls . . . ', he sees a reference to the 'presidents of the church of God, composed of "foreigners and aliens", who surround (the church) with rational teachings'.[27] The gates of the city of God are the 'elementary and introductory teaching, which are "open day and night" to welcome all those from the nations who choose true religion'.[28]

This kind of allegorization of the renewed Jerusalem as the institutional church is carried out most fully in Eusebius' exegesis of Isa. 54: 11–13, a passage to which we have already drawn attention.[29] The allegorical differentiation of tasks in the godly polity summarizes what we have said thus far: the foundations of the *politeuma* which God has built are the prophets and apostles (Eph. 2: 20), on whom the structure of the present church rests. The parapets of the walls represent 'those gifted with thought and wisdom', who are best equipped for the rational defence of the faith. Considering what Eusebius says about the clergy's right to speak to those who are intellectually endowed, we should infer that he means the bishops here, though he doesn't name them. The gates of the new Jerusalem

---

[23] See discussion of this verse in Ch. III.2.

[24] Ibid. 133. 2–16.

[25] Ibid. 316. 2–8.

[26] Ibid. 376. 30–4.

[27] Ibid. 374. 31–375. 1.

[28] Ibid. 375. 14–17.

[29] Ibid. 341. 27–343. 10. See Ch. IV.5. Compare the use of this passage from Isaiah which Eusebius made in the panegyric for Paulinus of Tyre (*HE* 10. 4. 61–8), where the application of the allegory is to the physical building.

are, once again, those who are being tutored in elementary instruction. The walls, now differentiated as parapets, are those who encircle and protect the church by their prayers. It may be relevant to recall the ascetic élite discussed in Book 1 of the *The Proof of the Gospel*, who are engaged in constant meditation on things divine and in seeking the divine propitiation.[30] Finally, the masses of those who are enrolled as citizens in this celestial city may be identified with the rapidly growing rank and file in the church. As pointed out in Ch. IV, the allegory probably derives from Origen, though this can be said with certainty only of the equation of the prophets and apostles with the sapphires of the prophecy.[31]

Another lengthy allegory, with a more overtly social intent, is found in the discussion of Isa. 60: 5–7.[32] The text lent itself to a fulfilment in the calling of the Gentiles, and Eusebius saw a precise meaning in each of the items of tribute that would be offered at the altar of the Lord. The 'abundance of the sea' is the conversion of the Gentiles itself. The animals symbolize 'those less initiated and less intelligent ones' in the church. 'Camels' are the wealthy, since their wealth is a burden and they are bent (*skolion*) under it. Eusebius recognizes that according to Jesus' words it is exceedingly difficult, if not impossible, for a rich man to be saved (Matt. 19: 24–6). The miracle of God which makes this possible is that the rich can pass through the narrow way into eternal life without giving up their burden, provided that they offer their gifts to God. The social utility of such a message is obvious: the wealthy will enjoy a place in the church, if only as members of the second rank, by sharing their abundance. 'Sheep', being 'most tame and simple', are the immature in the church whom the Logos has illuminated. The rams are 'the more lordly ones' (*archikôteroi*) who convert from the Gentiles. One would not be surprised if a text like this applied to the newly Christian emperor or his subordinates, but Eusebius says instead that these Gentiles with a natural propensity for leadership are the bishops, 'who have dedicated themselves to the preaching of piety and who preside at the liturgy of the altar of sacrifice'. He continues:

For the church of God is glorified especially by the conversion of men of this sort. This is the fulfilment of 'And my house of prayer will be glorified'. This promise was made to the Jerusalem of old, the mother of the new city,

---

[30] *DE* 1. 8.
[31] Origen, *Comm. Lam.*, 4. 7 (*PG* xiii. 653B).
[32] *CI* 371. 28–374. 4.

which I have said is the ensemble of those in the old people who lived rightly, prophets and patriarchs, saints and righteous men, to whom the Logos first proclaimed the coming of Christ.[33]

The overall effect of the allegory is once again to portray a church under episcopal domination, open to mass conversion, and heir to the Old Testament promises.

A critical condition of the church's emergence as a church of the empire was its ability to absorb large numbers of converts whose motivation or dedication were often less than ideal. The drag of resistant human nature against Christian rigorism by no means began in the fourth century, but the problem it posed entered a new stage of seriousness. We have already pointed to *The Proof of the Gospel's* distinction between ascetic and worldly Christians. Just as the godly polity of old had made a place for large numbers of people incapable of the exalted spiritual religion of the pre-Mosaic Hebrew patriarchs, so the new godly polity contained two classes of Christians. The key passage is Eusebius' commentary on Isa. 61: 10–11.[34] Eusebius puts the words of rejoicing in the mouth of the church, since the reference to the rejoicing of bride and bridegroom suggested the analogy of Christ and the church expounded in Ephesians 5: 25–7 and shaped for Eusebius by Origen.[35] Characteristically, he is interested not in Origen's psychological interpretation of the marriage of the individual soul with Christ, but in the ecclesiastical exploitation of the biblical image. The joy of the bride consists in her adornment at the resurrection with those alone who have been formed according to the likeness of the bridegroom, the perfect (*teleioi*). No longer will there be among her those who stand in the second rank of the good (*en deuterôi tôn agathôn tagmati*). At the time when the church becomes merged with the heavenly Jerusalem, she will be purified of all those who have not attained 'to mature manhood, to the measure of the stature of the fullness of Christ' (Eph. 4: 13).

This expression of the eschatological purification of the church (others could be cited[36]) raises the question of the institutional church's relation to the heavenly Jerusalem.

---

[33] *CI* 373. 34–374. 4.

[34] Ibid. 382. 12–35.

[35] Especially in Origen's exegesis of the Song of Songs (e.g. *Comm. Songs*, 2. 7; *Hom. Songs*, 1. 1). See the study of Jacques Chênevert, *L'Église dans le Commentaire d'Origène sur le Cantique des Cantiques* (Brussels and Paris, 1969).

[36] Cf. ibid. 121. 20–122. 38 (on Isa. 18: 5–6), 205. 20–7 (on Isa. 31: 9), and 383. 32–384. 22 (on Isa. 65: 5–6).

2. The Godly Polity *in via*: The Church and the Heavenly Jerusalem

As noted in the last chapter, Eusebius twice tells his readers that Jerusalem stands for three distinct entities: the historic city of the Jews, the godly polity of the church, and the community of the saints and angels in heaven.[37] A natural point to begin reflection on the relation between the historical church and the heavenly Jerusalem is Eusebius' interpretation of the two most important Jerusalem texts from the New Testament (aside from Revelation), Gal. 4: 26 and Heb. 12: 22.[38] The *Commentary on Isaiah* shows much more interest in the latter, the most frequently cited biblical verse in the entire commentary. Why did this verse appeal to Eusebius? Besides employing a wider range of biblical symbols (Mt Sion, heavenly Jerusalem, city of God, ecclesia of the first-born enrolled in the heavens), the Hebrews passage expressed better the idea of movement towards a goal (*proselêluthate*) than the static *hê anô Ierousalêm* of Galatians. It also implied an intimate bond between the heavenly Jerusalem and the historical church, which appealed to his desire to equate the church with the city of God.[39] Despite his devotion to Heb. 12: 22, he never quotes Heb. 13: 14 ('For we have here no lasting city, but we seek the city which is to come'). The expectancy of this verse may have been too strong, since he tends to see in the godly polity 'an abiding city', the *patris* which Heb. 11: 16 says the Old Testament worthies yearned for. And if Heb. 13: 14 looks too much to the future, *a fortiori* the same applies to what the book of Revelation has to say about the new Jerusalem. Eusebius' opposition to millenarian hopes based on Revelation is well known, and he usually avoids alluding to the book in the *Commentary on Isaiah*.[40]

---

[37] Cf. *CI* 312. 32–313. 5.

[38] On patristic interpretation of the heavenly Jerusalem, see K. L. Schmidt, 'Jerusalem als Urbild und Abbild', *Eranos-Jahrbuch*, 18 (1950), 207–48; O. Rousseau, 'Quelques textes patristiques sur la Jérusalem céleste', *Vie spirituelle*, 86 (1952), 378–88; E. Lamirande, *L'Église céleste selon Saint Augustin* (Paris, 1963); and id., 'Jérusalem céleste', *Dictionaire de spiritualité*, viii. 947 f. For Origen see especially his *Commentary on the Song of Songs* and the study of J. Chênevert cited above in n. 35.

[39] See the table of citations below.

[40] See the table of biblical citations in the index. The only direct quote arises with reference to Isa. 48: 12, 'I am the first and I am eternal', rendered in the other Greek versions as, 'I am the first and the last', which Eusebius notes guardedly is said 'somewhere else' of the only-begotten Word, and that he is 'the Alpha and the

His own view relies on both the realized and the future dimensions of salvation, because he regards the church now as the carrier of the promises, the city of God spoken of in scripture, yet still unperfected (a mixed body, as stated above) and *in via* towards its final destiny of reunion with the Lord. Normally Eusebius reserves 'heavenly Jerusalem' for the eschatological vindication of the church, and 'city of God' or 'godly polity' for the church's existence in history. Neither of these terms is a fixed, however. Jerusalem or Sion, without the adjective heavenly, is often the church, and the city of God can be either on earth or in heaven. The crucial thing is not the names of these points of reference in salvation history, but their coherence in a unified historical scheme. The pages of Isaiah mirrored the history of the godly polity in its earthly and its heavenly existence.

The table is a partial summary of Eusebius' references to the city of God/godly polity and the heavenly/new/spiritual Jerusalem/Sion. The majority of instances refer to the church in history (H). A lesser number apply Jerusalem and Sion texts to the eschatological (E) manifestation of the city at the end of time. In connection with this usage of heavenly Jerusalem, Heb. 12: 22 is usually quoted. A few passages speak of the Jerusalem above as an already existing spiritual reality (S).

This completes our survey of the general features of Eusebius' doctrine of the church in the *Commentary on Isaiah*. We turn now to a more detailed consideration of the role of the episcopacy as the leaders of the city of God.

3. The Archons of the Godly Polity: The Episcopacy

W. Telfer devoted a chapter to Cyprian's doctrine of the episcopacy in his study of the office of the bishop in the church. I would like to quote at length his description of the Cyprianic 'bishop-magistrate' because of the unexpected similarities between his account and the view of Eusebius developed in this study. Telfer sees Cyprian

Omega'. His exegesis of these texts is remarkable: the Word is first in the sense that he is the *archê* of life, being life itself, and last in the sense that he emptied himself to the point of dying on the cross—no mention of his imminent return! The descent of the heavenly Jerusalem and the thousand-year reign of the saints are completely passed over. For Eusebius' attitude to Revelation, cf. Grant, *Eusebius as Church Historian*, 126–37.

TABLE 2. *References to the city of God and the heavenly Jerusalem in the* Commentary on Isaiah

	Isaiah	Summary
E	18: 7	The persecuted city of God to offer sacrifices under the High Priest, the Son of God, in the heavenly city after the consummation (Heb. 12: 22).
H	22: 1	The Jews have fallen from Mt Sion and the heights of the godly polity, which Sion is the heavenly Jerusalem spoken of in Heb. 12: 22.
E	26: 1	The Saviour to take up his kingdom in the supernatural mountain, in the heavenly Jerusalem, after the destruction of the Powers (Heb. 12: 22). There is the godly polity, the city of God.
H	33: 20	The historical Sion is addressed, but is asked to pay heed to another 'city of feasts', the church of God, founded on a rock.
H	33: 21–2	The new city is built on the Lord himself, its rock and also its river (Pss. 45: 5, 64: 10), encircling the city of God, the church.
H/E	35: 9–10	The earthly (*epigeion*) and the heavenly (*epouranion*) Sions: those in the pilgrim church (*en . . . hodôi*) have as end of their journey the latter (Heb. 12: 22). (An especially interesting text because of the journey motif, cf. Isa. 35: 8–9.)
H	41: 27–9	To the church, called Sion and Jerusalem, God will give charge over all those who are wayfarers towards God and his kingdom.
E	43: 5–6	Those reborn in the church will be gathered in the supernatural city (Heb. 12: 22), born aloft by angelic powers.
H/S	49: 11	Three meanings of Jerusalem: the Jewish city, the godly polity of souls, and the angelic polity in heaven.
H	49: 16	Sion is the godly polity of old among the Jews; since its fall, the true Sion is the indestructible and infallible godly polity/city of God, the church.
H	49: 17	Same as preceding.
H	49: 19	The new city of God is the church, from which the corrupt Jewish religious leadership is excluded.
H	51: 3	The fruitfulness of the new Sion, the godly polity, makes it God's garden, his *paradeisos*.

TABLE 2. *Continued*

	Isaiah	Summary
E	51: 11	Those who serve God will come to the heavenly Sion (Heb. 12: 22), where there will be neither grief, pain, nor suffering.
S/H	51: 17	Three Jerusalems: in heaven, whose king is God; the city of God on earth, the godly polity among men; the suffering city of the Jews.
H	52: 7	'God will reign' is directed to Sion, the godly community and the apostolic band, because they proclaim the kingdom of heaven to all men.
H	52: 9–10	Sion/Jerusalem = the city of God/godly polity among men.
H	54: 11–13	Allegory of the church as the rebuilt Jerusalem: this is the godly polity on earth, though it counts prophets and apostles among its members (the sapphires of the biblical text).
H	59: 20	Sion is the church, the godly polity.
H	60: 1–2	The city of God, called Jerusalem in the Bible, is the godly polity as it existed first among the Jews and now in the church.
H	60: 3	The city of God is the godly polity, constituted among the Jews by all who lived religiously, and by the Gentiles enlightened by Christ.
H	60: 14–15	The city of God is Sion, formed from two peoples, the ancient company of the saints of God, and the people from the Gentiles.
E	60: 19–21	An eschatological prophecy of the heavenly life to be lived by the heavenly and true Jerusalem (Heb. 12: 22).
H/E	62: 10–12	Both historical and eschatological: the demons shall not restrict entrance to the heavenly city (Heb. 12: 22); the daughter of Sion is the church, daughter of the former godly polity, to be called 'the city sought after'.
E	65: 19–20	Eschatological: Jerusalem is the godly polity of the future, of those in whose good deeds God will rejoice; resurrection references make the eschatological setting certain.
H	66: 7–9	Birth of the new Sion, the church, and its rapid maturation contrasted with the slow maturation of Judaism.

TABLE 2. *Continued*

	Isaiah	Summary
H	66: 10–13	New Sion = the godly polity = the church. New Jerusalem = the church. The river of peace in the city of God is the Logos (cf. Pss. 45: 5, 64: 10).
E/S	66: 23	Eschatological: the spiritual Jerusalem is where the Saviour will erect his kingdom; the heavenly city (*ouranopolis*), the kingdom of God, is the place of the true Sabbath, the rest of souls (Eusebius' future tenses suggest the eschatological interpretation, but *hê katô Ierousalêm* is certainly a reminiscence of Gal. 4: 26, and suggests a present spiritual reality).

working to deal with a recalcitrant *plebs* by religious law, on the analogy of the Old Testament *sacerdotium*.

And the Cyprianic bishop . . . came to be magistrate and governor of the lives of his people, while they lived under him as citizens of a City of God beleaguered round about by the heathen and secular 'city' of the empire. Thus whereas the Christians of Irenaeus appear as pilgrims making their journey by the light of heaven through a strange land, the Christians of Cyprian appear as enfranchised members of what was coming to be conceived as a shadow-empire. This polity was within the empire, and yet had a life separate from it. And it was destined to become the empire of Christ, when he should give the word for this age to pass away. It was, in short, an eschatology that was interpreting the actualities of the Church in the world.[41]

Much the same could be said of Eusebius' view of the bishop, except for the important new circumstance of a Christian emperor. Henceforth the emperor too would be a member of the church. But otherwise Telfer's description of the bishop's relation to the church in political terms resembles the exalted place Eusebius gives to the bishop as the first officer in the city of God. Eusebius too thinks of the church as a polity 'destined to become the empire of Christ when he should give the word for this age to pass away'. He too realized that in the meantime the church would have to accommodate members of widely differing degrees of enthusiasm and commitment.

[41] W. Telfer, *The Office of a Bishop* (London, 1962), 128.

Eusebius describes the office and status of the bishop in the commentary in a variety of capacities: governmental, judicial, liturgical, and eschatological. Although none of these is described in great detail, which would be inappropriate in a biblical commentary, they cumulatively give the episcopacy a high visibility in his exegesis. Most of this section will illustrate this centrality by demonstrating the bishop's usurpation of messianic and eschatological prophecies. Many of the passages discussed in the first section are also relevant to the present topic.

Eusebius did not suddenly discover the episcopacy when he sat down to write his commentary. His other works show a very high estimation of the episcopal office in the church. The opening lines of the *Church History* proclaim that the first theme of his pathbreaking work is the successions (*diadochai*) stretching from the apostles to his own time, and of those who had been most illustrious in the leadership and governance of the church.[42] In Book 10 of the *Church History* his speech at the rededication of the cathedral of Tyre develops an elaborate allegory of the new church and the renewed community, at the centre of which is the person of the bishop, Paulinus: 'In the ruler [*archôn*] of all, as is right, the entire Christ has taken his seat, and in those who have the second place after him [this bounty] is apportioned to each one's capacity, by gifts of the power of Christ and the Holy Spirit.'[43] He also says of Paulinus: '. . . this man also, bearing in his own soul the image of Christ entire, the Word, the Wisdom, the Light, hath formed this magnificent temple of God most high . . .'[44] This strong assertion of the bishop's Christic identity shows that Eusebius is deeply rooted in an Eastern tradition of monarchical episcopacy which goes back to Ignatius of Antioch.[45] Ignatius had spoken of the bishop as a type (*typos*) of God himself, and had also compared him to Jesus Christ.[46]

---

[42] *HE* 1. 1. See Grant, *Eusebius as Church Historian*, 45–59, on Eusebius' handling of the apostolic succession.

[43] Ibid. 10. 4. 67.

[44] Ibid. 10. 4. 26.

[45] Telfer, *The Office of a Bishop*, 67. Telfer devoted ch. 4 to a discussion of the significance of Ignatius and his letters as evidence for the history of the monarchical episcopate. See also R. M. Grant, *The Apostolic Fathers: A New Translation and Commentary*, i: *An Introduction* (New York, 1964), 166–73.

[46] The bishop as a type of God: *Letter to the Trallians*, 3: 1; compared to Christ: *Letter to the Trallians*, 2: 1, *Letter to the Romans*, 9: 1. Cited in Grant, *The Apostolic Fathers*, i. 167. W. Schoedel, *Ignatius of Antioch* (Philadelphia, 1985), 22–3, is more sceptical about how strictly such language should be taken.

A hierarchical typology of the sort found in Ignatius' letters survived in the church of Antioch, and may well be the background for Eusebius' own doctrine of the episcopacy, although the normal version of the typology, as found for instance in the third-century Syriac *Didascalia*, called for the bishop to stand for God and the deacons for Christ.[47]

In any event, Eusebius' assertion that the bishop takes the place of Christ is the starting point for understanding his exegetical legitimation of the hierarchy. For the *Commentary on Isaiah* shows a marked tendency for the bishop to displace the person of Christ in messianic texts or to be invested with eschatological authority in texts that bear, or seem to bear, on the end of all things or on the restoration of Jerusalem. An excellent example of this displacement, especially because it can be compared with Eusebius' earlier and more traditional understanding and because of the heavily juridical flavour of the passage, is the interpretation of Isa. 16: 5 ('Then a throne will be established in mercy and there will take his seat on it with truth in the tent of David one who judges and seeks justice and is swift to do righteousness'). In the *Prophetic Selections* he said of this verse:

This is a prophecy about the second coming of Christ, when the Word of God shall take his seat in the tent of David and judge with truth, his kingdom having been established over all with mercy and love, that is [by his kingdom], I believe is meant the church of the saints and the firstborn enrolled in heaven [cf. Heb 12: 23], and all the saints who have come under the portion of the Word of God.[48]

In the commentary the key word *thronos* suggested an ecclesiastical interpretation in which the Christian bishop, in whom Eusebius had already said in the *Church History* the whole Christ is seated, holds the place of Christ and dispenses justice in the church.[49] This is a very clear investment of the bishop with the power and authority of Christ at his second coming.[50]

---

[47] Per Beskow, *Rex Gloriae: The Kingship of Christ in the Early Church* (Uppsala, 1962), 167 f. Beskow cites *Didascalia*, 2. 26. 4–8. See Grant, *The Apostolic Fathers*, i. 167, for explanations of the unsymmetrical typology which would see, as both Ignatius and the *Didascalia* do, the deacons as Christ and the presbyters as merely the apostles; also Beskow, *Rex Gloriae*, 169.

[48] *EP* 4. 9 (188. 10–20).

[49] *CI* 109. 4–110. 11. The contrast with the *Selections* was already noted by Sirinelli, *Les vues historiques*, 482 f.

[50] Jerome tells us in his *Commentary on Isaiah* that the Jews were accustomed to apply this verse to Hezekiah. He gives as a Christian alternative a reading which sees

The eschatological aura surrounding the bishop's judicial function is a further link with the style of episcopal leadership that Telfer identified in Cyprian as typically Western, in the quotation with which we began. Telfer suggested that Constantine himself saw the juridical authority of the bishop in an eschatological light, perhaps under the influence of Hosius.[51] Although Constantine's legislation recognizing the secular competence of an episcopal audience was passed before Eusebius met him, this convergence of Constantinian and Eusebian thought on church authority perhaps makes intelligible Eusebius' statement in the *Life of Constantine* that the emperor rated the priests of God higher than judges of any kind.[52] Eusebius' association of the bishop's throne with the throne of Christ may be the earliest example of this, if Per Beskow is right in claiming that this connection had not been made in pre-Constantinian times.[53]

Another remarkable example of messianic displacement is Eusebius' explanation of the great prophecy of the peace of the animal kingdom in the messianic age (Isa. 11: 6–9).[54] Alexandrian exegesis traditionally allegorized scriptural references to animals as symbolizing human traits. Passages like this were applied to the civilizing consequences of the spread of the Gospel. The *Commentary on Isaiah* contains abundant examples. But the little child who will lead this peaceable kingdom is not Christ, as we might expect, but the Christian bishop, whom Eusebius says is appropriately called a *paidion mikron* because of his innocence and purity of soul.

Isa. 60: 17–18 describes the rebuilding of Jerusalem with gold and silver instead of bronze and iron, under leaders and overseers who would rule in peace and righteousness (*tous archontas sou en eirênêi*

---

the text fulfilled in the first coming of the Saviour, as well as in his second; in his first he rules through the church's penitential discipline, in the second he will rule as judge of all men; cf. *Comm. Is.* 5. 16. 5 (*CCL* lxxiii. 180. 4–181. 15), 6. 16. 1–5 (*CCL* lxxiii. 260. 49–64). Eusebius speaks only of the judgement of the church and omits the eschatological judgement.

[51] Telfer, *The Office of a Bishop*, 132–6.

[52] The legal decision is reported by Sozomen (*Hist. eccl.* 1. 9) and inferred from subsequent enactments preserved in the *Theodosian Code* (*CT* 1. 27. 1, dated 318) and the *Sirmondian Constitutions*, i. Discussions of the legislation in Barnes, *Constantine and Eusebius*, 51, 312, and A. H. M. Jones, *The Later Roman Empire: A Social Economic and Administrative Survey 284–602*, 2 vols. (Norman, Okla., 1964), i. 90 f. Eusebius reports Constantine's esteem of the priests of God as judges in *VC* 4. 27.

[53] Beskow, *Rex Gloriae*, 170.

[54] *CI* 83. 33–84. 17.

kai tous episkopous sou en dikaiosynêi).[55] Here as elsewhere the convergence of Septuagint vocabulary with technical Christian vocabulary served Eusebius' apologetic needs. He allegorizes the building materials as various types of moral character to be directed by the overseer/bishops (*episkopoi*) towards the construction of the new Jerusalem here on earth, in the shape of the morally renewed life of Christian converts. A similar prophecy of the restoration of Jerusalem is found in Isa. 61: 6–7:

But you shall be called priests [*hiereis*] of the Lord, ministers [*leitourguoi*] of God. You will consume the wealth of the nations, and in their riches you shall marvel. Thus they [i.e. the priests] will inherit the earth twofold, and an eternal joy will be upon them.

According to Eusebius' gloss the text refers to the leaders (*proestôtes*) of the church, a reading he reinforces with a traditional Christological proof text, Ps. 2: 7–8 ('You are my son, today I have begotten you; ask of me and I will give the nations as your inheritance, and as your possession the ends of the earth').[56] The bishops possess the nations as their inheritance in a twofold fashion: in the present life they already enjoy the wealth and riches of the nations, and they can also look forward to an 'eternal joy' in the life to come.[57]

Another exegetical device by which Eusebius legitimates the episcopacy is the identification of the bishops as the successors of the religious officers of the godly polity among the Jews. The apostles and their disciples, for example, are the successors of the prophets, according to Eusebius' interpretation of Isa. 52: 8 in the versions of Aquila, Symmachus, and Theodotion: 'The voice of your watchmen [*skopoi*] gave voice, they will rejoice together'.[58] They are rightly called *skopoi* because of their imitation of the prophetic office among the Jews, in the new Sion, the church of God, the godly polity. Although Eusebius does not explicitly mention the bishops here, the etymological play on *epi-skopoi* explains his preference for the other Greek versions over the Septuagint. The mention of the church of God and the godly polity proves that he is thinking of the text in an ecclesiastical context, not merely a New Testament one.

---

[55] *CI* 377. 5–19. Already in 1 Clement, 42:5 and Irenaeus, *Adv. Haer.* 4. 41. 2.
[56] Given a Christological demonstration by Eusebius himself in *DE* 4. 16.
[57] *CI* 381. 22–9.
[58] Ibid. 331. 16–33. The LXX has, 'The voice of those who guard you has been lifted up . . .'

Eusebius explores the relation between old and new priesthood in other places in the *Commentary on Isaiah*. As noted in the previous chapter, he showed great interest in Jewish exegetical lore about the person of the deposed Somnas (Isa. 22: 15–25). From his Jewish informant Eusebius learned the non-biblical tradition that Somnas, a royal steward or major-domo according to Isa. 22 (a secretary in 36: 22), had actually been a high priest. Isaiah's description of the duties and honours of his position matched Eusebius' own expectations of the Christian ministry:

And I will clothe him [Eliakim] with your robe [Somnas'] and I will give your crown to him, and I will put your power and ministry [*oikonomia*] in his hands, and he will be like a father to those who dwell in Jerusalem and who dwell in Judaea. And I will give him the glory of David, and he will rule, and there will be no one to contradict him. And I will establish him as a leader [*archōn*] in a sure position. And he will be a throne of glory to the house of his father. And every glorious person in the house of his father will trust in him, from the least even to the greatest, and they will depend on him [22: 21–4, LXX].

In place of the disgraced Somnas, Isaiah announced that God would establish Eliakim. Eusebius blends the biblical text with his Midrashic source to portray the nature of the high office Eliakim would assume in place of Somnas.

For all these things [sc. Somnas' excesses, cf. Isa. 22: 16] will work for your destruction, since you have been deposed and rejected from the high priest-hood, of which you showed yourself unworthy, God being a just judge who gives to each according to his worth. On you, then, he will bring these things; but on the other, Eliakim, whom he has assessed as his good servant and slave, he will invest with your robe and will honour by placing on him the crown of the high priesthood, whose ministry [*oikonomia*] you had hitherto been entrusted with. For he is a man worthy of it. And since he has been promoted [*proachtheis*] by God, unlike you he will not be proud and boastful. He will hold the place of a father towards all those who are going to be governed by him. Therefore, as to one who is soothing and gentle, [God] will give the glory of David, the most just and gentle king, in order to rule [*archein*] the people with great authority [*exousia*], so that none will gainsay his deeds. He will be rooted, established, and placed securely at his ministry [*leitourgia*], so that no glorious member of the people shall contend or contrive envy, nor shall jealousy ever come into being on his account, but they shall 'trust in him as in a father'.[59]

***

[59] *CI* 148. 6–20.

This passage describes the high priest in terms commonly applied to the Christian priesthood, as a check of the entries in *PGL* will show for the transliterated words. *Proagô* (to promote in clerical rank) and *exousia* both appeared in the recently proclaimed canons of Nicaea.[60] The paternalist theme was also congenial.[61] Eusebius believed that a successful bishop ruled without arousing envy and jealousy; in the *Church History* he explained the outbreak of persecution under Diocletian as a divine punishment for the envy and reviling in which the bishops had indulged.[62] The contemporary application of this miniature portrait of the ideal bishop is stated explicitly: God chastened and disciplined Somnas 'for our sake'.[63] His fate is a warning against those who would be arrogant in the exercise of their dominion (*en tais archais*).

The Somnas pericope is more than an *exemplum* for the proper conduct of a powerful and confident episcopacy. Eusebius adds another interpretation that very likely comes from Origen, but which he adapts in characteristic ways. The optative mood of the main clause (*synapseie tis ta prokeimena . . .*) suggests that he is introducing someone else's opinion. The same interpretation shows up in Jerome's *Commentary on Isaiah*, where Jerome attributes it to those who like to take everything according to *anagôgê*, most probably a reference to Origen.[64] Eusebius says that Somnas and Eliakim are images and symbols (*eikôn, symbolon*) of the priesthood of the new covenant. Borrowing either from Origen or from *The Interpretation of Hebrew Names*, he observes that Eliakim means 'the resurrection of God', symbolizing the passing away of the old priesthood after the passion of the Saviour and the establishment of the new priesthood in the church by virtue of his resurrection.[65] Origen was surprisingly fond of seeing anticipations of Christian institutions and customs in the Old Testament law; according to R. P. C. Hanson, he was the first Christian writer to make a direct correlation between the threefold Christian ministry of bishop, presbyter, and deacon, and the high priest, priests, and Levites of the Old

---

[60] Canons 1 and 6 respectively; *proagô* also means clerical advancement in canon 12 of the Synod of Ancyra (314), E. J. Jonkers (ed.), *Acta et symbola conciliorum quae saeculo quarto habita sunt* (Leiden, 1954).
[61] Ibid. 316. 6–8; 404. 24–5.
[62] *HE* 8. 1. 7.
[63] *CI* 148. 27.
[64] Jerome, *Comm. Is.* 5. 22. 15–22 (*CCL* lxxiii. 215. 84–216. 1).
[65] *CI* 148. 30–149. 4.

Testament.[66] But Origen also regarded the Christian ministry itself as an image of spiritual realities.[67] By comparison, Eusebius has no interest in extending the relation of image and reality beyond its fulfilment in the Christian priesthood. Quite typically he stops with the application of the Jewish type to its counterpart in the Christian church.

Other interpretations of the Jewish priesthood as referring to the Christian clergy occur in Eusebius' exegesis of the climactic prophecy in Isa. 66: 18–23, in which the nations gather in Jerusalem amidst a renewed creation to make their offerings to God. Discussion of this passage introduces another aspect of Eusebius' legitimation of the hierarchy, its perdurance and function in the *eschaton*.[68] The orders (*tagmata*) which marked the Christian polity on earth will survive in the heavenly Jerusalem. According to the biblical text, the prophet had predicted that God would take some of the Gentiles as his priests and Levites (66: 21), a passage open to Christian exploitation. The election (*eklogê*) of a new Gentile priesthood was proclaimed in an explicitly eschatological setting, God's creation of a new heaven and a new earth, unlike the Jewish priesthood, which Eusebius saw as part of the old order that was passing away. The hierarchical differentiation of the Christian community on earth is now projected into its post-historical existence.

This may be illustrated by a comparison of Eusebius' description of life in the heavenly Jerusalem and the kingdom of Christ with Origen's. Origen was accustomed to interpret biblical prophecies of the new heaven and the new earth (Isa. 65: 17, 66: 22, Rev. 21: 1), and of the promised land generally, cf. the 'good land' (*gê agathê*) of Deut. 8: 7–10, as the transcendent world described by Socrates in the *Phaedo* (110A). Origen believed that in the creation story God revealed the existence of a heaven and an earth beyond the heaven and earth of human experience. The Hellenistic cosmos of the eight spheres, from the moon to the sphere of the fixed stars,

---

[66] Hanson, *Allegory and Event*, 303. But the passage which he cites speaks only of a correlation of presbyter-priest and deacon-Levite, and says nothing about the bishop. Cf. Origen, *Hom. Jer.* 12. 3 (SC 238: 20. 16–20). He cites other passages on this subject at p. 330 n. 1, but these are not really convincing either (*Homilies on Joshua*, 4. 1; *On Prayer*, 28. 9 f.).

[67] *Commentary on Matthew*, 14. 22, cited in Hanson, *Allegory and Event*, 330. See Hanson's comments there on Origen's allegorical interpretation of the Christian ministry, 329 f.

[68] For what follows, cf. Eusebius' remarks in *CI* 408. 14–410. 17.

corresponded to the firmament of the biblical account. Invisible and beyond this was a supercelestial sphere that comprised the new earth and new heaven where the promises of scripture would be fulfilled for the saints.[69] Justifying himself on the basis of texts like John 14: 2 ('In my father's house there are many mansions'), Origen taught a doctrine of progressive enlightenment and purification of souls in the next life, where there would be degrees of virtue and reward—stations, *monai* (John 14: 2)—through which souls passed in their ascent to the ultimate restoration in God.[70] The 'earth' and 'heaven' of the supercelestial sphere represented the penultimate and ultimate stages of this ascent. In the parts of *On First Principles* where he expounds these views, he commonly cites Matt. 5: 5 ('Blessed are the meek, for they shall inherit the earth') and interprets it to mean that the *praeis* of the Beatitudes will possess the earthly part of the supercelestial sphere, where they will be prepared for life under the perfect commandments of the eternal Gospel in heaven.[71]

Origen's favourite metaphor for heavenly life is the school or lecture-room, in which souls will learn the reasons behind the divine dispensation of the cosmos as part of their progressive post-mortem enlightenment.[72] Eusebius' favourite metaphor is the liturgy. In his exegesis of the closing verses of Isaiah we find the same distinction of a supercelestial heaven and earth, the same scriptural proof texts (John 14: 2, Matt. 5: 5), and a heavenly hierarchy, as in Origen. But the centre-piece of his picture of heavenly life is a heavenly liturgy conducted by Jesus Christ as high priest, with his subordinate ministers, the clergy. The priestly and liturgical language of the Isaian text assists this interpretation. He tells us, apropos of the new heaven and the new earth, that they are the earth and the kingdom of heaven which the Lord promised to the meek in the Beatitudes, and that they will last forever. Furthermore, the prophecy reveals that there will be a variety of places in the kingdom of heaven, according to the words of Christ in John 14: 2. This interpretation of John 14: 2 became a commonplace in patristic exegesis as a justification of the degrees of reward to be apportioned to the saints in heaven, commensurate with their deeds on earth.[73] We might be puzzled to

---

[69] Origen describes this picture of the created order in *De Princ.* 2. 3. 6–7; 2. 11. 5–7; 3. 6. 8–9; *C. Cels.* 7. 28–31.
[70] *De Princ.* 2. 11. 6.
[71] Ibid. 2. 3. 6; 3. 6. 8.
[72] Ibid. 2. 11. 7.   [73] See the citations in *PGL* s.v. *monê.*

understand why Eusebius introduced it at this juncture if we did not know Origen's idea that the new earth and the new heaven represented the final stage of the soul's purification and enlightenment after death. Eusebius does not subscribe to the Origenist doctrine that there is an eternal Gospel beyond the commands of the Sermon on the Mount, and that only those who were prepared for the perfect commandments of the eternal Gospel would win entry to the supercelestial heaven. What he says is a bit different: first, that the *monai* on earth will have an analogy in heaven; and that the heavenly *monai* will possess their glory (*doxa*) in descending fashion.[74] He appears to be saying that the hierarchical distinctions among Christians on earth will be duplicated in heaven. This is supported by references elsewhere to the privileged role of the clergy in sharing the eschatological glory of Christ in his kingdom. Thus at Isa. 66: 15 Eusebius says that at his second coming Christ will take as his bride those of his priests who are worthy of the *doxa* of his kingdom.[75] He alludes here to an earlier eschatological prophecy in the little apocalypse in chs. 24–7: 'The brick will be melted and the wall will fall, when the Lord shall reign in Sion and Jerusalem and shall be glorified before his priests [*enôpion tôn presbyterôn*]' (Isa. 24: 23). Of this verse he says: 'For those whom Christ has honoured in the present life with ecclesiastical dignities, having made them priests, these same ones he will make worthy of his divinity.'[76] The clergy are the saints of the Most High whom Daniel says will receive the kingdom.[77]

Unlike Origen, Eusebius does not seem to think of souls as mobile and their stations as mere resting places on a perpetual ascent; rather, they are as it were permanent addresses in the next life. Eusebius does not share Origen's view of the afterlife as a progressive purification. He describes these stations as residences from which souls emerge periodically for liturgical assemblies at which they are refreshed by the ineffable joys and good things of heaven.[78] The prophet referred to these occasional assemblies as the 'new moons and Sabbaths' of the old law (66: 23), which Christians regard as types and symbols of the true feasts in the heavenly Jerusalem. Just

---

[74] *CI* 409. 3–6.
[75] Ibid. 405. 25–9.
[76] Ibid. 161. 17–18.
[77] Ibid. 161. 32–6.
[78] Ibid. 409. 32–410. 4.

as the Israelites gathered from throughout the whole country to assemble at the Jerusalem sanctuary, so the saints gather from their heavenly stations for worship at the appointed seasons, 'however we ought to construe the "years" and "seasons" there'.[79] As in the Jewish system only the high priest himself, Jesus Christ, has access to the innermost sanctum of the temple, that is, the true divinity of the Father, but Eusebius' remark quoted above suggests that the priests may share this right, having been made worthy of his divinity. Unlike those who come to worship at appointed times, the actual citizens of Jerusalem itself, the 'myriads of angels and church of the firstborn' (Heb 12: 23), have perpetual enjoyment of the good things of heaven, serving as the priests and ministers of the high priest, the Son of God.[80] It is unclear whether Eusebius is speaking here just of the angels, or whether the human priests and ministers of the Son of God have this right of permanent, not merely occasional possession of heavenly joy. In light of the passages cited on the previous page, this is at least a possible interpretation. In any case, we have demonstrated how Eusebius projected the privileged position of the clerical leadership of the church into the next world, where they would share in a pre-eminent way the glory of Christ's kingdom and continue to lead the whole people in the liturgies of the heavenly Jerusalem.

4. The Roman Empire in the *Commentary on Isaiah*

Our presentation of Eusebius' view of the church as the godly polity in the *Commentary on Isaiah* is largely complete, now that we have shown by close reference to the text of the commentary how Eusebius read into Isaiah the threefold history—pre-Incarnational, post-Incarnational, eschatological—of the community of the saints, and how he justified the hierarchical eminence of the clergy in that community. Now we must consider the question, first raised in Ch. II, of the place he gives to the Roman Empire. His well-known accommodations to the exigencies of the Constantinian settlement do not at first sight fit easily with the strong view of the church as the godly polity, the city of God, which has been documented in the *Commentary on Isaiah*. The commentary thus offers valuable evi-

---

[79] *CI* 409. 27–8.
[80] Ibid. 410. 11–17.

dence for a full and balanced appreciation of his thought on church and empire.[81]

The nature of Eusebius' theological *rapprochement* of Christianity and the Roman Empire can be briefly summarized.[82] Eusebius stands in a line of thought originating in the Acts of the Apostles[83] and developed by the second century Apologists and by Origen, who argued that Roman persecution was based on a tragic misconception. Christianity was actually compatible with the best ideals of the empire, whose origins and prosperity lay under God's dispensation.[84] An important theme in the Apologists' programme for reconciliation between the two was the co-ordination of the birth of Christ with Augustus' inauguration of the Pax Romana.[85] Origen, despite his general lack of interest in politics, espoused the same idea, with additional refinements. In *Against Celsus* he observed that Augustus' unification of the diverse kingdoms of the world under his sole rule enhanced the fulfilment of the Lord's command to

[81] See my presentation of this argument in 'Religion and Politics in the Writings of Eusebius of Caesarea: Reassessing the First "Court Theologian"', *CH* 59 (1990), 309–25.

[82] Among the many works dealing with Eusebius' political theology, I have consulted the following: N. H. Baynes, 'Eusebius and the Christian Empire', in *Byzantine Studies and Other Essays* (London, 1955), 168–72; H. G. Opitz, 'Euseb von Caesarea als Theologe', *ZNW* 34 (1935), 1–19; Erik Peterson, *Monotheismus als politisches Problem: Ein Beitrag zur Geschichte der politischen Theologie im Imperium Romanum* (Leipzig, 1935), repr. in *Theologische Traktate* (Munich, 1951), 45–157 (86–94 on Eusebius; references are to this printing); Hans Eger, 'Kaiser und Kirche in der Geschichtstheologie Eusebs von Cäsarea', *ZNW* 38 (1939), 97–115; Chesnut, *The First Christian Histories*, 91–118, 133–66; Berkhof, *Kirche und Kaiser*, 100–4, and id., *Die Theologie des Eusebius von Caesarea*, 53–9; George H. Williams, 'Christology and Church–State Relations in the Fourth Century', *CH* 20/3 (1951), 1–33 and 20/4 (1951), 1–26; Beskow, *Rex Gloriae*, 261–75; Gerhard Ruhbach, 'Die politische Theologie Eusebs von Caesarea', in *Die Kirche angesichts der Konstantinischen Wende*, 236–58; Carl Schmitt, 'Euseb als Prototyp politischer Theologie', *Politische Theologie II* (Berlin, 1970), repr. in *Die Kirche angesichts der Konstantinischen Wende*, 220–35; Kurt Aland, 'Kaiser und Kirche von Konstantin bis Byzanz', *Kirchen-geschichtliche Entwürfe* (Gütersloh, 1960), 257–79, repr. in *Die Kirche angesichts der Konstantinischen Wende*, 42–73; Gerard E. Caspary, *Politics and Exegesis: Origen and the Two Swords* (Berkeley, 1979); F. E. Cranz, 'Kingdom and Polity in Eusebius of Caesarea', *HTR* 45 (1962), 47–66.

[83] See Haenchen, *Apostelgeschichte*, 92.

[84] The literature on attitudes and relations between church and empire is immense. A good survey may be found in the relevant chapters of R. M. Grant, *From Augustus to Constantine: The Thrust of the Christian Movement into the Roman World* (New York, 1970).

[85] For a fine statement of this outlook, see Melito of Sardis, *To Antoninus*, in Eusebius, *HE* 4. 26. 7–10. Further discussion of this theme in Peterson, *Monotheismus*, 66 ff.

spread the Gospel to all nations (Matt. 28: 19), because of the ease and security of world travel and the liberation of men from the hitherto necessary burden of military service, so incompatible with the spirit of the Gospel.[86]

As Erik Peterson has noted, Eusebius gave a rich development to what in Origen were only motifs and indications.[87] Especially in his apologetic treatise *The Proof of the Gospel*, we find Eusebius writing in similar terms as Origen but going beyond him in important ways. Like Origen, he appealed to Augustus' pacification of warring nations and cities, but he fleshed out his conception with a wide range of historical data, such as the end of native kingship in Judaea, Ptolemaic Egypt, Cappadocia, Macedonia, Bithynia, and Greece.[88] More importantly, he considered the hegemony of the Roman Empire a religious as well as a political fact, because of the intimate bond he saw between nationalism—what he called 'polyarchy'—and polytheism. The Pax Romana meant not only the end of national and political pluralism, but of religious pluralism as well, of the worship of many gods. Eusebius echoes Origen in saying that the empire enabled the easier spread of the Gospel. But whereas Origen had simply meant that the new internationalism brought freer commerce between former antagonists and lessened friction and suspicion, Eusebius believed that the empire was now interposed as a bulwark against the religiously inspired hostility of pagan polytheism.

But when these [i.e. the governments of the nations] were abolished, they [the apostles] could accomplish their projects quite fearlessly and safely, since the Supreme God had smoothed the way before them, and subdued the spirit of the more superstitious citizens under the fear of a strong central government. For consider, how if there had been no force available to hinder [*to kôluon*] those who in the power of polytheistic error were contending with Christian education, that you would have long ago seen civil revolutions, and extraordinarily bitter persecutions and wars, if the superstitious had had the power to do as they willed with them. Now this must have been the work of God Almighty, this subordination of the enemies of His own Word to a greater fear of a supreme ruler.[89]

[86] Origen, *C. Cels.* 2. 30, with discussion in Peterson, *Monotheismus*, 82 ff., and also Caspary, *Politics and Exegesis*, 129 ff.

[87] *Monotheismus*, 86.

[88] *DE* 3. 2. 37 (Judaea, where native kingship ended with the coming to power of Herod the Great, in fulfilment of Gen. 49: 10); 3. 7. 30–5 (Egypt, where the death of Cleopatra marked the end of the Ptolemaic dynasty; also cited here is the subjection of Cappadocia, Macedonia, Bithynia, and Greece under Roman rule).

[89] *DE* 3. 7. 33–5, trans. Ferrar, i. 161–2.

The hindering force of the empire (*to kôluon*) could be 'the re-strainer' (*ho katechôn*) of 2 Thess. 2: 7, but more likely it refers to Luke's final verse in Acts, according to which Paul preached the kingdom of God in Rome 'unhindered' (*akôlutôs*).[90] The empire hindered only those who were hostile to the Gospel. Like apologists before him, Eusebius had to account for the manifest hostility of at least some of these supreme rulers, as indeed he does in the lines which immediately follow the quoted passage. But fundamentally he thought of the empire as an ally of Christianity because it was the agent of peace and the repressor of anarchic political and national pluralism.[91] Parallels to this passage can be multiplied.[92] In the Preface to Book 8 of the *Proof* Eusebius gave sharp expression to his co-ordination of the supersession of pagan polytheism by Christian monotheism, with the defeat of international pluralism by the single authority of the Roman Empire. The Old Testament prophecies, he wrote, foresaw this astounding reversal in international affairs as a sign of the coming of the Saviour:

They suggest other signs of the same times as well, an abundance of peace, the overturning in nation and city of immemorial local and national forms of government [*toparchias kai polyarchias*], the conquest of polytheistic and demonic idolatry, the knowledge of the religion of God the one Supreme Creator.[93]

According to Peterson, this application of biblical eschatological prophecy to secular history demonstrated a striking lack of exegetical tact. But Eusebius went further than this in his panegyrical works on Constantine. The emperor's Christian sympathies stimulated him to even more explicit correlations of politics and religion. Speaking before the emperor at Constantine's tricennial celebration in 336, Eusebius described in rhetorically extravagant language how Constantine imitated on earth the rule of the Logos in heaven.[94] In an especially bold passage he declaimed,

Once more, having harnessed, as it were, under the self-same yoke the four most noble Caesars as horses in the imperial chariot, he sits on high and

[90] Haenchen, *Apostelgeschichte*, 655 f.

[91] Peterson, *Monotheismus*, 89.

[92] Ibid.; citations, 135 f. Note especially the lengthy development of this theme in Eusebius' *Treatise on the Holy Sepulchre* (*LC* 16).

[93] *DE* 8. Prol. 3, trans. Ferrar, ii. 96–7.

[94] *LC* 2. 1–5. See the translation and commentary of H. A. Drake, *In Praise of Constantine* (Berkeley, 1976).

directs their course by the reins of holy harmony and concord; and, himself everywhere present and observant of every event, thus traverses every region of the world. Lastly, invested as he is with a semblance of heavenly sovereignty, he directs his gaze above, and frames his earthly government according to the pattern of the divine original, feeling strength in its conformity to the monarchy of God. And this conformity is granted by the universal Sovereign to man alone of all the creatures on the earth: for he only is the author of sovereign power, who decrees that all should be subject to the power of one.[95]

Here Eusebius combines biblical solar imagery from the psalms (Ps. 18: 5–7) and the prophets (Mal. 3: 20, the sun of righteousness) which was traditionally ascribed to Christ and applied it to Constantine. He also has drawn on Hellenistic philosophy of kingship in which the king imitates the divine government in the heavens.[96] Eusebius seems to come perilously close to eliminating a role for the incarnate Christ in his parallelism of the cosmic rule of the Logos in heaven and the political rule of Constantine on earth.

It is not surprising that language of this kind has led some to the harsh verdict that Eusebius allowed himself in his late works to be reduced to a political propagandist.[97] The modern tradition of Eusebius the flatterer of kings goes back at least to Jacob Burckhardt, who condemned him as 'the first thoroughly dishonest historian of antiquity'.[98] In the twentieth century more restrained critics have called him a political publicist, a herald of Byzantinism, a political theologian, and a political metaphysician.[99] Whether approving or critical, modern scholars have been preoccupied with the political relevance of Eusebius' thought.[100] Scholars like Hans Eger and H.-G. Opitz, influenced by the classical philologist Eduard Schwartz, applauded Eusebius' effort at relating Christianity to the

[95] *LC* 3. 4–5 (rev. trans. E. C. Richardson, in *Eusebius: Church History, Life of Constantine, Oration in Praise of Constantine*, i in *A Select Library of Nicene and Post-Nicene Fathers of the Christian Church*, 2nd Ser. (repr. Grand Rapids, Mich., 1982), 584). See Drake's annotations, *In Praise of Constantine*, 159 n. 11.

[96] See Baynes, 'Eusebius and the Christian Empire', 168–72, and Chesnut, *The First Christian Histories*, 133–55, for discussions of the background of Hellenistic political and philosophical speculation in Eusebius' thought.

[97] See Peterson's summary judgement on Eusebius' ideas, *Monotheismus*, 91–3, and their enormous influence (93 ff).

[98] Burckhardt, *Constantine the Great*, 283.

[99] Respectively, Peterson, *Monotheismus*, 91; Berkhof, *Die Theologie des Eusebius*, 21 f.; Eger, 'Kaiser und Kirche', 115; and Beskow, *Rex Gloriae*, 318.

[100] See the overview of Ruhbach, 'Die politische Theologie Eusebs von Caesarea', 236–9.

broader stream of world history.[101] Though writing from a very different theological orientation, Jean Sirinelli has emphasized the same aspect of Eusebius as an apologetic historian and theologian who sought a positive relationship between Christianity and culture. The Catholic convert Erik Peterson and the Reformed theologian Hendrik Berkhof have, on the other hand, strongly criticized Eusebius' role in providing a theological rationale for the Constantinian settlement, which they blame especially on his subordinationist Christology. They are followed in the main by G. H. Williams and Per Beskow.[102] The studies of Gerhard Ruhbach and T. D. Barnes have sought a more balanced judgement. Barnes tried to free Eusebius from the charge of mere opportunism by demonstrating the strong continuity in his thinking on the place of Christianity in the Roman Empire, since in his view Eusebius' fundamental attitude was already shaped by the end of the third century and reflected a broad Christian optimism about the future.[103] Ruhbach takes Eusebius' sincerity at face value and sees him as an apologetic historian with good, if misguided intentions, who always saw political events from a religious perspective and never for their own sake.[104]

Barnes' and Ruhbach's contributions have the important merit of directing attention away from too narrow a preoccupation with the immediately political implications and motivations of Eusebius' life and work. Given modern obsession with the political, the risk of distortion is considerable. Much of the work on Eusebius has been done with one eye on the crisis which convulsed Europe in the 1930s and 1940s; the involvement of Christianity in the fate of the Third Reich has left its mark on scholarship. Ruhbach especially has made an important contribution by seeing Eusebius in the light of his heritage as an Origenist apologetic theologian with a strongly historical and biblical bent. However, he does not discuss Eusebius' exegesis; the evidence in the *Commentary on Isaiah* complements his analysis by demonstrating how a bishop-apologist viewed the practical needs of the church.

---

[101] For Schwartz's views on Eusebius, see especially his Pauly-Wissowa article, *RE* vi. 1370–439.

[102] See the books and articles cited above.

[103] Barnes, *Constantine and Eusebius*, 186, 249, and *passim*.

[104] Ruhbach, 'Die politische Theologie Eusebs von Caesarea', summarizes his Heidelberg dissertation, *Apologetik und Geschichte: Untersuchungen zur Theologie Eusebs von Caesarea* (1962), which I have not examined.

In the *Commentary* we can find most, though not all, of the apologetic themes mentioned earlier in our summary of Eusebius' political theology. In the *Commentary on Isaiah* Eusebius notes that the birth of the Saviour was contemporary with the Augustan peace and the disappearance of autonomous national kingdoms, and that universal peace made evangelization easier.[105] The swords-to-ploughshares prophecy in Isa. 2: 1–4 appears to be applied to the reign of Constantine.[106] We discussed in Ch. II the probable allusions in this passage to Constantinian slogans of *eirênê* and *homonoia*. But what is conspicuously absent in the *Commentary on Isaiah* is the idea of the emperor's imitation of the Logos. Eusebius omitted it partly because it was inappropriate to the genre of the commentary but also because it clashed with his emphasis on the bishops as the leaders of the godly polity. There is less room for the emperor as the usurper of the eschatological glory of Christ, as he sometimes seems in the panegyrical literature, because that role had already been co-opted by the bishops.

The emperor and his entourage are certainly not absent from the commentary, though Constantine, unlike Augustus, is nowhere mentioned by name.[107] References take the form of passing allusions or vignettes. The emperor and his officials attend sacred services. Eusebius sees the literal fulfilment of Isa. 49: 23 ('Kings shall be your foster-fathers, and queens your nursemaids') in the presence in church of the supreme rulers and their governors, genuflecting and resting their brows upon the ground (!).[108] Besides attending the liturgy, they prove they are loyal benefactors of the church by making rich offerings and by succouring the poor through gifts of grain to the church.[109] Finally, his officials fulfil the prophecy of 2: 20–1 by their confiscation of idols, to melt them down for their precious metals.[110] This statement repeats an assertion Eusebius makes elsewhere in trying to prove that Constantine embarked on a vigorous repression of paganism.[111]

[105] *CI* 91. 21–92. 5 (end of the Ptolemaic dynasty); 114. 7–115. 16 (Damascus and Syria); 126. 28–127. 16 (Egypt again, with specific identification of Augustus as the mighty king mentioned by Aquila, Symmachus, and Theodotion, he being the sole ruler (*monarchêsanta*) of the empire); 14. 32–15. 14 (the destruction of toparchies and polyarchies).

[106] Ibid. 14. 32–15. 14.

[107] Ibid. 127. 7.

[108] Ibid. 316. 17–25.   [109] Ibid. 316. 10–16.   [110] Ibid. 20. 29–21. 5.

[111] *VC* 3. 54. 4; *LC* 8. 1–5, 9. 6. See Barnes, *Constantine and Eusebius*, for the most recent summary of Constantine's religious policies for the unified empire, especially

From this rather meagre list of references one could not deduce the extravagant imperial adulation of the panegyrics. There is nothing about the person of the emperor or the empire in this commentary which could not as easily have come from the pen of Ambrose of Milan or any of the great fourth-century ecclesiastics who were convinced, like Ambrose, that the emperor was in the church but not over the church. Eusebius' conception of the role of the Christian emperor, on the evidence presented by the *Commentary on Isaiah*, amounts to attending the liturgy, donating to the support of the poor and the church, and repressing religious error, none of which were controversial expectations by fourth-century standards.

It is telling that the *Commentary on Isaiah* has much more to say about the pagan Roman Empire of Augustus, Vespasian, and Hadrian than the incipiently Christian empire of Constantine. When Eusebius refers to the Roman Empire, he usually is addressing the events of AD 70 and 135, when the emperors acted as divinely appointed scourges of the Jews.[112] This deeply biblical notion, which suited Eusebius' anti-Jewish apologetic so well, regarded the Romans as no different than previous rods of God's anger and staffs of his fury: his chosen instruments to execute judgement against his people. Had Eusebius wished, Isaiah offered him rich material for developing a favourable and flattering portrait of the emperor, most obviously in the person of Cyrus, the Lord's anointed.[113] But the Cyrus passages are given a scrupulously historical interpretation, as noted in the last chapter.

To summarize: the *Commentary on Isaiah* contains Eusebius' typical apologetic themes concerning the Roman Empire, but without the patina of Hellenistic political speculation and rhetoric that surrounds his portrait of Constantine in the other works written in the decade before his death. Eusebius' exegesis of Isaiah is certainly

246–8, where Barnes makes a strong case for the veracity of Eusebius' assertion that Constantine intended, and inaugurated, a campaign of religious coercion against paganism. A. H. M. Jones, *The Later Roman Empire*, i. 92, also believes that Eusebius reflects a genuine intention on Constantine's part to repress the pagan cult.

[112] *CI* 10. 12–20; 14. 13–25; 18. 23–8; 25. 29–36; 31. 4–5; 31. 27–32. 17; 35. 5–6; 42. 30–44. 11; 117. 13–23; 188. 34–189. 8; 189. 19–27; 219. 34–220. 3; 224. 22–6; 327. 16–21.

[113] As was recognized by the late Professor Arnaldo Momigliano, who in conversation with the author ventured the prediction that Eusebius' commentary would somehow link Constantine with Cyrus. The text did not bear out this expectation.

marked by the new position of the church under a Christian emperor, and in places this influence is quite frank. Nevertheless, the Roman Empire itself, especially the Christian empire, is only a minor theme in the *Commentary*. It is regarded mostly from the vantage point of the needs and structures of the Christian church. Eusebius was not dazzled by the splendour of the Constantinian regime to the same degree in all his works. The rhetorician who praised the deeds of the first Christian emperor did not cease to be a Christian bishop whose first point of orientation was his church, the city of God on earth.[114] Future study of Eusebius should not be misled into seeing the Constantinian literature as the exhaustive expression of Eusebius' thought, even after the Council of Nicaea.

5. Eschatology

A corollary of the conventional wisdom on Eusebius' political theology is that he succumbed to a fully realized eschatology which saw the apotheosis of history in the now Christian Roman Empire.[115] The evidence for his eschatological interpretation of the Empire is convincing, as far as it goes.[116] It would certainly be justified,

[114] Contrary to peremptory judgements such as that of Gerhard Ladner, *The Idea of Reform: Its Impact on Thought and Action in the Age of the Fathers*, rev. edn. (New York, 1967), 123 f., who opined that Eusebius did not distinguish between empire and church.

[115] Again, Peterson's analysis has been highly influential. See also R. Farina, *L'impero e imperatore cristiano in Eusebio di Cesarea: La prima teologia politica del cristianesimo* (Zürich, 1966), 161–3; Sirinelli, *Les vues historiques*, 482; Opitz, 'Eusebius von Caesarea als Theologe', 14; Eger, 'Kaiser und Kirche', 114. Glenn Chesnut has tried to balance overly immanentist interpretations of Eusebius' eschatology by drawing attention to elements of apocalyptic eschatology embedded in his thought, even in his picture of Constantine; cf. *The First Christian Histories*, 156–66. His fine analysis is not, however, completely convincing; see my remarks in 'Religion and Politics in Eusebius', 310 n. 3, and 316 n. 33. C. Odahl, 'The Use of Apocalyptic Imagery in Constantine's Christian Propaganda', *Centerpoint*, 4 (1981), 9–20, creates a false problem by equating the doctrine of the second return of Christ with apocalypticism *tout court*; as noted below, it was possible to hold the former without holding the latter. F. Thielmann, 'Another Look at the Eschatology of Eusebius of Caesarea', *VC* 41 (1987), 226–37, correctly stresses the more conventional aspects of Eusebius' eschatology.

[116] See the passages cited by Chesnut, 160 n. 117. Once again, the most explicit identification of the empire as the bearer of eschatological peace is probably to be found in the panegyrical literature, *LC* 16. 7–8 (Ps. 71: 7–8 and Isa. 2: 4), though the *Commentary on Isaiah* has a circumspect parallel mentioned in Section 4 above (*CI* 14. 32–15. 14, also referring to Isa. 2: 4).

for example, to regard as realized eschatology Eusebius' description in the *Life of Constantine* of the new Church of the Holy Sepulchre in Jerusalem as the biblical New Jerusalem, predicted by the prophets.[117] Nevertheless, as Glenn Chesnut has rightly pointed out, Eusebius' eschatology is too flexible to be confined to the present prosperity of the Constantinian regime. He is just as fond of regarding the missionary spread of the church as an eschatological sign.[118] In Section 2 of the present chapter we pointed to passages in the *Commentary on Isaiah* which see the leaders of the institutional church as the fulfillers of eschatological prophecy. So once again we must conclude that it would be misleading to take what Eusebius says in the Constantinian literature too exclusively, apart from what he says in his other works.

An examination of the eschatological doctrine of the *Commentary on Isaiah* shows that Eusebius retained the main lines of New Testament eschatology, while making certain adaptations of details that collided too directly with Alexandrian sensibilities. Our contention is that the ideas of the Second Coming and the final judgement expounded in the commentary are instrumental to Eusebius' whole scheme of thought, not extraneous or vestigial carry-overs from a more naïve age. The relevant material is found mainly in connection with the chapters of Isaiah that deal with apocalyptic and eschatological themes.

Given the number of eschatological passages in the book of Isaiah, Eusebius would have had to resort to drastic allegorizing to avoid the subject altogether. He had no desire to resort to a thorough spiritualization of the biblical prophecies, because the themes of ultimate judgement and vindication were compatible and even necessary to round off his history of the godly polity. The parts of Isaiah where his eschatologically inclined exegesis tends to cluster are the prophecies against the nations (13–23), the little apocalypse in chs. 24–7, chs. 33–4, and the eschatological prophecies of chs. 65–6. Consistent with the prophet's predictions of woes against the nations, Eusebius read chs. 13–23 as foreseeing historical ruin and chastisement for the designated peoples and nations. But he believed that a universal judgement (*katholikê krisis*) was intended as well. His extrapolation from limited and national to ultimate and universal judgement, for which Jerome was to criticize

---

[117] *VC* 3. 33.

[118] Again, see Chesnut's citations, 160 n. 116. Interestingly, all the cites in the *DE* are based on texts from Isaiah: *DE* 2. 3. 67–73; 2. 3. 111–12; 6. 13. 19–20.

him,[119] was justified in his eyes in light of the pronouncements on universal judgement in the following chs. 24–7. The exegesis of chs. 13–14 and chs. 24–7 is largely, though not exclusively, given to the punishment of the wicked and the constraint of the wicked powers. In discussing chs. 65–6, Eusebius tends to speak more of the rewards of the righteous. We bring together now his comments on the end of all things, pointing out where he seems to introduce typical Alexandrian adaptations, and explaining why his biblically based eschatology is central to his thought.

The basic historical framework of Eusebius' commentary is thoroughly traditional. The age of the church is the age between the times of Christ's comings, his first in humility and suffering, his second in power and glory.[120] Eusebius gives no indication when this will take place.[121] The return of Christ with his angels, the avenging powers, is the first act in the apocalyptic scenario, though Eusebius gives no description of Christ's descent, perhaps because of his dislike of millenarianism. The second act is the shaking of the cosmic order. 'The earth is laid waste' (Isa. 24: 3) is allegorized to mean that the souls of the wicked will be punished by the avenging powers for having clung to the things of the earth.[122] This sort of spiritualization of destruction, and the reference to the earthiness of Adam, the first man, would seem to derive from Origen. The wicked have condemned the image of God in them by their fondness for pleasure and the body.

As for the heavenly bodies, the prophet proclaimed that 'God will strike the cosmos of heaven with his hand' (Isa. 24: 21), in confirmation of the Lord's own prediction (Matt. 24: 29 f.), but here too Eusebius seems to demythologize the graphic description of biblical apocalyptic. 'The sun will be confounded, and the moon put to shame' (24: 23) meant that these heavenly bodies, which had been God's ministers, will blush to see the fate of those wicked ones on whom they had shone before the consummation. Noting that the references to sun and moon are absent from the Septuagint, though contained in the Hebrew and the other Greek versions, Eusebius

---

[119] Jerome, *Comm. Is.* 5. 13. 3 (*CCL* lxxiii. 161. 3–6).

[120] Christ's second coming is glorious: *CI* 201. 27; 216. 17; 228. 13; 405. 15. The conventional contrast between first and second comings (e.g. Justin, *Dial.* 110. 5, 111; Origen, *C. Cels.* 1. 56) is made at *CI* 228. 13 and 25. 7–10.

[121] But see Chesnut's interesting speculation on just how much time Eusebius may have foreseen before the end (*The First Christian Histories*, 159 f).

[122] *CI* 155. 1–8.

explains that the LXX had omitted them, speaking cryptically of melting bricks and falling walls (Isa. 24: 23, LXX), because their version was destined to be published for the Greeks, and the biblical diction was inappropriate (*dia to apemphainon tês lexeôs*).[123] His manipulation of the different versions of this verse shows his anxiety lest crudities in the biblical account offend educated sensibilities.

In another place Eusebius says that the sun, moon, and stars will be liberated for a better fate, freed from serving the vanity of bodily needs, and endowed with regeneration,[124] an exegesis which may owe as much to Paul as to Origen (cf. Rom. 8: 21). There is probably an allusion to Origen's eschatology in Eusebius' comment on Isa. 34: 5–6, where he uses his usual formula *allos d'an eipoi* to introduce an interpretation not his own: someone else might say that at the end of the world the heavenly bodies will put off their physical garments and enter a higher existence.[125]

Then follows the resurrection of the dead, who are gathered in separate assemblies (Isa. 26: 19–20). The prophet advises the saints to retreat to their chambers (*tamieia*) and to lock the doors, so that, safely tucked away in these shelters, they will be spared the sight of the fate of the wicked when the wrath of God passes by. These chambers are identified as the separate mansions (*monai*, cf. John 14: 2) reserved for each order of the saints (see the discussion in the previous section).[126] The avenging angels execute God's wrath, though in forms of punishment that are rarely made explicit by Eusebius. The sword of Isa. 66: 16 is spiritualized, and similarly the consuming worm of 66: 24, which becomes the worm of conscience.[127] It is unclear whether the inextinguishable fire of 66: 24 is physical or not, but since Eusebius identifies it as the fire prepared for the devil and his angels (Matt. 25: 41), which are incorporeal beings, he apparently does not think of it as physical; the wicked burn with suffering from seeing too late the good things enjoyed by the saints.[128] The souls of the saints, sometimes equated with the martyrs, sometimes simply called the meek (Matt. 5: 5), are roused

---

[123] Ibid. 159. 14–161. 4. Also see his exegesis of Isa. 34: 3–4 (220. 31–222. 16).
[124] Ibid. 97. 26–36.
[125] Cf. *CI* 222. 19–25. This passage was omitted from the catenae edited by Montfaucon. It survived only in the Florentine MS discovered by von Möhle. For the teaching of Origen on the redemption of the heavenly bodies, see *De Princ.* 1. 7. 4–5.
[126] *CI* 170. 22–171. 26.
[127] Ibid. 405. 32–4; 410. 28–32.
[128] Ibid. 168. 13–15.

from sleep by the dropping of the dew of the Logos upon them.[129]
They are taken to the fortified city (Isa. 26: 1), the heavenly Jerusalem, where the godly polity is, the city of God, to sing a new song of triumph.[130] Eusebius allegorizes Isaiah's prophecy that in the new Jerusalem there will no longer be premature deaths (65: 20) to mean that all those destined to rebirth will be full-grown and mature in their souls at the time of the resurrection, and that the resurrection of the wicked to the second death will take place at the same time.[131] The saved will be taken to Jerusalem by horses and chariots (Isa. 66: 20), i.e. the angelic powers, and on mules, i.e. the resurrection bodies, on the etymological grounds that *lampnai* (actually covered chariots) stands for the shining glory of the resurrection body.[132]

The last feature of Eusebius' scenario, and one which interested him a great deal, was Christ's subjugation of the evil powers, variously identified as death, Satan, Leviathan, or the dragon-serpent of Isa. 27: 1, the great fish of Job 3: 8, the devil, the lion, and the basilisk.[133] The dragon-serpent is the one with whom the martyrs struggled. With the coming of Christ's kingdom, he and all the evil powers, Paul's rulers of this age (1 Cor. 2: 6), will be confined to prison (Isa. 24: 22).[134] This was the expression of Christ's ultimate triumph, as foreseen by Paul in 1 Cor. 15: 24–8, when God would put all his enemies under his feet, every rule and authority and power, death would be destroyed, and God would be all in all. Christ would rule forever, glorified by his priests, and all his saints co-ruling with him.[135]

Although many of the details of this summary reflect the influence of Alexandrian allegory, it is easy to see that Eusebius has preserved the basic structure of traditional biblical eschatology, in which Christ returns at the end of time to judge all men after a universal resurrection, and to consign them to their respective fates for eternity, the saints with him in bliss, the wicked with the imprisoned and subjugated hostile powers. There is no sense here either that a prolonged process of purification will bring a final *apokatastasis*, or that Eusebius had backed away from the future orientation of traditional

[129] *CI* 170. 30–171. 10; 166. 23–167. 12.
[130] Ibid. 166. 1–15.
[131] Ibid. 397. 25–398. 4.
[132] Ibid. 407. 24–32.
[133] Ibid. 172.5–174.19.
[134] Ibid. 160. 4–16. Cf. also 95. 15–28.
[135] Ibid. 161. 16–35.

eschatology and its expectation of a second parousia.[136] The sufferings of the martyrs, and the fate of all Christians who attempted to live as the meek ones of the Beatitudes, called for vindication by God in a future life, the goal towards which the godly polity journeyed during its tenure in this world before the consummation. Eusebius was undoubtedly too intellectually fastidious to express these hopes in the naïve fashion of the millenarians. Nor would it have been congenial to him to regard the Roman Empire as the domain of Antichrist. Nevertheless, the *Commentary on Isaiah* shows that he was fully committed to the idea of a climactic and definitive consummation of history, in which the church would be purified of all but the saints, and would be joined with her Lord for all eternity.

Finally, we ought to note that if the category of realized eschatology is applicable to Eusebius, in the *Commentary on Isaiah* it fits his view of the institutional church better than it does the empire. The Christian church herself, under the leadership of the bishops, is the godly polity, the city of God on earth, and the fulfilment of the inspired utterances of the greatest of the prophets.

6. Conclusion

The present chapter has shown how Eusebius read back into the text of Isaiah the present-day needs and situation of the Christian church, convinced as he was that this historic community was the Sion and Jerusalem spoken of by the prophet. We have demonstrated in particular how Eusebius directed his exegesis towards the illustration of the hierarchical principle in the church; the character and centrality of the episcopacy; the juxtaposition of two classes of Christians, the totally committed and the nominal; the relation of the church on earth to the heavenly Jerusalem; its relation to the Roman Empire and its Christian emperor; and his expectations of the end of the world and of history.

The cumulative result of this research is to portray Eusebius in a more conventional capacity as a bishop-scholar-apologist devoted to advancing an adequate self-understanding for the church in the face of the new situation created by Constantine's unification of the

---

[136] Implied by Sirinelli, *Les vues historiques*, 482, who sees the parousia as an outmoded relic without actual relevance to Eusebius' real concerns.

empire and his Christian affiliation. The conclusions we have reached call for retouching, though not painting over, the portrait drawn by students of the *Life of Constantine*, the *Tricennial Oration*, the *Treatise on the Holy Sepulchre*, and Book 10 of the *Church History*. The overly sharp lines of that portrait need to be softened by the recognition that the literary conventions of the genre of panegyric disposed Eusebius to formulations and statements that did not preclude his entertainment of other, superficially contradictory ideas.[137]

A promising comprehensive assessment of Eusebius has been proposed by Gerhard Ruhbach.[138] Ruhbach presents Eusebius as a man whose views were fundamentally shaped during the third century— in this respect agreeing with Barnes—but were forced under the pressure of events into a new mould, so that Eusebius is treated as a transitional figure (*Übergangsgestalt*). He shared Origen's theological views and apologetic programme, but lacked his speculative talent and preferred to shape his apologetics in terms of evidence provided by history.[139] For Ruhbach, Eusebius saw the acts of God in history as the best proof of the Gospel.[140] His theological and apologetic outlook was shaped by the Old Testament and its idea of a God who intervenes in history on behalf of his people.[141] This is precisely the outlook of the *Commentary on Isaiah*. Ruhbach insists that Eusebius never abandoned the viewpoint of *Heilsgeschichte* in favour of a secularized and immanent eschatology even in the late works on Constantine. He never became a political theologian in the sense of one who shaped his ideas to justify political policies or was interested in political events for their own sake, but always saw them from a theological and an ecclesiastical perspective.[142] Ruhbach reminds us of the genre limitations of official panegyric and points out, as have others, how Eusebius created a distinctively Christian version of rulership that emphasizes the humanity and moral responsibility of the ruler.[143] He concedes that Eusebius lacked the critical

---

[137] Cf. J. Straub, 'Konstantin als *episkopos tôn ektos*', in *Regeneratio Imperii*, 127 n. 35. See the useful study of G. Vigna, *The Influence of Epideictic Rhetoric on the Political Theology of Eusebius of Caesarea* (Northwestern University diss., 1980).
[138] Ruhbach, 'Die politische Theologie Eusebs von Caesarea', 236–58.
[139] Ibid. 253 f.
[140] Ibid. 241.
[141] Ibid. 253.
[142] Ibid. 248, 250.
[143] Ibid. 248, citing J. Straub, *Vom Herrscherideal in der Spätantike* (Stuttgart, 1939), 129.

capacity to fashion a truly adequate theology of history which saw events fully in the round, from varied perspectives, so that a certain flatness and moralizing quality attaches to his description of contemporary history.[144] He also admits that Eusebius' preoccupation with the needs and interests of the church was seriously inadequate, and certainly paved the way for imperial exploitation.[145] But his basic perspective remained a biblically grounded conviction that God manifested himself in his deeds, the *magnalia Dei*. His enthusiastic and naïve assessment of the new situation presented contemporary history for Christians as the fruit of the long-foreseen designs of God, anticipated in the Old Testament and inaugurated in the Incarnation. The fulfilment of prophecy irradiated the present and suffused it with a sense of realized eschatology that extended to the empire as well as the church, but the latter, not the former, remained the key reference point.

The ecclesiastical orientation which Ruhbach discerned as the dominant theme in Eusebius, and the key to his uncritical praise of Constantine as the instrument of the Logos, also underlies the *Commentary on Isaiah*. Freed from the immediate and distorting presence of the imperial court, Eusebius reveals in this work how the bishop of a large Christian community created a scholarly exegesis that was sensitive and attuned to the radically new situation of the church in the Constantinian era.

---

[144] Ruhbach, 'Die politische Theologie Eusebs von Caesarea', 253.
[145] Ibid. 257.

BIBLIOGRAPHY

Primary Sources

Acta et symbola conciliorum quae saeculo quarto habita sunt, ed. E. J. Jonkers (Leiden: E. J. Brill, 1954).

Analecta sacra spicilegio Solesmensi parata, ed. J. B. Pitra, 8 vols. (Paris: Typis Tusculanis, 1876–83).

Athanasius of Alexandria, *Opera Omnia*, PG xxv.

Barnabas, Letter of, in *Patres apostolici*, ed. F. X. Funk (Tübingen: In Libraria H. Laupp, 1901), 38–98.

The Babylonian Talmud, ed. I. Epstein, 18 vols. (London: Soncino, 1948).

Biblia Hebraica Stuttgartensia, ed. K. Elliger and W. Rudolph (Stuttgart: Deutsche Bibelstiftung, 1977).

Clemens Alexandrinus, ed. O. Stählin, 4 vols. (GCS, nos. 12, 15, 17, 39; Leipzig: J. C. Hinrichs, 1905–36).

Clement, First Letter of, in *Patres apostolici*, ed. F. X. Funk (Tübingen: In Libraria H. Laupp, 1901), 98–184.

——*Second Letter of*, in *Patres apostolici*, ed. F. X. Funk (Tübingen: In Libraria H. Laupp, 1901), 184–211.

Cyprian, *Ad Quirinum*, ed. R. Weber (*CCL* iii; Turnholti: Brepols, 1972), 1–179.

Didascalia Apostolorum, ed. R. H. Connolly (Oxford: Clarendon Press, 1929).

Epictetus, trans. W. A. Oldfather, 2 vols. (LCL; Cambridge, Mass.: Harvard University Press, 1926–8).

Epiphanius of Salamis, *Panarion*, ed. K. Holl, 3 vols. (GCS nos. 25, 31, 37; Leipzig: J. C. Hinrichs, 1915–33).

Epistolographi Graeci, ed. R. Hercher (Paris: A. Firmin Didot, 1873).

Eusebius of Caesarea, *Church History, Life of Constantine, Oration in Praise of Constantine*, trans. A. C. McGiffert and E. C. Richardson, in *A Select Library of Nicene and Post-Nicene Fathers of the Christian Church*, i (repr. Grand Rapids, Mich.: W. Eerdmans, 1982).

——*Commentarii in Psalmos*, PG xxiii and xxiv. 9–76.

——*Die Demonstratio Evangelica*, ed. I. A. Heikel, vi of *Eusebius' Werke* (GCS no. 23; Leipzig: J. C. Hinrichs, 1913).

——*The Ecclesiastical History*, ed. and trans. Kirsopp Lake and J. E. L. Oulton, 2 vols. (LCL; Cambridge, Mass.: Harvard University Press, 1972).

Eusebius of Caesarea, *Eclogae propheticae*, ed. T. Gaisford (Oxford, 1842).

——*Gegen Markell*, ed. E. Klostermann, iv of *Eusebius' Werke* (GCS no. 14; Leipzig: J. C. Hinrichs, 1906).

——*Der Jesajakommentar*, ed. J. Ziegler, ix of *Eusebius' Werke* (GCS; Berlin: Akademie-Verlag, 1975).

——*Die Kirchengeschichte: Über die Märtyrer in Palestina*, ed. E. Schwartz, ii, pts. 1–3 of *Eusebius' Werke* (GCS no. 9, pts. 1–3; Leipzig: J. C. Hinrichs, 1903–9).

——*Das Onomastikon der biblischen Ortsnamen*, ed. E. Klostermann, iii, pt. 1 of *Eusebius' Werke* (GCS no. 11, pt. 1; Leipzig: J. C. Hinrichs, 1904).

——*Die Praeparatio Evangelica*, ed. K. Mras, viii, pts. 1–2 of *Eusebius' Werke* (GCS no. 43, pts. 1–2; Berlin: Akademie-Verlag, 1954, 1956).

——*La Préparation évangélique*, ed. J. Sirinelli, G. Schroeder, E. des Places, *et al.*, Books 1–15 in 9 vols. (SC nos. 206, 215, 228, 262, 266, 292, 307, 338, 369; Paris: Les Éditions du Cerf, 1974–91).

——*Preparation for the Gospel*, trans. with intro. by E. H. Gifford, 2 pts. (repr. Grand Rapids, Mich.: Baker, 1981).

——*The Proof of the Gospel*, ed. and trans. W. J. Ferrar, 2 vols., repr. as one (Grand Rapids, Mich.: Baker, 1981).

——*Die Theophanie*, ed. H. Gressman, iii, pt. 2 of *Eusebius' Werke* (GCS no. 11, pt. 2; Leipzig: J. C. Hinrichs, 1903).

——*Tricennatsrede an Constantin*, ed. I. A. Heikel, i of *Eusebius' Werke* (GCS no. 7; Leipzig: J. C. Hinrichs, 1902), 195–295.

——*Über das Leben des Kaiser Konstantins*, ed. F. Winkelmann, i, pt. 1 of *Eusebius' Werke* (2nd edn., GCS; Berlin: Akademie-Verlag, 1975).

Evagrius Scholasticus, *The Ecclesiastical History of Evagrius*, ed. J. Bidez and L. Parmentier (London: Methuen & Co., 1898).

Hesychius of Alexandria, *Lexicon*, ed. M. Schmidt, 5 vols. (repr. of 1858 edn.; Amsterdam: A. M. Hakkert, 1965).

Historia monachorum in Aegypto, ed. A. J. Festugière (Subsidia Hagiographica, no. 53; Brussels: Société des Bollandistes, 1971).

John Chrysostom, *Opera Omnia*, ed. B. Montfaucon, rev. G. R. L. von Sinner, 13 vols. (Paris: Gaume Brothers, 1834–40).

Irenaeus of Lyons, *Contre les hérésies*, ed. A. Rousseau, L. Doutreleau, *et al.* (SC no. 100, 152, 153, 210, 211, 263, 264; Paris: Les Éditions du Cerf, 1965–82).

——*Démonstration de la prédication apostolique*, trans. with intro. and notes by L. M. Froidevaux (SC no. 62; Paris: Les Éditions du Cerf, 1959).

Isaias, ed. Joseph Ziegler, *Septuaginta: Vetus Testamentum Graecum*, xiv (2nd rev. edn.; Göttingen: Vandenhoeck & Ruprecht, 1967).

Jerome, *Commentariorum in Esaiam libri I–XVIII*, in S. Hieronymi Presbyteri, *Opera*, pt. 1: *Opera Exegetica*, 2 and 2A., ed. M. Adriaen (*CCL* lxxiii–lxxiiiA; Turnholti: Brepols, 1963).

Josephus, ed. and trans. H. St. J. Thackeray, R. Marcus, A. Wikgren, L. H. Feldman, 9 vols. (LCL; Cambridge, Mass.: Harvard University Press, 1929–63).

Justin Martyr, *Die Apologien Justins des Märtyrers*, ed. G. Krüger (Sammlung ausgewählter kirchen- und dogmengeschichtlichen Quellenschriften, i, pt. 1., 4th rev. edn.; Tübingen: J. C. B. Mohr, 1915; repr., Frankfurt: Minerva, 1968).

——*Dialogue avec Tryphon*, introduction, notes, and index by Georges Archambault, 2 vols. (Textes et documents pour l'étude historique du christianisme, nos. 8, 11; Paris: A. Picard, 1909–14).

Lactantius, *Institutions divines*, introduction, text, and trans. by P. Monat (SC nos. 204–5, 326, 337, 377; Paris: Les Éditions du Cerf, 1973–92).

Liber Interpretationis Hebraicorum Nominum, in Paul de Lagarde (ed.), *Onomastica sacra* (2nd edn.; Göttingen, 1887, 26–111; repr. in S. Hieronymi Presbyteri, *Opera*, pt. 1: *Opera Exegetica*, 1; CCL lxxii; Turnholti: Brepols, 1969), 59–161.

Macarius the Egyptian, *Die fünfzigen geistlichen Homilien des Macarius*, ed. H. Dörries, E. Klostermann, and M. Kroeger (Patristische Texte und Studien, no. 4; Berlin, 1964).

Martyrdom of Polycarp, in *Patres apostolici*, ed. F. X. Funk (Tübingen: In Libraria H. Laupp, 1901), 314–42.

Midrash Rabbah, ed. H. Freedman and M. Simon, 10 vols. (London: Soncino Press, 1939).

The New Oxford Annotated Bible with the Apocrypha: New Revised Standard Version, ed. Bruce M. Metzger and Roland M. Murphy (New York: Oxford University Press, 1991).

Novatian, *Opera*, ed. G. F. Diercks (CCL iv; Turnholti: Brepols, 1972).

Novum Testamentum Graece, ed. E. Nestle and K. Aland, *et al.* (26th revd. edn.; Stuttgart: Deutsche Bibelstiftung, 1979).

Origen of Alexandria, *Commentaire sur S. Jean*, Books VI and X, ed. C. Blanc (SC no. 157; Paris: Les Éditions du Cerf, 1970).

——*Commentary and Homilies on the Song of Songs*, trans. and annotated by R. P. Lawson (Ancient Christian Writers, xxvi; Westminster, Md.: Newman, 1957).

——*Contra Celsum*, trans. with introduction and notes by Henry Chadwick (Cambridge: Cambridge University Press, 1965).

——*Commentaire sur le Cantique des Cantiques*, introduction, trans., and notes by L. Brésard, H. Crouzel, and M. Borret (SC nos. 375–6; Paris: Les Éditions du Cerf, 1991–2).

——*Contre Celse*, introduction, text, trans., and notes by M. Borret (SC nos. 132, 136, 147, 150, 227; Paris: Les Éditions du Cerf, 1967–76).

——*Homélies sur Jérémie*, trans. P. Husson and P. Nautin, with Introduction and notes by P. Nautin, 2 vols. (SC nos. 232, 238; Paris: Les Éditions du Cerf, 1976–7).

Origen of Alexandria, *Homélies sur Josué*, ed. A. Jaubert (SC no. 71; Paris: Les Éditions du Cerf, 1960).

—— *Homélies sur S. Luc*, ed. H. Crouzel, F. Fournier, and P. Périchon (SC no. 87; Paris: Les Éditions du Cerf, 1962).

—— *Homiliae in Isaiam*, PG xiii. 219–53.

—— *Der Johanneskommentar*, ed. E. Preuschen, iv of *Origenes' Werke* (GCS no. 10; Leipzig: J. C. Hinrichs, 1903), 1–574.

—— *Klageliederkommentar*, ed. E. Klostermann, iii of *Origenes' Werke* (GCS no. 6; Leipzig: J. C. Hinrichs, 1901), 233–79.

—— *On First Principles*, trans. with Introduction and notes by G. W. Butterworth (New York: Harper & Row, 1966).

—— *Philocalie 21–27 (Sur le libre arbitre)*, ed. E. Junod (SC no. 226; Paris: Les Éditions du Cerf, 1976).

—— *Traité des principes*, introduction, critical text, trans., notes, fragments, by H. Crouzel and M. Simonetti (SC nos. 252, 253, 268, 269, 312; Paris: Les Éditions du Cerf, 1978–84).

Palladius, *Historia Lausiaca*, PG xxxiv. 991–1262.

Pamphilus of Caesarea, *Apologia Pamphili Martyri pro Origene*, PG xvii. 539–616.

Patrologiae cursus completus... Series Graeca, ed. J. P. Migne, 161 vols. (Paris: Seu Petit-Montrouge, 1857–66).

Patrologiae cursus completus... Series Latina, ed. J. P. Migne, 221 vols. (Paris: Garnier, 1841–1905).

Patres apostolici, ed. F. X. Funk (Tübingen: In Libraria H. Laupp, 1901).

Philo, 10 vols. with 2 suppl., trans. F. H. Colson and G. H. Whitaker; suppl. from the Armenian by R. Marcus (LCL; Cambridge, Mass.: Harvard University Press, 1924–62).

Plutarch, *Moralia*, 16 vols. (LCL; Cambridge, Mass.: Harvard University Press, 1927–69).

Die Pseudoklementinischen Homilien, ed. B. Rehm (GCS no. 41; Berlin: Akademie-Verlag, 1953).

Septuaginta: Vetus Testamentum graece iuxta LXX interpretes, ed. Alfred Rahlfs, 2 vols. (9th edn.; Stuttgart: Deutsche Bibelstiftung, 1935).

Socrates, *Historia ecclesiastica*, PG lxvii. 29–872.

Tatian, *Oratio contra Graecos*, ed. E. Schwartz (TU, no. 4, pt. 1; Berlin, 1888).

Tertullian, *Adversus Iudaeos*, ed. H. Tränkle (Wiesbaden: Franz Steiner Verlag, 1964).

—— *Adversus Marcionem*, ed. A. Kroymann (*CSEL* xlvii; Vienna: F. Tempsky, 1906), 290–650.

—— *Adversus Praxean*, ed. A. Kroymann and E. Evans (*CCL* ii; Turnholti: Brepols, 1954), 1157–1205.

Theodoret of Cyrus, *Commentaire sur Isaie*, ed. J.-N. Guinot (SC no. 276, 295, 315; Paris: Les Éditions du Cerf, 1980–4).

——*Interpretatio in Isaiam*, *PG* lxxxi.

——*Kirchengeschichte*, ed. L. Parmentier (2nd edn., F. Scheidweiler, GCS no. 44; Berlin: Akademie-Verlag, 1954).

——*Kommentar zu Jesaia*, ed. A. von Möhle (Mitteilungen des Septuaginta-Unternehmens der Gesellschaft der Wissenschaften zu Göttingen, 5; Berlin: Wiedemann, 1932).

The Theodosian Code and the Novels, and the Sirmondian Constitutions, ed. and trans. Clyde Pharr (Princeton: Princeton University Press, 1952).

Victorinus of Pettau, *Opera*, ed. and annotated with Introduction by J. Haussleiter (*CSEL* xlix; Vienna: F. Tempsky, 1916).

Urkunden der Ptolemäerzeit, ed. Ulrich Wilken, 2 vols. (Berlin: Walter de Gruyter, 1927–57).

Secondary Sources

Ackroyd, P. R., and Evans, C. F. (eds.), *The Cambridge History of the Bible*, i: *From the Beginnings to Jerome* (Cambridge: Cambridge University Press, 1970).

Aland, Kurt, 'Die Christen und der Staat nach Phil. 3: 20', in *Paganisme, Judaisme, Christianisme: Influences et affrontements dans le monde antique: Mélanges offerts à Marcel Simon* (Paris: Éditions E. de Boccard, 1978), 247–59.

——'Die religiöse Haltung Kaiser Konstantins', *SP* 1. TU, no. 63 (Berlin: Akademie-Verlag, 1957), 549–600.

——'Kaiser und Kirche von Konstantin bis Byzanz', in Ruhbach (ed.), *Die Kirche angesichts der Konstantinischen Wende* (Darmstadt: Wissenschaftliche Buchgesellschaft, 1976), 42–73.

Altaner, B., and Stuiber, A. (eds.), *Patrologie: Leben Schriften und Lehre der Kirchenväter* (9th edn.; Freiburg: Herder, 1980).

Anastos, Milton V., 'Porphyry's Attack on the Bible', in Luitpold Wallach (ed.), *The Classical Tradition: Studies in Honor of Harry Caplan* (Ithaca, NY: Cornell University Press, 1966), 421–50.

The Anchor Bible Dictionary, ed. D. N. Freedman *et al.*, 6 vols. (New York: Doubleday, 1992).

Attridge, Harold, and Hata, Gohei (eds.), *Eusebius, Christianity, and Judaism* (Detroit: Wayne State University Press, 1992).

Avi-Yonah, Michael, *The Jews of Palestine: A Political History from the Bar Kochba War to the Arab Conquest* (New York: Schocken Books, 1976).

Baehrens, W. A., 'Die neunte fragmentarische Jesaiahomilie des Origenes eine Fälschung', *Theologische Literaturzeitung*, 49 (1924), 263–4.

Bardy, G., 'La Littérature patristique des Quaestiones et Responsiones sur l'Écriture sainte', *RB* 41 (1932), 228–36.

Bardy, G., 'La Théologie d'Eusèbe de Césarée d'après *l'Histoire ecclésiastique*', *RHE* 50 (1935), 5–20.

——'Les Traditions Juives dans l'œuvre d'Origène', *RB* 34 (1925), 217–52.

Barnes, Timothy D., 'Constantine and the Christians of Persia', *Journal of Roman Studies*, 75 (1985), 126–36.

——*Constantine and Eusebius* (Cambridge, Mass.: Harvard University Press, 1981).

——*The New Empire of Diocletian and Constantine* (Cambridge, Mass.: Harvard University Press, 1982).

——'Origen, Aquila and Eusebius', *Harvard Studies in Classical Philology*, 74 (1970), 313–16.

——'Panegyric, History and Hagiography in Eusebius' *Life of Constantine*', in R. Williams (ed.), *The Making of Orthodoxy: Essays in Honour of Henry Chadwick* (Cambridge: Cambridge University Press, 1989), 94–123.

——'Two Speeches by Eusebius', *Greek, Roman and Byzantine Studies*, 18 (1977), 341–2.

Barrett, C. K., 'The Interpretation of the Old Testament in the New', in Ackroyd and Evans (eds.), *The Cambridge History of the Bible* (Cambridge: Cambridge University Press, 1970), i. 377–411.

Barthélemy, D., 'Eusèbe, la Septante, et les "autres"', in André Benoit (ed.), *La Bible et les pères* (Colloque de Strasbourg, 1969; Paris: Presses universitaires de France, 1971), 51–65.

Bate, H. N., 'Some Technical Terms of Greek Exegesis', *JTS* 24 (1922–3), 59–66.

Bauer, J. B., 'Zions Flüsse, Ps. 45(46), 5', in J. B. Bauer and J. Marbock (eds.), *Memoria Jerusalem: Freundesgabe Franz Sauer zum 70. Geburtstag* (Graz: Akademischer Druck, 1977), 59–91.

Baynes, N. H., *Constantine the Great and the Christian Church* (repr. from *Proceedings of the British Academy*, 15 (1929); London: Oxford University Press, 1931), 341–442.

——'Eusebius and the Christian Empire', in *Byzantine Studies and Other Essays*; repr. from *Mélanges Bidez* (Annuaire de l'Institut de Philologie et d'Histoire Orientales et Slaves, 2; Brussels, 1934; London: Athlone Press, 1955), 168–72.

Berkhof, Hendrik, *Kirche und Kaiser: Eine Untersuchung der byzantinischen und der theokratischen Staatsauffassung im vierten Jahrhundert* (Zürich: Evangelischer Verlag, 1947).

——*Die Theologie des Eusebius von Caesarea* (Amsterdam, 1939).

Beskow, Per, *Rex Gloriae: The Kingship of Christ in the Early Church*, trans. Eric J. Sharpe (Uppsala: Almquist & Wiksell, 1962).

Beumer, Johannes, S. J., 'Die altchristliche Idee einer präexistierenden Kirche und ihre theologische Anwendung', *Wissenschaft und Weisheit*, 9 (1942), 13–22.

Biblia Patristica: Index des citations et allusions bibliques dans la littérature patristique, 6 vols. (Centre d'analyse et de documentation patristique; Paris: Éditions du centre national de la recherche scientifique, 1975–).

Bieder, Werner, *Ekklesia und Polis im Neuen Testament und in der alten Kirche: Zugleich eine Auseinandersetzung mit Erik Petersons Kirchenbegriff* (Zürich: Zwingli Verlag, 1941).

Bienert, Wolfgang A., *'Allêgoria' und 'Anagôgê' bei Didymos dem Blinden von Alexandrien* (Patristische Texte und Studien, no. 13; Berlin: Walter de Gruyter, 1972).

Bietenhard, Hans, *Caesarea, Origenes und die Juden* (Franz Delitzsch Vorlesungen, 1972; Stuttgart: Verlag W. Kohlhammer, 1974).

Boer, W. den, 'Allegory and History', in W. den Boer *et al.* (eds.), *Romanitas et Christianitas. Studia Iano Henrico Waszink A. D. VI Kal. Nov. A. MCMLXXIII XIII lustra complenti oblata* (Amsterdam: North-Holland Publishing Co., 1973), 15–27.

Bonwetsch, N., 'Der Schriftbeweis für die Kirche aus den Heiden als das wahre Israel bis auf Hippolyt', in *Theologische Studien Theodor Zahn dargebracht* (Leipzig: Deichert, 1908), 1–22.

Bowersock, Glen, 'The Arabian Ares', in Gabba (ed.), *Tria Corda* (Como: Edizioni New Press, 1983), 43–7.

Brown, Francis, Driver, S. R., and Briggs, C. A. (eds.), *Hebrew and English Lexicon of the Old Testament* (Oxford: Clarendon Press, 1977).

Brown, Raymond, Donfried, Karl, and Reumann, John (eds.), *Peter in the New Testament: A Collaborative Assessment by Protestant and Roman Catholic Scholars* (Minneapolis: Augsburg Publishing House, 1973).

Burckhardt, Jacob, *The Age of Constantine the Great*, trans. Moses Hadas (New York: Vintage Books, 1967).

Cameron, Averil, 'Eusebius of Caesarea and the Re-Thinking of History' in Gabba (ed.), *Tria Corda* (Como: Edizioni New Press, 1983), 82–8.

——*Christianity and the Rhetoric of Empire: The Development of Christian Discourse* (Sather Classical Lectures, no. 55; Berkeley: University of California Press, 1991).

Campenhausen, Hans Freiherr von, *The Formation of the Christian Bible*, trans. J. A. Baker (Philadelphia: Fortress Press, 1972).

Cangh, Jean-Marie van, 'Nouveaux fragments hexaplaires: *Commentaire sur Isaïe* d'Eusèbe de Césarée', *RB* 78 (1971), 384–91.

Caspary, Gerard E., *Politics and Exegesis: Origen and the Two Swords* (Berkeley: University of California Press, 1979).

Causse, A., 'De la Jérusalem terrestre à la Jérusalem céleste', *Revue de l'histoire et de la philosophie religieuse*, 27 (1942), 12–36.

——'Le mythe de la nouvelle Jérusalem du Deutero-Esaie à la IIIe Sibylle', *Revue de l'histoire et de la philosophie religieuse*, 18 (1938), 376–414.

Chadwick, Henry, 'Evidences of Christianity in the Apologetic of Origen', *SP* 2. TU, no. 64 (Berlin: Akademie-Verlag, 1957), 331–9.

Chadwick, Henry, 'The Fall of Eustathius of Antioch', *JTS* 49 (1948), 27–35.

Chênevert, Jacques, S. J., *L'Église dans le Commentaire d'Origène sur le Cantique des Cantiques* (Studia: Travaux de recherche, 24; Brussels: Desclée de Brouwer, 1969).

Chesnut, Glenn, *The First Christian Histories. Eusebius, Socrates, Sozomen, Theodoret and Evagrius* (Théologie historique, 46; Paris: Éditions Beauchesnes, 1977; rev. edn. Macon, Ga.: Mercer University Press, 1986).

Cohen, J., 'Roman Imperial Policy toward the Jews from Constantine until the End of the Palestinian Patriarchate (ca. 429)', *Byzantine Studies*, 3 (1976), 1–29.

Congar, Y.-M.-J., 'Ecclesia ab Abel', in *Abhandlungen über Theologie und Kirche: Festschrift für Karl Adam* (Düsseldorf: Patmos Verlag, 1952), 79–108.

Cox, Patricia, *Biography in Late Antiquity* (Berkeley: University of California, 1983).

Cranz, F. E., 'Kingdom and Polity in the Theology of Eusebius of Caesarea', *HTR* 45 (1952), 47–66.

Crouzel, Henri, 'La distinction de la "typologie" et "d'allégorie"', *Bulletin de la littérature ecclésiastique*, 65 (1964), 161–74.

——*Origen: The Life and Thought of the First Great Theologian*, trans. A. W. Worrell (San Francisco: Harper and Row, 1989).

Curti, C., 'Eusebio di Caesarea', *Dizionario patristico e di antichità cristiane* (1983), i. 1285–93.

——'Il linguaggio relativo al Padre e al Figlio in alcuni passi dei "Commentarii in Psalmos" di Eusebio di Caesarea', *Augustinianum*, 13 (1973), 483–506.

——'L'interpretazione di Ps. 67: 14 in Eusebio di Caesarea', in *Paradoxa politeia: Studi patristici in onore di Giuseppe Lazzati* (Milan: Vita e pensiero, 1979), 195–207.

Daniélou, Jean, *A History of Early Christian Doctrine before the Council of Nicaea*, trans. John A. Baker, 3 vols. (London: Darton, Longman & Todd, 1964–77).

——*Origen*, trans. Walter Mitchell (New York: Sheed & Ward, 1955).

Decker, D. de, and Dupuis-Masay, G., '"L'Épiscopat" de l'empereur Constantin', *Byzantion*, 50 (1980), 118–57.

Devreesse, Robert, *Essai sur Théodore de Mopsueste* (Studi e Testi, no. 141; Vatican City: Vatican Library, 1984).

——'L'Édition du commentaire d'Eusèbe de Césarée sur Isaïe: Interpolations et omissions', *RB* 42 (1933), 540–55.

Dictionnaire de spiritualité ascetique et mystique, doctrine et histoire, ed. Marcel Viller *et al.*, 12 vols. to date (Paris: Beauchesne, 1932–).

Dizionario patristico e di antichità cristiane, ed. Angelo Di Berardino, 3 vols. (Casale Monferrato: Marietti, 1983–8).

Dodd, C. H., *According to the Scriptures* (London: Nisbet, 1952).

Dodds, E. R., *The Greeks and the Irrational* (Sather Classical Lectures, no. 25; Berkeley: University of California Press, 1951).

Dörries, H., *Das Selbstzeugnis Kaiser Konstantins* (Abhandlungen der Akademie der Wissenschaften in Göttingen; Philologisch-historische Klasse, 3rd ser., no. 34; Göttingen: Vandenhoeck & Ruprecht, 1954).

Drake, H. A., *In Praise of Constantine: A Historical Study and New Translation* (Classical Studies, no. 15; Berkeley: University of California, 1976).

—— 'What Eusebius Knew: The Genesis of the *Vita Constantini*', *Classical Philology*, 83 (1988), 20–38.

Dummer, J., 'Zwei neue Bände des Eusebius-Ausgabe in den Griechischen Christlichen Schriftstellern', *Klio*, 62 (1980), 597–601.

Dvornik, Francis, *Early Christian and Byzantine Political Philosophy*, 2 vols. (Washington, DC: Dumbarton Oaks, 1966).

Eger, Hans, 'Kaiser und Kirche in der Geschichtstheologie Eusebs von Cäsarea', *ZNW* 38 (1939), 97–115.

Ehrhardt, A. A. T., 'Constantin d. Gr. Religionspolitik und Gesetzgebung', *Zeitschrift der Savigny-Stiftung, Romanistische Abteilung*, 72 (1955), 127–90.

—— 'Constantine, Rome, and the Rabbis', *Bulletin of the John Rylands Library*, 42 (1959–60), 288–312.

—— 'Das Corpus Christi und die Korporationen im spätrömischen Recht', *Zeitschrift der Savigny-Stiftung, Romanistische Abteilung*, 70 (1953), 299–347; 71 (1954), 25–40.

Encyclopedia Judaica, 16 vols. (Jerusalem: Macmillan, 1972).

Fascher, E., 'Jerusalems Untergang in der urchristlichen und altkirchlichen Überlieferung', *Theologische Literaturzeitung*, 89 (1964), 81–98.

Faulhaber, Michael von, *Biblische Studien*, iv, pts. 2 and 3: *Die Propheten-Catenen nach römischen Handschriften* (Freiburg: Herder, 1899).

Fox, Robin Lane, *Pagans and Christians* (New York: Alfred Knopf, 1987).

Gabba, E., (ed.), *Tria Corda: Scritti in onore di Arnaldo Momigliano* (Como: Edizioni New Press, 1983).

Gager, John, *Moses in Greco-Roman Paganism* (Society of Biblical Literature Monograph Series, 16; Nashville: Abingdon Press, 1972).

—— *The Origins of Anti-Semitism* (Oxford: Oxford University Press, 1985).

Geerard, Maurits (ed.), *Clavis patrum Graecorum: qua optimae quaeque scriptorum patrum Graecorum recensiones a primaevis saeculis usque ad octavum commode recluduntur*, 5 vols. (Turnhout: Brepols, 1974–87).

Gerber, W. E., 'Exegese III (NT u. Alte Kirche)', *Reallexikon für Antike und Christentum*, vi. 1211–29.

Ginzberg, L., 'Die Haggada bei den Kirchenvätern, VI: Der Kommentar des Hieronymus zu Jesaja', in S. W. Baron and A. Marx (eds.), *Jewish Studies in Memory of George A. Kohut* (New York: Alexander Kohut Memorial Foundation, 1935), 279–314.

Ginzberg, L., *The Legends of the Jews*, trans. Henrietta Szold, 7 vols. (Philadelphia: Jewish Publication Society of America, 1946–64).

Gozzo, S., 'De Hieronymi commentario in Isaiae librum', *Antonianum*, 35 (1960), 49–78, 168–214.

Grant, Robert M., *The Apostolic Fathers: A New Translation and Commentary*, i: *An Introduction* (New York: Thomas Nelson & Sons, 1964).

——'Early Alexandrian Christianity', *CH* 40 (1971), 133–44.

——'Eusebius and His Lives of Origen', in *Forma Futuri: Studi in onore del Cardinale M. Pellegrino* (Turin: Bottega d'Erasmo, 1975), 635–49.

——*Eusebius as Church Historian* (Oxford: Clarendon Press, 1980).

——*From Augustus to Constantine: The Thrust of the Christian Movement into the Roman World* (New York: Harper & Row, 1970).

——*The Letter and the Spirit* (London: SPCK, 1957).

——'Porphyry Among the Early Christians', in den Boer *et al.* (eds.), *Romanitas et Christianitas* (Amsterdam: North-Holland Publishing Co., 1973), 181–7.

——'The Religion of Maximin Daia', in *Christianity, Judaism, and Other Graeco-Roman Cults: Studies for M. Smith*, 4 vols. (Studies in Judaism and Late Antiquity, no. 12; Leiden: E. J. Brill, 1975), iv. 143–66.

——*A Short History of Biblical Interpretation* (New York: Macmillan, 1948).

——'The Stromateis of Origen', in J. Fontaine and C. Kannengiesser (eds.), *EPEKTASIS: Mélanges patristiques offerts au Cardinal Jean Daniélou* (Paris: Beauchesne, 1972), 285–92.

Grillmeier, Aloys, *Christ in Christian Tradition: From the Apostolic Age to Chalcedon (451)*, trans. J. S. Bowden (New York: Sheed & Ward, 1965).

Groh, Dennis, 'The *Onomasticon* of Eusebius and the Rise of Christian Palestine', *SP* 18 (1983), 23–32.

Gryson, Roger, and Szmatula, Dominique, 'Les commentaires patristiques sur Isaïe d'Origène à Jérôme', *Revue des Études Augustiniennes*, 35 (1990), 3–41.

Guillet, J., 'Les exégèses d'Alexandrie et d'Antioche: Conflit ou malentendu?', *RSR* 34 (1947), 257–302.

Haenchen, Ernst, *Die Apostelgeschichte* (Kritisch-exegetischer Kommentar über das Neue Testament, begründet von H. A. W. Meyer, 3rd division, 10th edn.; Göttingen: Vandenhoeck and Ruprecht, 1956).

Hanson, R. P. C., *Allegory and Event: A Study of the Sources and the Significance of Origen's Interpretation of Scripture* (Richmond: John Knox, 1959).

——'Biblical Exegesis in the Early Church', in Ackroyd and Evans (eds.), *The Cambridge History of the Bible* (Cambridge: Cambridge University Press, 1970), i. 412–53.

—— *The Search for the Christian Doctrine of God: The Arian Controversy 318–81 AD* (Edinburgh: T & T. Clark, 1991).

Harl, M., 'L'histoire de l'humanité racontée par un écrivain chrétien au debut du IVe siècle', *Revue des études grecques*, 75 (1962), 522–31.

Harnack, Adolf von, *Geschichte der altchristlichen Literatur bis Eusebius*, 2 vols. (Leipzig: J. C. Hinrichs, 1958).

—— *History of Dogma*, trans. from the 3rd German edn. by Neil Buchanan, 7 vols. bound as 4 (New York: Dover, 1961).

——*Judentum und Juden-christentum in Justins Dialog mit Tryphon*, TU, 39 (Leipzig: J. C. Hinrichs, 1913), 47–98.

—— *The Mission and Expansion of Christianity in the First Three Centuries*, trans. and ed. by James Moffatt of i of 2nd German edn. of 1906 (London: Williams and Norgate, 1908; repr. with intro. by Jaroslav Pelikan, New York: Harper Torchbooks, 1961).

Harris, J. Rendel, *Testimonies*, 2 vols. (Cambridge: Cambridge University Press, 1916–20).

Hefele, C. J., and Leclercq, H., *Histoire des conciles d'après les documents*, 12 vols. in 21 parts (Paris: Letouzey et Ané, 1907–52).

Hollerich, Michael, 'Myth and History in Eusebius' *De vita Constantini*: *Vit. Const.* 1.12 in its Contemporary Setting', *HTR* 82 (1989), 421–45.

—— 'Origen's Exegetical Heritage in the Early Fourth Century: The Evidence of Eusebius', in Robert J. Daly (ed.), *Origeniana Quinta* (Leuven: Peeters Press, 1992), 542–8.

—— 'Religion and Politics in the Writings of Eusebius of Caesarea: Reassessing the First "Court Theologian" ', *CH* 59 (1990), 309–25.

Huber, W., *Passa und Ostern: Untersuchungen zur Osterfeier der alten Kirche* (Beihefte zur Zeitschrift für die neutestamentliche Wissenschaft, no. 35; Berlin, 1969).

Hulen, A. B., 'The Dialogues with the Jews', *JBL* (1932), 58–70.

Hunt, E. D., *Holy Land Pilgrimage in the Later Roman Empire 312–460* (Oxford: Clarendon Press, 1982).

The Interpreter's Dictionary of the Bible, ed. George Arthur Buttrick, 4 vols. (Nashville: Abingdon, 1962).

Jay, Pierre, *L'exégèse de Saint Jérôme, d'après son 'Commentaire sur Isaïe'* (Paris: Études Augustiniennes, 1985).

Jellicoe, Sidney, *The Septuagint and Modern Study* (Oxford: Clarendon Press, 1968)

Jones, A. H. M., *Constantine and the Conversion of Europe* (rev. edn., New York: Collier Books, 1962).

—— *The Later Roman Empire. A Social Economic and Administrative Survey, 284–602*, 2 vols. (Norman, Okla.: University of Oklahoma Press, 1964).

Kee, Alistair, *Constantine versus Christ: The Triumph of Ideology* (London: SCM Press, 1982).

Kelly, J. N. D., *Early Christian Creeds* (3rd edn.; New York: Longmans, 1972).

——*Early Christian Doctrines* (London: A. & C. Black, 1958).

——*Jerome: His Life, Writings, and Controversies* (New York: Harper & Row, 1975).

Klostermann, E., 'Formen der exegetischen Arbeiten des Origenes', *Theologische Literaturzeitung*, 72 (1947), 203–8.

Kraft, Heinz, *Kaiser Konstantins religiöse Entwicklung* (Beiträge zur historischen Theologie, 20; Tübingen: J. C. B. Mohr, 1955).

——(ed.), *Konstantin der Grosse* (Wege der Forschung, 131; Darmstadt: Wissenschaftliche Buchgesellschaft, 1974).

——'Zur Taufe Kaiser Konstantins', *SP* 1. TU, no. 63 (Berlin: Akademie-Verlag, 1957), 642–8.

Kraft, Robert A., 'Barnabas' Isaiah Text and the "Testimony Book" Hypothesis', *JBL* 79 (1960), 336–50.

de Labriolle, Pierre, 'La polemique antimontaniste contre la prophétie extatique', *Revue d'histoire et de littérature religieuses*, 11 (1906), 97–145.

Ladner, Gernard, *The Idea of Reform: Its Impact on Thought and Action in the Age of the Fathers* (rev. edn.; New York: Harper & Row, 1967).

Lamirande, Émilien, O. M. I., *L'Église céleste selon Saint Augustin* (Paris: Études Augustiniennes, 1963).

——'Jérusalem céleste', *Dictionnaire de spiritualité* (1974), viii. 944–58.

Lampe, G. W. H. (ed.), *A Patristic Greek Lexicon* (Oxford: Clarendon Press, 1968).

Lange, Nicholas de, *Origen and the Jews: Studies in Jewish–Christian Relations in Third-Century Palestine* (University of Cambridge Oriental Publications, no. 25; Cambridge: Cambridge University Press, 1976).

Laurin, Joseph-Rheal, O. M. I., *Orientations maîtresses des apologistes chrétiens de 270 à 361* (Analecta Gregoriana, 61; Rome: apud aedes univ. Gregorianae, 1954).

Levine, Lee I., *Caesarea Under Roman Rule* (Studies in Judaism in Late Antiquity, 7; Leiden: E. J. Brill, 1975).

Lightfoot, J. B., 'Eusebius of Caesarea', *Dictionary of Christian Biography* (1880), ii. 308–48.

Linder, Amnon, *The Jews in Roman Imperial Legislation* (Detroit: Wayne State University Press, 1987).

Lohmeyer, Ernst, *Philipper-, Kolosser-, Philemon-Briefe* (Kritisch-exegetischer Kommentar über das neue Testament, begründet von H. A. W. Meyer, 9th division, 13th edn.; Göttingen: Vandenhoeck & Ruprecht, 1964).

Lohse, Bernhard, *Das Passafest der Quartadecimaner* (Gütersloh: C. Bertelsmann, 1953).

Lohse, Eduard, '*Siôn, Ierousalêm*', *Theological Dictionary of the New Testament* (1971), vii. 292–338.

Louth, Andrew, 'The Date of Eusebius' *Historia Ecclesiastica*', *JTS* NS 41 (1990), 111–23.

de Lubac, Henri, *Exégèse médiévale: Les Quatre sens de l'écriture*, 4 vols. in 3 parts (Théologie, nos. 41–2, 59; Paris: Aubier, 1959–64).

——*Histoire et esprit. L'Intelligence de l'écriture d'après d'Origène* (Théologie, no. 16; Paris: Aubier, 1950).

——'Sens spirituel', *RSR* 36 (1949), 542–76.

——' "Typologie" et "Allégorisme" ', *RSR* 34 (1947), 180–226.

Luibheid, Colm, *Eusebius of Caesarea and the Arian Crisis* (Dublin: Irish Academic Press, 1978).

McArthur, Harvey D., 'The Eusebian Sections and Canons', *CBQ* 27 (1975), 250–6.

Mercati, Giovanni, *Opere minori*, 5 vols. (Studi e Testi, nos. 76–80; Vatican City: Vatican Library, 1937–41).

Möhle, A., 'Der Jesaia-kommentar des Eusebius von Kaisareia fast vollständig wieder aufgefunden', *ZNW* 33 (1934), 87–9.

Momigliano, Arnaldo, 'Pagan and Christian Historiography in the Fourth Century', in Momigliano, *The Conflict between Paganism and Christianity in the Fourth Century* (Oxford: Clarendon Press, 1963), 79–99.

Moore, George F., *Judaism in the First Centuries of the Christian Era: The Age of the Tannaim*, 3 vols. (Cambridge, Mass.: Harvard University Press, 1955).

Moreau, J., 'Eusebius von Caesarea', *Reallexikon für Antike and Christentum*, vi. 1052–88.

Nautin, Pierre, *Origène: Sa vie et son œuvre* (Christianisme antique, no. 1; Paris: Beauchesne, 1977).

Nestle, Eberhard, 'Alttestamentliches aus Eusebius', *Zeitschrift für die alttestamentliche Wissenschaft*, 29 (1909), 57–62.

Odahl, Charles M., 'The Use of Apocalyptic Imagery in Constantine's Christian Propaganda', *Centerpoint*, 4 (1981), 9–20.

Olsen, Glen, 'Allegory, Typology, and Symbol: The *sensus spiritualis*, pt. I: Definitions and Earliest History; pt. II: Early Church through Origen', *Communio*, 4 (1977), 161–79, 357–84.

Opitz, Hans-Georg, 'Euseb von Caesarea als Theologe', *ZNW* 34 (1935), 1–19.

Papazoglou, F., 'Une signification tardive du mot *politeia*', *Revue des études grecques*, 72 (1959), 100–5.

Parkes, James William, *The Conflict of the Church and the Synagogue: A Study in the Origins of Antisemitism* (London: Soncino Press, 1934).

Paulys Realencyclopädie der classischen Altertumswissenschaft (new edn. begun by Georg Wissowa, continued by Wilhelm Kroll and Karl Mittelhaus, with the collaboration of numerous specialists, ed. Konrat Ziegler; Stuttgart and Munich: Alfred Druckenmüller, 1894–1980).

Pelikan, Jaroslav, *The Christian Tradition: A History of the Development of Doctrine*, i: *The Emergence of the Catholic Tradition 100–600* (Chicago: University of Chicago Press, 1971).

Pepin, Jean, *Mythe et allégorie: Les origines grecques et les contestations judéo-chrétiennes* (2nd rev. edn.; Paris: Études Augustiniennes, 1976).

Peterson, Erik, *Der Monotheismus als politisches Problem: Ein Beitrag zur Geschichte der politischen Theologie im Imperium Romanum* (Leipzig: Jakob Hegner, 1935; repr. in *Theologische Traktate*; Munich: Hochland Bücherei, 1951), 45–147.

des Places, Eduard, *Eusèbe de Césarée commentateur: Platonisme et écriture sainte* (Théologie historique, no. 63; Paris: Éditions Beauchesnes, 1982).

——'Numénius et Eusèbe de Césarée', *SP* 13. TU, no. 116 (Berlin: Akademie-Verlag, 1975), 19–28.

Preisigke, Friederich (ed.), *Wörterbuch der griechischen Papyrusurkunden*, 3 vols. (Berlin: Selbstverlag der Erben, 1925–31).

Prestige, G. L., *God in Patristic Thought* (London: SPCK, 1952).

Prigent, Pierre, *Justin et l'ancien Testament* (Études bibliques; Paris: Librairie Lecoffre, 1964).

——*Les testimonia dans le christianisme primitif: L'Épitre de Barnabé (I à XVI) et ses sources* (Paris: J. Gabalda, 1961).

Quasten, Johannes, *Patrology*, 3 vols. (repr. Westminster, Md.: Christian Classics, 1983); iv ed. A. Di Berardino (Westminster, Md.: Christian Classics, 1986).

Rad, Gerhard von, *Old Testament Theology*, ii: *The Theology of Israel's Prophetic Traditions*, trans. D. M. G. Stalker (New York: Harper & Row, 1965).

Rahner, Hugo, 'Flumina de ventre Christi: Die patristische Auslegung von Joh 7: 37–38', *Biblia*, 22 (1941), 269–302, 367–403.

Reallexikon für Antike und Christentum: Sachwörterbuch zur Auseinandersetzung des Christentums mit der antiken Welt, ed. Theodor Klauser, Hans Lietzmann, J. H. Waszink, Leopold Wenger, F. J. Dölger (in progress, Leipzig: K. W. Hiersemann, 1941–).

Ricken, F., 'Die Logoslehre des Eusebios von Caesarea und der Mittelplatonismus', *Theologie und Philosophie*, 42 (1967), 341–56.

——'Nikaia als Krisis des altchristlichen Platonismus', *Theologie und Philosophie*, 44 (1969), 321–41.

Rondeau, M.-J., *Les commentaires patristiques du psautier (IIIe–Ve siècles)*, i: *Les travaux des pères grecs et latins sur le psautier: Recherches et bilans*, ii: *Exégèse prosopologique et théologie* (Orientalia Christiana Analecta, nos. 219, 220; Rome: Pont. institutum orientalium studiorum, 1982, 1985).

——and Kirchmeyer, J., 'Eusèbe de Césarée', *Dictionnaire de spiritualité*, vi, pt. 2, 1687–90.

Rousseau, O., 'Quelques textes patristiques sur la Jérusalem céleste', *Vie spirituelle*, 86 (1952), 378–88.

Ruhbach, Gerhard, *Apologetik und Geschichte: Untersuchungen zur Theologie Eusebs von Caesarea* (Heidelberg University diss., 1962).

——(ed.), *Die Kirche angesichts der Konstantinischen Wende* (Wege der Forschung, no. 306; Darmstadt: Wissenschaftliche Buchgesellschaft, 1976).

——'Die politische Theologie des Eusebs von Caesarea', in Ruhbach (ed.), *Die Kirche angesichts der Konstantinischen Wende*, 236–58.

Ruppel, W., 'Politeuma: Bedeutungsgeschichte eines staatsrechtlichen Terminus', *Philologus*, 82 (1926–7), 268–312, 434–54.

Saffrey, H. D., 'Un lecteur antique des œuvres de Numénius: Eusèbe de Césarée', in *Forma Futuri: Studi in onore del Cardinale M. Pellegrino* (Turin: Bottega d'Erasmo, 1975), 145–53.

Sansterre, J.-M., 'Eusèbe de Césarée et la naissance de la théorie "césaropapiste"', *Byzantion*, 42 (1972), 131–95, 532–94.

Schäublin, Christoph, *Untersuchungen zu Methode und Herkunft der Antiochenischen Exegese* (Theophaneia, Beiträge zur Religions- und Kirchengeschichte des Altertums, no. 23; Köln: Peter Hanstein Verlag, 1974).

Schmidt, Karl Ludwig, *Die Polis in Kirche und Welt: Eine lexicographische und exegetische Studie* (Rektoratsprogramm der Universität Basel für das Jahr 1939; Basel: Universitätsbuchdruckerei Friederich Reinhardt, 1939).

Schmitt, Carl, 'Eusebius als Prototyp politischer Theologie', in *Politische Theologie II* (Berlin: Duncker & Humblot, 1970), 68–88; repr. in Ruhbach (ed.), *Die Kirche angesichts der Konstantinischen Wende*, 220–35.

Schneemelcher, Wilhelm, *Kirche und Staat im vierten Jahrhundert* (Bonner akademische Reden, no. 37; Bonn: Hanstein-Verlag, 1970); repr. in Ruhbach (ed.), *Die Kirche angesichts der Konstantinischen Wende*, 122–48.

Schoedel, William, *Ignatius of Antioch* (Hermeneia Series; Philadelphia: Fortress Press, 1985).

Schoeps, Hans-Joachim, *Aus frühchristlicher Zeit: Religionsgeschichtliche Untersuchungen* (Tübingen: J. C. B. Mohr, 1950).

Schürer, Emil, *The History of the Jewish People in the Age of Jesus Christ (175 BC–AD 135)* (new English version rev. and ed. by Geza Vermes and Fergus Millar, 3 vols. in 4 pts.; Edinburgh: T. & T. Clark, 1973–88).

Schwartz, Eduard, 'Eusebios von Caesarea', *Realencyclopädie der classischen Altertumswissenschaft*, vi (1909), 1370–439; repr. in *Griechische Geschichtsschreiber* (Leipzig: Koehler and Amelang, 1957), 495–598.

——*Kaiser Constantin und die christliche Kirche* (2nd edn.; Berlin: B. G. Teubner, 1936).

Scott, Alan, *Origen and the Life of the Stars: A History of an Idea* (Oxford: Clarendon Press, 1991).

Seitz, Anton, *Die Heilsnotwendigkeit der Kirche nach der altchristlichen Literatur bis zur Zeit des hl. Augustinus* (Freiburg im Br.: Herdersche Verlagehandlung, 1903).

Shotwell, Willis, *The Biblical Exegesis of Justin Martyr* (London: SPCK, 1965).

Simon, Marcel, *Verus Israel: Étude sur les relations entre les chrétiens et Juifs dans l'empire romain (135–425)* (2nd edn.; Paris: Éditions E. de Boccard, 1964).

Simonetti, Manlio, 'Eusebio e Origene: Per una storia dell'Origenismo', *Augustinianum*, 26 (1986), 323–34.

—— 'Sulle fonti del *Commento a Isaia* di Girolamo', *Augustinianum*, 24 (1984), 451–69.

Sirinelli, Jean, *Les vues historiques d'Eusèbe de Césarée durant la période prénicéenne* (Publications de la section de langues et littératures, 10; Université de Dakar, Faculté des lettres et sciences humaines, 1961).

Skarsaune, Oskar, *The Proof from Prophecy: A Study in Justin Martyr's Proof-Text Tradition: Text-Type, Provenance, Theological Profile* (Novum Testamentum, Supplement 56; Leiden: E. J. Brill, 1987).

Smith, Sir William (ed.), *A Dictionary of Christian Biography, Literature, Sects, and Doctrines*, 4 vols. (London: J. Murray, 1877–87).

Sparks, H. F. D., 'Jerome as Biblical Scholar', in Ackroyd and Evans (eds.), *The Cambridge History of the Bible*, i. 510–40.

Spicq, Ceslas, O. P., *Notes de lexicographie néotestamentaire*, 2 vols. (Orbis Biblicus et Orientalis, no. 22; Fribourg: Éditions universitaires, 1978).

Stead, G. C., Review of *Der Jesajakommentar*, ed. Joseph Ziegler, *ix* of *Eusebius' Werke, Journal of Theological Studies*, 35 (1984), 230–32.

Stevenson, J., *Studies in Eusebius* (Cambridge: Cambridge University Press, 1929).

Storch, Rudolph H., 'The "Eusebian Constantine"', *CH* 40 (1971), 145–51.

Strack, H. L., and Billerbeck, P., *Kommentar zum Neuen Testament aus Talmud und Midrasch*, 6 vols. in 7 pts. (Munich: Beck, 1922–61).

Strathmann, W., '*Polis*', *Theological Dictionary of the New Testament* (1968) vi. 516–35.

Straub, J., 'Kaiser Konstantin als *episkopos tôn ektos*', *SP* 1: 678–95. TU, no. 63 (Berlin, 1957; repr. in *Regeneratio Imperii: Aufsätze über Roms Kaisertum und Reich im Spiegel der heidnischen und christlichen Publizistik*; Darmstadt: Wissenschaftliche Buchgesellschaft, 1972), 119–33.

—— 'Konstantin als *koinos episkopos*', *Dumbarton Oaks Papers*, 21 (1967), 37–55; repr. in *Regeneratio Imperii* (Darmstadt, 1972), 70–88.

—— *Vom Herrscherideal in der Spätantike* (Forschungen zur Kirchen- und Geistesgeschichte, no. 18; Stuttgart: W. Kohlhammer, 1939).

Telfer, W., 'Constantine's Holy Land Plan', *SP* 1. TU, no. 63 (Berlin: Akademie-Verlag, 1957), 696–700.

—— *The Office of a Bishop* (London: Darton, Longman & Todd, 1962).

Theological Dictionary of the New Testament, ed. Gerhard Kittel, trans. and ed. by Geoffrey W. Bromiley, 10 vols. (Grand Rapids, Mich.: Wm. B. Eerdmans, 1964–76).

Thielmann, F., 'Another Look at the Eschatology of Eusebius of Caesarea', *VC* 41 (1987), 226–37.

Tigcheler, Jo, *Didyme l'Aveugle et l'exégèse allégorique: Étude semantique de quelques termes exégétiques importantes de son commentaire sur Zacharie* (Graecitas Christianorum Primaeva, 6; Nijmegen: Dekker & Vande Vegt, 1977).

Trigg, Joseph W., *Origen: The Bible and Philosophy in the Third-Century Church* (Atlanta: John Knox Press, 1983).

—— 'The Angel of Great Counsel: Christ and the Angelic Hierarchy in Origen's Theology', *JTS* 42 (1991), 35–51.

Ungern-Sternberg, Arthur Freiherr von, *Der traditionelle alttestamentliche Schriftbeweis 'De Christo' und 'De Evangelio' in der alten Kirche bis zur Zeit Eusebs von Caesarea* (Halle: Verlag von Max Niemeyer, 1913).

Vigna, Gerald, *The Influence of Epideictic Rhetoric on Eusebius of Caesarea's Political Theology* (Northwestern University doctoral diss., 1980).

Vogler, Chantal, 'Les Juifs dans le code théodosien', in Jacques LeBrun (ed.), *Les chrétiens devant le fait Juif* (Le point théologique, no. 33; Paris: Éditions Beauchesnes, 1979), 35–74.

Vogt, Joseph, 'Die Constantinische Frage: Die Bekehrung Constantins', in *Relazioni del X. Congresso Internazionale di Scienze Storiche* (Florence, 1955), vi. 733–79; repr. in H. Kraft (ed.), *Konstantin der Grosse*, 345–87.

Volz, Paul, *Die Eschatologie der Jüdischen Gemeinde im neutestamentlichen Zeitalter: Nach den Quellen der rabbinischen, apokalyptischen, und apokryphen Literatur* (Hildesheim: Georg Olms Verlagsbuchhandlung, 1966).

Walker, P. W. L., *Holy City, Holy Places? Christian Attitudes to Jerusalem and the Holy Land in the Fourth Century* (Oxford: Clarendon Press, 1990).

Wallace-Hadrill, D. S., *Eusebius of Caesarea* (London: A. R. Mowbray & Co., 1960).

—— 'Eusebius of Caesarea's *Commentary on Luke*: Its Origin and Early History', *HTR* 67 (1974), 55–63.

Warmington, B. H., 'Did Constantine Have Religious Advisers?' *SP* 19 (Leuven, 1989), 117–29.

Weber, Antonio, *ΑΡΧΗ. Ein Beitrag zur Christologie des Eusebius von Caesarea* (Rome: Pontificia Universitas Gregoriana, 1964).

Wiles, M. F., 'Origen as Biblical Scholar', in Ackroyd and Evans (eds.), *The Cambridge History of the Bible*, i. 454–88.

——'Theodore of Mopsuestia as Representative of the Antiochene School', in Ackroyd and Evans (eds.), *The Cambridge History of the Bible*, i. 489–510.

Wilken, Robert, *The Christians as the Romans Saw Them* (New Haven: Yale University Press, 1984).

——'Eusebius and the Christian Holy Land', in Attridge and Hata (eds.), *Eusebius, Christianity, and Judaism*, 736–60.

——*The Land Called Holy: Palestine in Christian History and Thought* (New Haven: Yale University Press, 1992).

Williams, A. Lukeyn., *Adversus Judaeos: A Bird's Eye View of Christian Apologiae until the Renaissance* (Cambridge: Cambridge University Press, 1935).

Williams, George H., 'Christology and Church–State Relations in the Fourth Century', *CH* 20/3 (1951), 1–33, and 20/4 (1951), 1–26.

Winkelmann, F., 'Zur Geschichte des Authentizitätsproblem der Vita Constantini', *Klio*, 40 (1962), 187–243.

Wutz, Franz, *Onomastica sacra: Untersuchungen zum Liber Interpretationis Hebraicorum Nominum des Hl. Hieronymus* (TU, no. 41, pts. 1 and 2; Leipzig: J. C. Hinrichs, 1914).

Young, Frances, *From Nicaea to Chalcedon: A Guide to the Literature and its Background* (Philadelphia: Fortress Press, 1983).

INDEX